Changing Governments
in India and China

Changing Governments
in India and China

Charles Bingman

CHANGING GOVERNMENTS IN INDIA AND CHINA

iUniverse books may be ordered through booksellers or by contacting:

iUniverse
1663 Liberty Drive
Bloomington, IN 47403
www.iuniverse.com
1-800-Authors (1-800-288-4677)

ISBN: 978-1-5320-1068-2 (sc)
ISBN: 978-1-5320-1069-9 (e)

Library of Congress Control Number: 2016918673

Print information available on the last page.

iUniverse rev. date: 11/07/2016

CONTENTS

INTRODUCTION

THE TWO MOST INTERESTING GOVERNMENTS in the world are those of India and China. In both countries, the governments are by far the most important national force, and they control the lives and well being of 2.5 billion people or about 37% of the total population of the world. These two Asian giants have much in common, and their approach to governance is strikingly similar. Consider the following:

1. Both entered initially into <u>seriously flawed governments</u>. "In China, it was initiated when the Communists came to power in 1949 under a dictatorship directed by Mao Zedong. It was enormous and breathtaking in its scope and impact, but it was also in many ways an enormous failure. Mao could not deal with poverty, distress, obsolescence, or hopelessness. He destroyed much – some of it needed destroying, but most of it was vital and now must be painfully reconstructed. After Mao's death in 1976, the Chinese Communist Party (CCP) was finally able to initiate its own broad range of reforms. Thus, China's modern history can be divided into two 30 year periods: 1949-1979 under Mao; and from 1979 to today during The CCP has had to abandon the Maoist legacy, redesign the economy, reform the government itself, and manage the consequences of these reforms for the Chinese people and society.

    In India too, its history divides into two significant periods. At the time of Independence in 1949, Prime Minister Pandit Jawaharal Nehru saw a country deeply divided with a Brahmin caste population of 20% at the top, 20% as Dalits or Untouchables, another 30% as "Backward" classes, and the rest in the middle in thousands of many castes, clans, religions and localized communities. 83% of the population is Hindu, but there are more than 160 million Muslims, plus Christians, Buddhists and others. This meant to him that the disparities within the country were so great that the government must control all from the center, and must of necessity own and control large parts of the economy. The private sector was not to be trusted to act beyond greed, for the general welfare. Thus, a three level economy was to emerge. The top level would be the extensive layer of state owned enterprises, controlling the "commanding heights" of the economy which would be developed and nurtured by the government, receiving the great bulk of whatever economic development funds the government could muster. The second level was to be the private sector, but mainly the traditional merchants, traders, and manufacturers who would be permitted to labor in the economic sectors not controlled by the government. But these private enterprises were not to be trusted, and would have to be controlled and regulated in almost strangling detail. The third level of the economy was the huge informal economy – millions of farmers, small shopkeepers, service providers, manual laborers, servants and artisans, many of them living in abject poverty, and most of them functioning in a huge, messy and often illegal economic environment so low on the totem pole that the government could not be bothered with them. For India, the watershed date was 1991, when the government under Prime Minister P. N. Rao and Finance Minister Manmohan Singh finally had the courage to initiate a series of reforms which tipped India over the brink toward economic liberalization, in a process that continues at a halting pace today.

2. <u>Development of the national economy is the single most important role of each government.</u> For most of the last 60 years, the philosophies of State Socialism have been dominant, and in both countries they have been substantial failures. In China, centrist socialist government control of the economy was absolute. In India, a two layer economy allowing a substantial private sector was tolerated as long as the State controlled the "commanding heights" of the economy.

3. Both countries put large proportions of economic activity in the hands of State Owned Enterprises (SOE) which were relatively new kinds of organizations that were capable of operating somewhat like private businesses, but were always intended to remain directly under the control of the government. Hundreds of thousands of these SOEs were created. The "good news" was supposed to be that they would generate revenue which would be captured by the government as income. The bad news is that they were a failed experience. They proved so inefficient that a many as 50% of them operated at a deficit, and many of the others managed only the slimmest of profit margins. Even at their peak, they could never provide a stable and profitable economy for more than about 20% of the workforce in China, and perhaps 7% in India. The gradual retreat from SOEs and indeed from State Socialism is one of the most compelling and difficult necessities for both countries, and the key to both economies remains not socialist theology but an inexhaustible supply of cheap labor.

4. As an adjunct to this centrist state socialist economic commitment, a whole range of economic policies were enacted. In China, essential control was exerted over the critical elements of the economy: what businesses were allowed to exist, what activities they could pursue, what prices they could charge and be charged, what supplies would cost. Prices were controlled, and people were simply told where they would be allowed work and live. This centrist control was, and remains in the firm grip of the Chinese Communist Party (CCP). India, by law, set aside whole major segments of the economy as the exclusive preserve of state owned and controlled enterprises, and the whole economy is endlessly and elaborately manipulated by a vast bureaucracy which came to be known as the License Raj.

5. Further, supposedly in order to protect and encourage the development of domestic enterprises, both governments made heavy commitments to what was known as import substitution policies, which usually involved official prohibition of imported goods or even services where foreign imports would compete with domestic products. Obviously, crucial things like oil or food had

to be admitted, but both governments seemed slow to realize that other imports such as high technology could be critical elements in the growth of the very enterprises that they sought to protect. At an increasing pace, both governments have started to loosen up the stringent import controls of the past. And both have also realized the wisdom of encouraging domestic enterprises to increase their exports instead of confining their business to domestic customers.

6. Socialist theory pretended that the government controlled economy was going to guarantee well paying jobs for all, but reality was that neither socialist economy ever came close, and huge numbers of people could never find "official" jobs in the government or the SOEs. <u>The real economy had three main elements</u>: hard scrabble agriculture, the informal economies in cities, and a "float" of as many as 180 million people who lived in slums, took what work they could find, and retreated to their villages in hard times. All of these real elements of the economy the government frankly ignored.

    But socialist theology made it impossible for the political leadership to ignore the fact that its socialist model wasn't working. It was not until 1979-85 in China and 1991 in India that the political leadership was forced by harsh economic reality to abandon this theology in favor of economic reality – that is, the reluctant shift to a whole new philosophy based on the emergence of a market based economy.

7. <u>Since this reversal of thinking, the economic results in both countries have been remarkable</u>. It is valuable to think in these terms: before this changed economic thinking and control had been centrist and "top down". After the change, the tides have been more disaggregated and <u>"bottom up."</u> Neither country has been fully able to abandon their economic past. The Chinese have, for 25 years been pursuing a careful, guarded, controlled conversion to something more like the Indian model – a broader, freer private sector including more foreign investment, side by side with a still powerful public sector with fewer but larger and more powerful SOEs. India, as in all things, is wild and chaotic. The government is increasingly turning to various forms of public- private enterprise

partnerships where the government provides most of the money, but none of the managerial skills, which it never really possessed anyway.

8. One of the compelling realities that has now become more recognize is that State Socialism was a complete and pervasive justification for <u>government regimes that were highly centrist and controlling</u>, and that were directed by a small and self appointed elite. In China, that elite has been the Chinese Communist Party (CCP) which has seized all power and will tolerate little or no opposition of any kind. India has created an elite of men of high caste, cloaked in the mantle of the British Raj, buttressed by sophisticated education and a sense of natural superiority. They believe that they have a right to rule and to receive preferment.

9. Governments in China are heavily and tightly integrated from top to bottom. The <u>central government controls provincial governments</u>, which in turn control townships and cities down to villages. In fact, China has two separate top-to-bottom governments: one of appointed government officials, and a second solely of parallel Party offices that are widely regarded as exercising the real authority. The Indian elite has been successfully challenged from time to time, but the Congress Party and the families of Pandit Nehru have had a grip on the hearts and minds and votes of India for more than 60 years, in a most extraordinary example of a family dynasty equaled only by the Kim family in North Korea and the Abdul-Aziz family in Saudi Arabia. This continuity in China has allowed the CCP to survive the 30 year catastrophe of the Maoist regime and the failures of the socialist economy, and enter a new 30 year period of a lot of economic reform, a little social reform and no political reform. The Chinese dictatorship survives and prospers because, whatever its sins and shortcomings, it is moving in the right directions and it is infinitely better than what it succeeded.

India's emergence as a world power is slower, messier, spastic, unplanned, and miserably led. It is the resurgence, from the bottom up, of powerful private and personal enterprise in spite of the government, and often in opposition to it. The old apparatus of SOEs and Statist control is withering in the face of its own inadequacies and the growing competition with the surging private sector.

10. The Chinese government control of the key elements of the economy has allowed it to <u>capture and control a remarkable proportion of the new wealth being generated.</u> This wealth is being deployed heavily into physical infrastructure like highways, ports, airports, power plants, dams and the acquisition of energy resources around the world. Wealth is not being deployed into education (except for a small elite), nor in health care, public welfare, pensions, housing for the poor, or a whole range of ominous and growing environmental threats. India has no such dictatorial control of wealth, and in fact, its government finances have always been inadequate, but it is following a development pattern similar to the Chinese. But very few people are expected to pay income taxes, and many of those manage to escape the burden. Politicians are pathologically inept and waste funds on pointless public subsidies and fritter money away through almost universal mismanagement. They join their Chinese counterparts as some of the most venal and corrupt officials in the world. India is the most populous democracy, but it almost manages to give democracy a bad name.

11. Corrosive politics and political leadership are extensively translated into <u>two horrible bureaucratic swamps</u>. In India, the demand for centrist control created and nurtured what became known as the License Raj, and more recently, the Regulation Raj. Hundreds of thousands of workers with narrow clerk-like mentalities administer thousands of laws and regulations designed to control, constrain, prevent, limit, delay and discourage. Modern India can no longer afford this still prevalent mentality, but it seems somehow extraordinarily difficult to eliminate or retrench it. China, in accordance with its nature, has evolved what it calls "vertical administration". That is, a finance officer for example at the municipal level must report vertically to the finance officer at the county level, who reports to the finance officer at the township level, who reports to the finance officer at the provincial level, who

reports to a ministry in Beijing, who reports to some official of the CCP. This vertical pattern is repeated endlessly for every public program and for every administrative function. The purpose of this vertical administration is, of course, to exercise control from the top in ways that are invisible to the general public. But ultimately, this too is seriously inhibiting, and will prove exceedingly difficult to reduce.

12. In both countries, the urge for centrist power led inevitably to <u>unwillingness to allow the evolution of truly effective local government</u>. Major responsibilities for social programs and for environmental protections were consigned to states/provinces and then down to cities, towns, and villages. But the central government always knew that the local governments had neither the funds nor the management competence to meet these burdens. Local governments in China remain under the control of the central government, but their arrogance, ruthlessness and corruption are widely hated. The most promising note has been that many of the "loser" SOEs offloaded by the national government onto local governments have shown a surprising capacity to recover and flourish under local government sponsorship and financing.

13. <u>Both countries remain heavily centered on farming and village life</u>. India has more than half a million villages, and more than 70% of the population still depends for their livelihoods on rural and village life. China has 678,000 villages and a population of almost 900 million who still live in or rely on rural areas. In both countries, it has been deliberate policy to ignore and even exploit the interests and wellbeing of the rural world, and use whatever funds have been available to concentrate on the development of new and higher value added elements of the economy. This has necessarily meant the emergence of cities as the driving force in both countries. More than 480 million of China's 1.3 billion people are now urban dwellers, both legal and illegal, in what has been the most extraordinary urbanization movement in world history. China has attempted without success to stem the tide of urban influx by permitting only a certain number of "official" residents, mostly employed in governments and SOEs, who are entitled to

public services, but the majority of residents have unofficially and illegally, living life at the margins and working in a huge informal economy. Millions return to their farms and villages when work is scarce or the government cracks down.

India parallels this pattern, except that its informal economy is less productive, and its slums in the larger cities are among the worst in the world. The Indian economy is less centered on industries that create large numbers of jobs, and the urban future seems to hinge on the size and success of the new middle class, drawing upon the denizens of the informal economy for small businesses, crafts and trades, and services provision. India cannot begin to match the pace of urban development, and the provision of urban infrastructure that China is now achieving.

In summary, in the modern era it has always been difficult to separate these governments from their economies. It has only been in the past 20 years or so that some degree of separation has been allowed to occur, and both countries seem to be in the midst of a great tide of retreat from government control and the advance of private enterprise. This in turn has permitted, and even demanded a rethinking of the roles of governments in both countries. The compelling logic until recently has been the almost total preoccupation with economic development. This is understandable, but it seems to have overwhelmed everything else. Whole major elements of each country have been more or less deliberately ignored to the great detriment of the people, and these neglects are the source of immeasurable resentment and stress from "the bottom up". Thus, both governments exist in growing turmoil, but for different reasons. China is a rigid, tyrannical top down regime, fearful of its future unless it can learn to provide a more humane and tolerant society. India is a wildly chaotic, disorganized mess seeking a political system that really works and is capable of making India into a modern economy and workable government.

CHAPTER I

Government Reform in India and China

THE TWO GREAT LEADERS WHO emerged in the period after WW II were Pandit Jawaharlal Nehru in India and Mao Zedong in China. In India, the revered Mohandas Gandhi perceived India as remaining a simple rural society made better by peace, harmony, morality and a far better commitment to basic human needs of health, education, and simple work. Nehru, on the other hand, introduced a whole new and more sophisticated level of thinking into both society in general and in the nature of the Indian government and economy. He saw European, and especially Soviet State Socialism, somewhat modified by British Fabian socialist thinking, as the perfect vehicle for carrying India into the modern world. India was to remain an elite society, ruled by the same elites, but now espousing and enforcing the principles of state socialism along with an overlay of democracy.

In China, Chairman Mao created an absolute dictatorship driven by rigid top down control in which "democracy" had no place and opposition was brutally suppressed. Unlike the Chinese, the Indian government and the whole of society has always supported genuine democracy, but Nehru saw it as guided forever by his Congress Party in ways that validated the leadership of the ruling elites, almost as a secular priesthood. India's glory is that it has the largest population of any genuine democracy in the world. India's shame is that its government is among the most incompetent in the world. It is built on noble sentiments and lousy performance.

Extraordinarily, both men, who were of very different character, often arrived at the same places. Both adopted state socialism. Both committed themselves powerfully to the instruments of state owned enterprises, and both lived just long enough to realize their inadequacies. Both turned their backs on the people's need for social services and never saw primary education and health care as worthy priorities. Both arrogantly believed that their personal visions of the world were not only correct, but that they must be mandated and enforced, and that those who opposed them were always intellectually and morally wrong. Both governments dumped the huge problems of primary education and basic health care onto local governments, fully aware they could not deal with them, lacking either the money or the civic delivery systems to do so.

There were differences as well, the greatest of which was that China sees government and indeed the world from the top down, and India sees the world from the bottom up.

INDIA: GOVERNMENT BY CHAOS

The Indian political system tends to produce administrations that are so beleaguered that they find it almost impossible to function. For almost 60 years, India's finest minds have produced valiant but totally unreal policies, plans and objectives. It is extraordinary how both China and India ended up suffering badly from arrogant misdirection of two of the most extraordinary men in modern history. It is not correct to say that Nehru and Mao were right, and that the lesser men and women who followed were not up to the challenge. In fact, both were wrong to begin with, and the history of the last 30 years has been one of struggles by their successors in both countries to rectify some huge errors. The bland bureaucratic language of the Indian government simply masks the enormous changes that are really taking place. The old State Socialist regime is dying. The private sector is emerging as the new hope for India. The economy is changing, and so too is the composition of national leadership, including the emergence of a new middle class of almost 200 million people who are slowly working out the nature of their political leadership role. When faced with real competition, the old SOEs have declined, and many have disappeared.

Nehru sincerely believed that India was so vastly complex, confusing and conflicting that the only way it could prosper or even survive was to be directed and guided from the top down. This meant to him that the government most own and control large parts of the economy. The private sector was not to be trusted to act beyond greed, for the general welfare. In general, he believed in:

1. The superiority of State Socialism in economic matters; a suspicion of the private sector; the absolute ownership of the "commanding heights" of the Indian economy, and the centrist control through regulation, of all significant elements of the economy.
2. The rightness of Fabian Socialism and Fabian economics, and also an admiration of the Soviet command and control system.
3. A general acceptance of the substitution of state owned enterprises (SOE) in place of private corporations, including SOE exclusive monopoly ownership of key elements of the economy including power, energy, communications, railways and airways, heavy industry including iron and steel, communications and suppliers of military weaponry.
4. A firm commitment to the rightness of State Owned Enterprises as the prime movers in the economy of the country -- and a stubborn unwillingness to recognize the reality of SOE failures and the general lack of success of centrist socialist policies.
5. A deep suspicion of an open economy which led to a broad policy of import substitution, export limitation, prohibitions of foreign direct investment, and subsidies for the development of domestic industry.
6. The necessity for the government to exert control over a wide range of national activities. This led to the emergence of the widely reviled License Raj and Regulation Raj.
7. Government provision of aid to farmers on the premise that the poor should share the benefits of the stronger economy, but often in ways that proved to be dysfunctional.
8. The need and desire to promote nationalism, plus recognition of its perceived political value.

Nehru saw a country deeply divided with a Brahmin caste population of 20% at the top, 20% as Dalits (former Untouchables), 30% as "Backward" castes, and the rest in the middle in thousands of castes. 83% of the population is Hindu, but there are more than 160 million Muslims, plus Christians, Buddhists and others. This meant to him that the disparities within the country were so great that the government must control all from the center, and must of necessity own and control large parts of the economy. Thus, a three level economy emerged. The top level was the extensive layer of state owned enterprises, controlling the "commanding heights" of the economy which would be developed and nurtured by the government, receiving the great bulk of whatever economic development funds the government could muster. The second level was the private sector, but mainly the traditional merchants, traders, and manufacturers who would be permitted to labor in the economic sectors not controlled by the government. But these private enterprises were not to be trusted, and would have to be controlled and regulated in almost strangling detail. In 1947, India's wealth resided with the landed gentry. After Independence, most of the wealth resided with the socialist government, in the senior civil service and the top State Owned Enterprises (SOE). Now, a large share of the wealth resides with a new generation of private sector entrepreneurs and India's new Middle Class.

The third level of the economy was the huge informal economy – millions of farmers, small shopkeepers, service providers, manual laborers, servants and artisans, many of them living in abject poverty, and most of them functioning in a huge, messy and often illegal economic environment so low on the totem pole that the government could not be bothered with them. In total, the Indian workforce is 470 million people. More recent governments have been granting major affirmative action concessions to categories of citizens called the Scheduled Castes and Tribes (former untouchables) who now are guaranteed admission to colleges and schools, and to 22.5% of all government jobs, including SOEs. Recent recommendations propose a further reservation of 10% of public sector jobs for Muslims, and a further reservation for women.

In addition, there are 85 seats out of 545 in Parliament set aside for Scheduled Castes and Tribes, and there is a current proposal to set aside an additional 33% of national and state assemblies for women. In 1991, census data indicated that there were about 140 million scheduled caste people and 66 million in the scheduled tribes, and about 500 million women. In addition there are those who are classified as Other Backward Classes who really range across the near poor and the lower middle classes involving more than 200 million people who claim a variety of preferences and quotas. And still, an estimated 300 million people live in absolute poverty, and there is little evidence that 60 years of such reservations have lifted up many dalits or women or Muslims. (See Appendix A: Ministries of the Central (Union) Government; Appendix B: Indian States and Union Territories; and Appendix C: Indian State Owned Enterprises).

Nehru and his associates faced other kinds of big policy choices. First was the practical problem that India was desperately poor, with an obsolete almost medieval economy. In earlier days, India along with China had been a great mercantile nation of producers, traders and bankers throughout the world. Its leaders had been among the great princes of the earth. But gradually the glory faded, the empires declined, the British Raj arrived, and India froze in time, a huge chaotic panorama of class, caste, religion, language and customs, and above all almost universal poverty. What resources existed were in the hands of the owners of land including various princely holdings, a very active but old style merchant class, and a elite middle class in the banks, the prestigious Indian Civil Service, and a small range of professional people. The great mass of Indians lived on small farms and in 680,000 villages. The elites were conservative, protective of their own interests, and unable and unwilling to concede the need for a world different from their own. In later days, the elite would become very devoted to the elimination of perverse caste differences, but in early days, this elite class of high caste Brahmins strongly believed that the enormous complexity of India would flow on forever, ruled – but not managed – by them.

Within the general framework then of state socialist philosophy, Nehru set out to acquire for the government the "commanding heights" elements of the economy, especially in steel, power, energy, banking, heavy industry, transport, shipping, and machine tools. Huge expansions of these sectors were undertaken, with emphasis on those that were thought to be "worker intensive", hoping to provide jobs for millions of India's congenitally unemployed. But at the same time, there was an inexplicable abandonment of whole segments of the population: farmers, villagers, women, the urban poor, those in the informal economy. Money was "saved" for economic development by almost wholly abandoning provision of vital social services such as health care, education, welfare and retirement assistance.

The socialist economic system, once launched became the main prop of the ruling Congress Party, and the system could not be allowed to fail. This in turn led to a whole series of major policy decisions designed to create an economic structure supporting centrist government control. Equally critical to Socialist control of the economy were dozens of key economic policies to extend and guarantee government authority. The banks were nationalized. No enterprise, public or private, could be created, expanded, redirected, or even terminated without the approval of the government. An extensive system was instituted which controlled critical prices at which goods and services had to be bought and sold, along with the cost of transfers between enterprises. In addition, to further enhance their economic position, some SOEs were made official monopolies, thus driving out any remaining private sector competition. India was later to discover that government monopolies were at least as perverse as private sector monopolies, and often were worse because there was seldom any recourse from government mistakes or oppression.

Nehru enthusiastically instituted a long term policy of what is generally called "import substitution". By various means, the government sought to encourage the domestic production of goods and services all the way from steel to shoes, and often, the state owned banks were required to lend money to such developing enterprises at subsidy rates. At the same time, the government enacted import controls to keep out foreign competition. Every government policy was specifically designed to favor domestic SOEs against foreign competitors and even against domestic private companies.

The perverse nature of this import substitution policy was soon apparent. Domestic producers were often less efficient and productive than their foreign competition, and thus Indian consumers were often forced to choose inferior goods and services at higher costs. Heads of SOEs were usually supportive of these policies because they were subsidized and protected. In fact, many private businesses felt the same way because they too could extract rich subsidies from the government. Meanwhile the traditional textile industry, which had, at one time been one of India's commercial strengths, was badly battered by machine based industrial competition in G. Britain and elsewhere. The Nehru regime foolishly tried to stem the tide by opposing industrialization (thru heavy special taxes) and textile imports. In fact, it appears that Nehru, for all of his sophistication, never really understood market demand. He was driven by his sense of what India could produce, and not by what the market wanted to buy.

Nehru was the ultimate elitist: he was absolutely convinced that the country would be better run by an elite. He thought democracy was a good thing because it would affirm the position of his elite. He thought competition was wasteful, and central planning was the only efficient way. The Industrial Policy Resolution of 1956 reserved 17 industries exclusively for public ownership, including iron and steel, mining, machine tool manufacture, and heavy electrical machinery manufacture. This policy was kept in force until 1991, and vestiges still remain, producing government ministries with dwindling roles and little to do except meddle. Meanwhile in places like Japan, S. Korea and even in China, more successful shifts had been made to open up the economy and encourage the private sector.

As an adjunct of this flawed policy, the License Raj was created, beginning with the Industries Development and Regulation Act of 1951 which sought to:

1. Create the approved pattern of official or permitted investment
2. To prevent private monopolies or concentrations of wealth (while permitting government monopolies and concentrations of government ownership and control)
3. Maintain regional balances in the allocation of industry location

4. Protect the interests of small-scale producers and encourage the
   entry of new entrepreneurs
5. Encourage optimum scale of plants and use of advanced technology.

Thus, government ownership was not considered control enough, and the government established and enforced industry production goals, and granted licenses to companies for their share of these goals. Violations of these production limits were severely punished. As one observer put it "government policies engendered state monopolies with uneconomic-scale plants employing too many people and second-rate technologies in remote, uncompetitive locations." The endless delays in clearing applications discouraged the truly efficient in favor of wily, inefficient producers who concentrated on the manipulation of the system. Licensing was an unmitigated disaster. It raised costs, brought delays, arbitrariness and corruption, and achieved nothing. The mixed economy ended in combining the worst features of socialism and capitalism. Nor did this mixed economy deliver social justice; it produced unsavory subsidies for the well off." [1]

India thus suffered, and still suffers, from a burdensome and intensively meddlesome government of politicians and bureaucrats and the special interests that directly support them. The state became an obscure amalgamation of special interests responsible to no one. The class with money and influence was tiny and came predominantly from the upper castes. It had monopolized power and privilege and the benefits from the few scarce facilities for education, health and infrastructure. The rest of the population was left out in the cold. Nehru's "noble vision" proved to be illusory and impossible to implement.

The exercise of power is always about money, but in India it is also about status, preferment, and a desire to appear superior. It is about preferential access to everything from official appointments to cricket match tickets. It is about pulling strings, jumping queues, evading traffic tickets, free government services, first class plane tickets, getting seated in the better restaurants, and avoiding income and all other taxes. As Luce so eloquently describes a popular program, "As for the Rural Employment

Guarantee Act, it is difficult to accept at face value the Congress Party's claim that it is a good faith attempt to eliminate poverty in India once and for all. It is hard to see how a scheme that requires the poor to provide twelve hours or more of backbreaking physical labor each day for just $1 or $2 will transform their conditions. If you wander around India's provincial capitals, you see perfectly cropped gardens surrounding the large public buildings and official residences. Often you will see gangs of twenty or thirty laborers, squatting in rows on their haunches, moving gradually forward in a line, plucking the lawns with their bare hands. Inside the buildings, there will be dozens of sweepers, keeping their bodies at all times lower than yours, rearranging the dust in a posture of time-honored submission. Occasionally, you pause and ask yourself: is this about employment? Or is it about reminding the sweepers and those for whom they sweep who possesses status in society and who does not?" Even when the government sets aside a certain percentage of jobs in the public sector for the Scheduled Castes and Tribes, somehow, the wealthier members of these groups end up monopolizing the quotas, not the really poor." [2]

After the death of Nehru, what India got was not a relaxation of Socialist centrism; what it got was Indira Gandhi. What it got after Indira Gandhi was hysterical self-destructive political madness.

Indira Gandhi had a far stronger practical sense of how the market functioned – through patronage! She seized the political high ground by basing her position of "poverty alleviation" as a populist political theme – which worked beautifully. Then, she "tampered with appointments in the civil service and the courts, dismissed troublesome chief ministers and appointed people from whom she demanded absolute loyalty. When she had control over the apparatus of government, every decision was based on patronage, influence peddling, bribery and power brokerage. She pressed a program of "land redistribution" which was supposed to help the farmers, but ended up helping the rich landholders acquire more land. [3]

She nationalized the banks (to "democratize lending"); provided grants or loans to various special interest groups; encouraged and subsidized labor unions; and extended political and military links with the Soviet Union.

She deliberately ignored many good inexpensive ideas for achieving rural development in favor for costly vote seeking subsidies. She failed to keep up with programs for infrastructure development so that she could say that she cut taxes – which she did not. Similarly, she refused funds to SOEs for modernization, but raised worker wages. This neglect of development/ modernization deteriorated the SOE base, made it less efficient, and ultimately worsened its ability to return a profit. Despite clear examples of success in places like Japan and S. Korea, she and her successors never really got beyond the old socialist theology of import substitution, and never discovered the value of export promotion. And while the whole economy suffered from a lack of investment money, the government continued stoutly to oppose foreign investment.

In the last analysis, Indira Gandhi never made any serious inroads against poverty and rural isolation. The failures of Indira Gandhi meant the failure of the Congress Party, and after her death in 1984 (assassinated) the Congress Party declined, and the nationalist/Hindu Bharitiya Janata Party (BJP) emerged very strongly. This emergence was local and bottom up, in contrast with Congress which remained national, centrist and elitist. There has been an absolute deluge of local parties, narrowly centering around some specific cause such as race or religion or geography or Untouchability. The Congress Party became tainted as the generator of endless corruption, and both it and its principal national rival the Hindu based BHP are widely seen as wallowing in petty political whining, complaining, back stabbing, bumbling, incompetence, favoritism, arrogance and downright craziness, while totally neglecting the serious issues the country faces. It is not coincidental that India is fighting several insurrections – in Kashmir, for two decades; against the Maoist Naxilites in northeastern states; against a "free Assam" insurgency in the far northeast, supported by Bangladesh; and against many other local struggles against the government and the police.

Finally, in the late 80s, there was the growing sense among leaders that past strategies were not enormously successful and that there was no alternative but to liberalize, which became the driving force behind the shift in India's development strategy. Yet India's economic policies still remain very "Statist" by global standards, and it is not clear that governments, despite many high sounding plans and policy statements, are yet ready to spend some it's their growing income on poverty alleviation, or even on vital social services.

State owned enterprises remain very important; liberalization, while now more widely permitted, is still not especially extensive. Growth in the 1980s was really public debt led; in the 80s and 90s, it is led by private investment. India is also improving its ability to offer consumer based goods and services, even as import barriers are being lifted. Even where India is losing out to newly allowed foreign competition, some of its domestic capability is meeting the challenge, as for example autos or machine tools. And there is still the feeling that investments in the affairs of SOEs are simply reinforcing inefficient enterprises that are either loss making or are producing very low financial returns on investment. Thus, public investment is slowly declining in many segments of the economy where private sector alternatives are feasible, thus getting the government out of economic ownership of production. And the government seems, reluctantly to accept that every retreat from the License Raj or the Regulation Raj, produces rapid, visible, and substantial economic benefits. Power and communications which used to be limited to the public sector have been opened up to the private sector, and the benefits, at least in communications, has been almost miraculous. Power is in terrible shape and will take longer to respond.

India's 604 Districts remain the grass roots of government and the District Officer is the chief administrator. He spends half of his time listening to petitioners. This is a paternalistic system, often very humane, but ultimately very inefficient. Much of the job consists of getting parts of the bureaucracy to do what they are supposed to do. The bureaucracy is a huge creaking and arrogant machine that soaks up, or siphons off much of the available funds. More and more, Indians give up on moving the machine, and both people and organizations have started to solve their own problems. [4]

India's central government employs around 17 million civil servants, and the 28 states and 7 union territories and the large number of local governments employ another 83 million including those working in state owned or directed enterprises. [5] Very few of these people are policy makers and their number "includes vast numbers of paper shuffling peons." Of these, perhaps 80,000 are in some form of supervisory of managerial positions, but just 5,600 are in the elite Indian Administrative Service (IAS). Increasingly, there is the real concern that the quality and authorities of the more senior people is declining. Some of the decline is due to the lure of more attractive jobs in the private sector. More is a function of the increasing usurpation of decision-making by ignorant second rate politicians, the growth of populist politics and the preference for "clout" rather than ability.

In recent years, the necessary abandonment of much of the old state socialist theology and the emergence of the new and more powerful market economy has meant that the power of the old bureaucracy and socialist politicians has waned, and nobody is sad to seem them decline. Power has shifted to a new class of private entrepreneurs, usually aided and abetted by foreign investors and companies. Bangalore, previously known mainly for its military arsenal, is the modern center of IT in India with companies like IBM, Texas Instruments, Group Bull, Motorola, Sun Microsystems and scores of new Indian firms, all of which are both rich and influential. There is a high degree of movement of top people from their Indian bases to the headquarters or other technical facilities of these companies. Many of the top people in the United States Silicon Valley near San Francisco are Indian. In India, education has shifted from sending the children of the wealthy to England, to sending (the smart ones) to one of the new technical or management institutes in India.

THE DECLINE AND FALL OF STATE OWNED ENTERPRISES

In addition to the role of state owned and controlled businesses– called Public Sector Undertakings in India and State Owned Enterprises (SOE) elsewhere – there was wide acceptance of the dark suspicions about private business, and the government expended much effort to keep private business confined to smaller and more local sectors of the economy, although not always successfully.

The more important elements of the economy were usually put under the control of more than 1300 SOEs which were creations of the government, supposedly to function like private companies, but under the control of some government ministry, and in total, they handle about 25% of the domestic output of the country employing about 19 million people. 85% of all SOEs are Central Public Sector Enterprises (CPSE) controlled by the national government. The rest are State Public Sector Enterprises (SPSE) which are controlled by the 28 States. Each SOE is required to produce comprehensive business plans, every element of which required the detailed evaluation and approval of the supervising ministry. The numbers of enterprises appear to have reached their peak about 1990 and then leveled off. The total investment by the government did not peak until 2000 and beyond.

In theory, SOEs were expected to generate income for the government, and government budgets initially optimistically included estimates of that income. But as in 80 other countries in the world, the actual performance of SOEs in India proved to be almost the direct opposite of this theory. Despite extensive government support and subsidy, a large percentage of SOEs operated at a loss, or at the slimmest of profit margins. Instead of revenues, the government found itself covering losses with money it could ill afford to divert.

In some cases, the government's power to control prices allowed it to beggar some SOEs while fattening up others. Most nationalized, state owned banks were forced to lend to SOEs at subsidized rates. These SOEs, counting on their political backers, might decline to repay these loans, even where they were financially able to do so. At times, the burden of toxic debts forced onto banks was so heavy that collapse of the whole banking system seemed probable, and the government was reluctantly forced to buy its way out of the crisis. But SOEs might be forced into a series of politically motivated bad decisions. Overstaffing was and remains common. As many as 25-40% of the workforce in some SOEs was redundant because "creating jobs" has been a popular political promise. Also, it is equally popular for the government to order SOEs to raise wages for these redundant workers just before the next election.

The government expects to run a deficit of about $4.2 billion for the next quarter and perhaps $17 billion for the full year. In addition, policy makers see little opportunity either to cut costs or to raise taxes (mostly for political reasons). Therefore, the government is expected to accelerate and expand its efforts to sell off SOEs to fill the gap, and would hope to realize more than $ 4 billion. The government has already approved the listing (for IPOs) of major SOEs: National Hydro Power Co., Oil India, Bharat Sanchar Nigram Ltd. (telecommunications), Coal India and United Bank of India. Of course, opposition political parties, and trade unions oppose the idea.

India like China wants to hang on to its commanding heights enterprises, but their rate of failure is just as bad as that of the Chinese. The difference is that India does not – and could not – control the private sector the way that the Chinese do. Thus, over time, a more effective private sector will drive out marginal SOEs despite the government. India's government which, like the Chinese began to retreat from State Socialist theology in the early 80s, has never succeeded in controlling the same high percentage of national wealth, nor do they seem to have the same grip on the commanding heights elements of the economy.

Today, the main elements of the present government policy towards Public Sector enterprises as contained in the National Common Minimum Programme (NCMP) are as follows:

1. To devolve full managerial and commercial autonomy to successful, profit making companies operating in a competitive environment.
2. But -- generally, profit making enterprises will not be privatized.
3. Every effort will be made to modernize and restructure sick public sector companies and revive sick industry.
4. Chronically loss making companies will either be sold off, or closed, after all workers have got their legitimate dues and compensation.
5. Private industry will be induced to turn around enterprises that have potential for revival.
6. Privatization revenues will be used for designated social sector schemes.

7. Public sector companies and nationalized banks will be encouraged to enter the capital market to raise resources and offer new investment avenues to retail investors. [7]

Despite these earnest commitments, nothing much is really allowed to change. For example, just this year (2010) Air India, a State Owned Enterprise recently had been losing so much money that it could not pay its fuel bills. So oil companies (which are also SOEs) threatened to stop delivery. Then, the government intervened, guaranteed a new loan (on top of tons of previous loans), directed oil companies to continue deliveries, and directed banks (also SOEs) to lend money to Air India. [8]

The collective judgment about India's publicly directed undertakings continues to be that the record seems to show that the managers of public assets doctor their books, hoard goods, evade taxes, hide profits, and collude with other enterprises to delude or defraud the government. They are poorly monitored, notoriously overstaffed, riddled with corruption, a big part of the patronage machine, chronic loss-makers, and financially sick in that their debts are often in excess of their real net worth.

The design and structure of the Indian government is generally laudable and it has produced it share of outstanding leaders, yet it functions with a style or character that runs somewhere between unwarranted arrogance and bumbling incompetence. Its politics has given democracy a bad name – irrational, chaotic, driven implacably by special interests, paternalistic, deliberately divisive, weakly populist, and eternally corrupt. Politics has descended to new depths, all too often infested by a combination of zealots, know-nothings, scoundrels and crooks. Political figures have often hired thugs to beat up opposition candidates and intimidate voters. [9]

This structure has forever been riddled with problems that emerged through a combination of bad policy and bad management. For example, as summarized by Das, [10] "The low level functionaries took months in the futile micro view of an application, and then sent it up the administrative chain to the headquarters of a ministry for final approval. The ministry then again spent several months reviewing the same data, then sent the application to an "inter ministerial licensing committee" of senior bureaucrats who were equally ignorant of entrepreneurial realities, who operated by ad hoc rules, and who lacked real sense of relative priority. Even after ministerial approval, the investor might have to seek approval for the import of machinery for the factory. If foreigners were involved, there was another apparatus for a "inter ministerial foreign affairs agreements committee". If a bank loan was involved, a whole new separate evaluation had to be conducted, despite the facts that the banks were state owned." In fact, Das continued, "Nehru's state owned companies were being managed by civil servants who had no training in running commercial enterprises. Their subsequent losses were defended by Nehru, saying 'their job is not to make a profit but to meet social objectives.'"

The highly centralized nature of the government and the almost absolute power exercised at the top invited insatiable demands for special interest preferment which were seldom resisted. But this is not petty larceny: the major long term, steady plundering of public funds has drained funds needed for critical public programs, destroyed confidence in the government, and necessitated serious interventions by the World Bank and the International Monetary Fund. Government structures from top to bottom are seen universally as corrupt, unfair, uncaring, and suffering from the insolence of office. India seems to rely heavily on huge public subsidies and populist programs to curry favor with a widely fragmented electorate. China need not bother, since there are scarcely any really contested elections.

The pathologies of Indian politics have been reflected in the operation and administration of the government ministries and agencies. The centrist nature of the government led inevitably to the urge to control, not only through the operations of SOEs but through the creation of hundreds of thousands of laws, regulations and administrative procedures which permitted the government to impact and even control almost every facet of Indian economy and society.

Intergovernmental relations – national, State, district and municipal – are still dominated by the urge toward centrist control. It is a philosophy directly the opposite to the U. S. structure where the

Constitution reserved to the states all powers not specifically assigned to the national government, and the states in turn have been motivated for both political and financial reasons to delegate very substantial powers to authorities in counties and municipalities. In India, the central (Union) government has always been reluctant to concede power by delegation, even when the Constitution requires it. The States in turn seem to see themselves in conflict and competition with municipalities, and resist power sharing even where the central government supposedly requires them to do so.

Two forms of local government have been mandated by the Constitution. Amendment 73 deals with rural governments, and Amendment 74 spells out the ground rules for urban governments. But note that 43 years passed between Independence and these amendments because politicians at the center never saw any compelling reason to let go of power. But the explosive growth of cities and their growing problems are now compelling reasons to strengthen and support cities rather than inhibit them. Urban growth is often disastrous. India now has more than 40 cities over one million in population, and six are over 5 million (Mumbai, 16 million; Kolkata, 13.2 million; New Delhi, 12.8 million; Chennai, 6.4 million; Bangalore, 5.7 million), and all suffer from high levels of slum living, poverty, filth, disease, and a scandalous shortage of even the most basic living facilities. Almost every Indian city suffers from the same problems, and the great fear is that urban life which is vital to the future of India, may be gaining a new middle class, but for most residents, life is getting worse rather than better.]11]

Another of Nehru's negative legacies was the long term indifference to, and lack of concern about public infrastructure. Its decline through old age and neglect continues to be a national crisis, and it has inhibited growth and economic development for both companies and communities. Even where the Indian government did undertake public projects, they often proved incapable of effective implementation and often produced little real results, as work petered out and money simply evaporated through graft, misallocation and monumental incompetence. The supposedly highly regarded Indian Administrative Service (IAS) is great at making plans and formulating policy, but seems incapable of any level of managerial effectiveness, nor did SOEs appear much better. In the implementation of infrastructure plans for example, a muddled bureaucracy seemed not to understand the need for fair and open competition among bidders for public contracts, and instead awarded them to favored SOEs or to friends, relations or simply those offering the largest bribes. A whole cottage industry of brokers, middle men, fixers and political influence peddlers grew up and flourished. Worthy projects were initiated, only to face serial bureaucratic delays in the application for an endless number of approvals, certifications, authorizations, clearances, inspections, modifications, amendments and technical questions. As with the Chinese bureaucracy, there were endless requirements to advance administrative actions up to higher levels in the chain of authority, where often the same application, containing the same material had to be re-submitted all over again, only to face the same questions that had already been answered at the lower level. Often, the result of such "vertical administration" delays was that projects often lost their support and their funding and just withered and died.

In many areas, the government created official purchasing organizations which had monopoly authority to buy and dispose of agricultural products, energy supplies, and manufactured goods. This gave the government the ability to dictate prices and often also the quality and quantity of the goods produced. As with the Soviets and the Chinese, this control was used for various political purposes. The profit margins of most producers were kept razor thin to allow the government to subsidize other more favored elements of the economy, favor some geographical areas and penalize others, or to favor SOEs over non-state private sector competitors. Domestic producers were always favored over foreign sources.

In a similar manner, the nationalization of the banking system by Indira Gandhi in 1969 gave the government a very disturbing degree of control over who could borrow money, and how much, for what purposes, and at what rates of interest. As always in India, the exercise of price controls and purchasing power were accompanied by the unsavory exercise of special interest politics, political and personal, preferment, and a lot of good old fashioned corruption.

The centrist state socialist economic system described above proved to have serious limitations. No matter how hard it tried, government could never produce an economic structure that met the needs of the whole nation. SOEs produced a reasonably stable manufacturing sector, but despite import substitution, enormous state subsidies, preferential bank loans and unfailing political support, SOEs in were able to provide reasonable employment and benefits for only about 20% of the workforce. And since socialist theology demanded the neglect of private enterprise, this sector did not begin to expand until well into the 90s. Huge populations were terribly under employed and lived in abject poverty on farms, in villages, in vast urban slums, in the informal economy, or as casual and intermittent labor. In the last analysis, Socialism failed to generate many jobs, just as it had failed in China and earlier, in the USSR. In the new India, the bottom up and consumer oriented economy has become the big job generator.

To be more explicit: the commitment to the centrally controlled economy, deployed through SOEs and supporting politics was mounted at great cost to 80% of the workforce, who got little or nothing from the government. It is strongly emphasized that this failure was the direct and explicit fault of the government, which did everything they could to conceal the nature of the growing failures, to throw money at hopeless situations, to cling far too long to wrong- headed policies, to back losers and neglect missed opportunities, and to neglect their citizens in almost every vital way. In China, subsidies to SOEs cost the government more than 50 billion Yuan each year. And the trend away from SOEs is world-wide: around the world, since 1980, more than 80 countries have launched ambitious efforts to divest themselves of most of their SOEs.

ENVIRONMENTAL THREATS

Neither Nehru nor Mao paid anything more than lip service to environmental problems and threats, and in China especially, Mao pursued a whole series of policies disastrous for the environment, and their problems are now the worst in the world. India is home to many of the world's most polluted cities. The air in Mumbai or Kolkata or New Delhi is all but unbreathable especially in winter when exhaust fumes, unchecked industrial emissions, and smoke from countless charcoal braziers in the street rise and are trapped by descending mist and fog. Thus, respiratory diseases are rife in India. Factories belch noxious black clouds; effluents pour untreated into rivers; sewage systems reek and overflow. Deforestation, over- cultivation, and excessive use of chemicals take their own environmental toll in rural India. Environmental consciousness remains very low. [12] Even when governments get around to passing regulations, they are largely ignored. And the whole pattern of the emerging problems of a new economy seen in China is repeated in India. Billions of dollars each year, amounting to more than 4.5% of GDP, are incurred in health costs because of air and water pollution. Yet green politicians still try to use environmental threats for political leverage. Welcome to environmentalism Indian style.

India, with about 1.2 billion people continues to justify much of its official policy on food self sufficiency. But tragically – and typically – this obsolete fear has driven the government into a whole series of wrong and dysfunctional policies affecting its agricultural and village world, and leading to the worst ecological consequences: degradation of agricultural land, over usage of fertilizers, pesticides, and insecticides, overgrazing, deforestation, squandering of precious water, give away electric power leading to more coal driven power plants – all at huge public cost while actually reducing rather than increasing the ability of the country to feed itself.

In fact, it is perhaps the most compelling irony that, in both China and India, economic expansion is absolutely vital, and India has finally joined China in recognizing that fact and abandoning the old socialist past as rapidly as possible. But the financial demands of economic development leave little money for curing the problems of the environment and natural resources, all of which are being made worse by the burgeoning economies. In both countries, this inherent conflict will play out for several more decades.

But for a long time, the response of the Indian government to environmental concerns was hypocritical and rather foolish. The government found it convenient to assert that environmental issues were a Western problem, especially relating to global warming, and that India was a victim rather than a perpetrator, and some extreme opinions were that the whole thing was somehow a Western, mostly European, plot against India. The Kyoto treaty was rejected, and it was thought that the 2% reduction target by the end of the century was pointless. Official Indian thought has been slowly changing, but as usual, change in official utterances is not the same as action. India's leaders see the current world pressures as coming at a very bad time for India, just when their new economic policies are paying off. But they concede that economic development is in fact making many environmental problems even worse. In reality, the effects of environmental neglect are so serious and obvious that even the government can now see them, usually through heavy banks of polluted air. What has been hypocritical has been the cheap skate policies of financial neglect, and the assignment of responsibility for environmental concerns to local governments ill prepared to deal with them. There is a growing recognition that past neglect now means that India lacks the political will, the money, and the managerial competence to deal with any of its environmental problems. Nor can it stop or mitigate industrial growth and heavy urbanization.

India enacted the National Climate Action Plan in 2008. The real issue is whether this is another example of mere rhetoric, or whether something – anything -- will actually be done. The plan would require really drastic action and a lot of trauma, political and otherwise, and environmental regulations are hard to enforce when a very large proportion of economic activities are very small and concealed in the secretive informal economy. Illiteracy remains high, bureaucratic process is muddled, and most people do not trust the government to begin with. How do you enforce anything in such a situation?

China has 85 million enterprises of all kinds; India is not far behind. The difference is that China is run from the top down and has heavy forces to enforce its will; India is bottom up and light on enforcement capabilities, much less the skill or political will to do anything unpopular. In both countries, SOEs are notoriously exempted from most government regulations. Environmental impact statements in both countries are a joke, and are generally ignored.

Most areas of India centralize all water functions at the State level, where they are further centralized into a single ministry: policy, regulation, financing, construction and maintenance, and service delivery. "Within the work culture of the Indian bureaucracy, this bundling virtually guarantees poor performance." Indian performance is said to compare poorly even with other Asian developing nations. Often when a pipe is damaged, whole neighborhoods are without water for weeks. Economists strongly urge the unbundling of these functions and more competition from the private sector. They also urge greater delegation of financial authority from the State to local communities. Many customers would pay for better service than hand pumps or communal pumps, but the socialist bureaucracy won't let them! Regulation should be independent and should be as free as possible from traditional political corruption and pressuring. There is apparently a substantial history to show that heavy subsidizing of water supplies is not necessary and simply leads to a lot of water wastage.

REFORM OF THE INDIAN CIVIL SERVICE

As with Mao and China, India had to wait for the death of Indira Gandhi to begin the belated and confused processes of economic reform. In 1975, Indira Gandhi had declared a formal State of Emergency which lasted for almost 2 years. She and her son Rajiv used this augmented authority to disrupt the top civil service – mostly through suspensions, retrenchments, early retirements and reassignments. In many situations, there was little public sympathy because of the arrogant and self-serving nature of the bureaucracy. There are many analysts who feel that retrenchment at all levels of the service is well warranted and desirable. A law has been passed to fix minimum job tenure in a given position to two years, but it is largely ignored in many places. There is also the strong feeling that the whole pay structure is obsolete and dysfunctional – some officials are paid too little, but many more are paid too much. A pay commission set of recommendations in 2008 proposed increases of about 28%, with more money at the top and the bottom, and little for the middle range of jobs. There is the usual blather about "pay for performance".

The Constitution written after Independence replaced the colonial Indian Civil Service with the Indian Administrative Service, but it is still a small elite of senior officials – about 5,000 out of a total of more than 17 million central government employees. This is a very structured and controlled body of officials: selected after a rigorous series of tests; trained in one central academy in Mussoorie, put through a program of probation/apprenticeship, and a series of increasingly more responsible junior positions. The IAS is one of three services. The others are the Indian Police Service and the Indian Forest Service, and then there are many separate organizations such as the Postal Service and the Indian National Railways.

Until very recently, the IAS has been characterized as a small elite drawn from the upper castes and the more affluent families. The changing politics of India created a spirit of reform, which set aside a certain number of positions for the Scheduled Castes, the Scheduled Tribes, and separately for women. Increasingly, the implementation of these laws has led to some substantial increases in the diversity of the government workforce. But it is still dominated by a somewhat arrogant elite. States have their own services under the professional leadership of a State Public Service Commission. However, many of the top people in these State services are cadres drawn from the central government IAS, and there is a lot of sympathy for running three levels of more clearly separate public services: national, state and local/municipal.

In India, the Indian Administrative Service has descended into lower levels of value and respect, and the reasons are very important. First and foremost, under Nehru, the government ran the country, and every ministry exerted extraordinary power over their sector of the economy. The arrogance that this bred was complete and unshakable. The IAS became the career of choice for the brightest and the best, but it was also the stalwart perpetuator of the undemocratic caste and class distinctions that have torn Indian society apart for centuries. But as the politics of India have changed, this arrogance became unacceptable and it tarnished the reputation of government officialdom.

Then, starting in the early 1990s, the very nature of the government's role began to change. The government was forced to abandon or mitigate the heavy handed centrist control over the economy, and with it, huge portions of the power wielded by the IAS. The private sector, released from the oppressive controls of the License Raj, surged forward, and for the first time since Independence, had the leverage to ignore, fend off, or out-maneuver their government overseers. Soon, the "brightest and best" of the young graduates began ignoring the government as a career choice in favor of many new and attractive jobs developing in the private sector, and many government enterprises, including SOEs and government controlled banks began to shrivel and decline. The prestige of the IAS has declined. Also, the IAS has long suffered from the widely held public opinion that they are unresponsive to public needs, and that they have allowed government to be widely corrupt. Recently, Transparency International's Corruption Perception Index ranked the Indian government 85th in a listing of 128 governments.

In fact, the tides running in India today are truly remarkable, and they all reflect the repudiation of the dominant role of the government(s) in the country. The long term abject failure of the government to provide adequate social services for the people has gradually led them to abandon the hope of service from the government, and has led communities to the realization that the government is hopeless and they must provide for themselves in every community from small villages to high rise urban apartments. As cities become more crowded, almost inevitably public services have fallen farther behind the demands placed on them. The urban rich now protect their homes in gated communities with private security guards, their own water, electricity and sewer systems, trash collection and transportation. And like the slum dwellers that surround them, they hold public schools in contempt and send their children to private schools, and guard their health in private hospitals. To quote Mishra, "Most middle class people, looking at political races, are worried more about the uncollected garbage on the streets, the lack of drainage, the pot-holed roads, the power and water breakdowns. They talk about growing corruption and crime in the city, about the recent murder of a young female doctor, the rise of mafia dons, the deteriorating environment outside their homes, and the general atmosphere of insecurity." [13]

The government is now moving toward more useful forms of partnership with the private sector. But where would the private sector be willing to invest in public/private sector joint ventures? Certainly, it will do so in the arena of public infrastructure either as contractors or in some form of joint venture such as build/operate/sell programs. Such infrastructure projects could include airports, airlines, other transportation capabilities such as ports, shipping, toll roads; energy development and distribution, fuels, communications, housing, and such government needs as office buildings or warehouses or military support facilities. In services sectors of the economy, the private sector is already active in medical/health care facilities, health insurance, pension systems, both elementary and higher education, adult training, facilities management, and entertainment.

The costs of the Indian civil service are considered very high by international standards – 18% of the government's general budget, plus another 6% for pensions. Many elements of the public service are notorious for absenteeism, lateness, and lax performance. It is widely felt, even by many in government that the staffs of agencies are vastly over blown and a major downsizing would be perfectly feasible and warranted if the politics could be solved. Many elements of the civil service – again see education and health care -- have very powerful unions that oppose any form of rationalization or modernization. People see that pensions for civil servants are far too generous, and meanwhile, retirement insurance for the rest of the country is virtually nonexistent.

NEGLECT OF PUBLIC INFRASTRUCTURE

States and local governments share responsibility for provision of public infrastructure, but few have managed to find either the money or the professional staff and organizations needed to develop and sustain infrastructure systems. As a consequence, most jurisdictions, both rural and urban, are decades behind their needs, and cities can only get worse with the great influx of new residents.

India's roads, ports, railroads, airports and trucking facilities are all operating at over capacity; most are run down and near failure. India's road network has more than two million miles – the world's second biggest. But only 5,000 miles are dual highways, compared to about 32,800 miles in China. The average speed of traffic in Delhi is just over 6 miles per hour.

Some miraculous change of fortune will be required to bring these facilities up to an adequate level of capability, and few believe in miracles.

Power shortages are now endemic. Peak demand last year outstripped supply by more than 15%, and growth is about to make this into a genuine crisis. This is a big problem for industry, but 600 million individual Indian homes have no electrical power connection at all.

Largely as a consequence of all kinds of political intervention, there is a growing gap between the cost of power and charges to users. This gap has been covered by subsidy, but losses are now less covered by budget subsidy and more by borrowing, with ominous long term financial implications. The power sector is seen as plagued by inefficient operations, underinvestment, technical inadequacies, and the theft of power. Among customers, farmers and many urban households enjoy the biggest subsidies. Households pay about 60% of actual costs, and farmers only about 10%. Furthermore, lacking reliable population estimates or metering in many places, the power companies have been accused of "inventing" rural customers to justify government subsidy payments.

Even when the Indian government undertakes a program, few expect it to succeed. When the National Rural Employment Guarantee Act (NREGA) was initiated in 2005, most praised its intent as a means to reduce rural poverty. The act guarantees 100 days of employment a year for at least one member of any rural family who is willing to perform usually unskilled labor for a minimum wage. It also supposedly committed the government to a program of "rural development" although what that meant was never very clear beyond the usual promises of better education and health care. Critics however suggest that this is Indian politics as usual; the act is more about currying favor in rural areas for the Congress Party which saw itself losing out to local political interests.

But the results to date are very frustrating. It is not clear how much help has actually reached the poor. In some States, only about half of the people performing the work were rated as "poor", and women, who had been one of the main hopeful targets, have not participated nearly enough.

It also appeared that too little work was actually offered – or accepted – because the majority of workers worked less than 30 days. Of even greater concern has been the persistent perception that much of the work has gone to the "non- poor" because they offered bribes to officials. Meanwhile, questions have been raised over whether many of the projects financed by NREGA contributed at all to rural development. Field investigations revealed hardly any activity in many locations. Roads have been built that have no chance of surviving the rains, and there has been spending on non-existent projects. Many wells in rural areas have been "dug" time and time again, but still do not exist.

THE REFORM OF INDIA'S FINANCES: BACK FROM THE BRINK

India, even while expanding its economy remains a poor country when its income is cast against its huge human demands. Revenues will always be far too small, and this fact should drive the whole issue of how the government manages its finances, both income and expenditure. The expansion and enrichment of the economy is providing the government with more revenue, and this permits it to make some important decisions about how to capture it and how to spend it.

To begin with, the government must first get its hands on the added revenue through changes in how it handles its tax system, and the collection of other revenues. That is the first urgent reform. In some jurisdictions, only about 10% of the population pays income taxes. Then, these skimpy revenues must be used to better target public budgets which, in India, are very much a process of the allocation of scarcity. There are two philosophies for the allocation of funds in a government budget – the rational and the "political". Right now, the Indian government rejects the rational and favors the political, and the second great reform would involve a reversal of these preferences. This means first that governments at all levels will need to make major changes in the policies that drive their budget allocation decisions in ways that mitigate many current budget costs that are wasteful, ineffective, or simply stupid. If this can be done, then even without increasing taxes, the public budget can be allocated instead to a whole new range of vital priorities that the government now deliberately and shamefully neglects. For India now, the problem is not so much one of deficit, but one of finding the courage to set rational priorities.

As discussed later, the tax system is a vast, complex and utterly chaotic cauldron of political warfare, special interest pressuring, bureaucratic aggrandizement, and government yearnings and frustrations. Important potential revenues escape taxation. Other taxes are fumbled and usurped. Much is never even collected because the system is so incompetent. Tax avoidance is a widely admired and practiced skill, and huge sums owed the government are simply dodged. Other income is just plain stolen. Obviously, such a tax system is a disgrace for any government. India's is worse than most and urgently needs major reform. But the cause of this catastrophe has been pitiful, bumbling, craven and incorrigible politics, and the way out of the mess would be to find intelligent, courageous politics, and it is almost impossible to find anybody in India or elsewhere who believes that such a miracle can ever happen.

The political system seems almost deliberately designed to be fatally vulnerable to special interest penetration. Even when the Congress Party ruled supreme, its policies of import substitution, import and export controls, price fixing, and its highly dependent SOEs created thousands of enterprises and interests which could be enriched or harmed by the actions of some government official. For almost 40 years, SOEs maneuvered successfully to extract the maximum subsidy from a government deeply committed not only to their protection but to concealment of their vast inefficiencies. Even true private companies could so successfully play the subsidy game that they found it more profitable to support the government's distortions than to sharpen their competitive abilities. Huge sums in the budget, more or less concealed, were expended with little clear evidence that they had achieved any discernable purpose other than to enrich the recipients.

A second budget burden over almost 60 years has been one that should, theoretically never have happened. It is really impossible to calculate the money spent, and the money wasted, on the operations of India's state owned enterprises. Each enterprise of course has its own budget and business plan, both exhaustively reviewed and approved by some supervising government ministry. But every element of these budgets may conceal some financial maneuver. For example, a manufacturing enterprise must purchase electric power, but that power will come from a power utility which is also a state owned enterprise. If the manufacturing enterprise is losing money, the government may decide to reduce its costs by instructing the power utility to sell it power at a substantially reduced price, or even at a loss. The same pattern might be enforced for supplies and materials, and for transport. Local governments may be pressured to lighten the tax burden of the favored SOE. Banks, which have long been nationalized, may be "encouraged" to lend money at subsidy rates, or to forgive loans. Prices for the sale of the enterprise goods and services may be fixed at excessive levels, so that the public itself is forced to pay some part of the SOE's inefficiencies. Consumers may also be denied the potentially lower costs or greater values of foreign goods and services they will never be allowed to buy.

Finally, even where the government does attempt to collect taxes and fees, it has a horrendous reputation for incompetence in collection. Tax avoidance is outrageous – ubiquitous, bold, blatant and highly successful – so successful that it there is widespread speculation that the political leadership is not unhappy when friends and supporters escape the net. And of course there is always the time honored recourse of bribing the tax and customs collectors.

India's farms and villages remain the bedrock of Indian life, and 70% of India's population lives in rural areas, compared to 8-10% in Japan or the United States. The real policy for agriculture was not stimulation of higher productivity or crop prices, but huge subsidy programs, and farmers have always been virtually free of formal taxes. There is a big subsidy for fertilizers, and an even bigger one for food distribution. Other subsidies are for LPG (cooking gas), kerosene for heating, cheap power, irrigation and housing. There is even a substantial "Food for Work" program.

In a sense, it is difficult to argue that spending money to help Indian poor is a bad thing. These subsidies demand billions of rupees each year, and are apparently forever. Especially under Indira Gandhi, they expanded, and then of course, they began to have a life of their own, and no politician had the guts to suggest any retrenchments. As a consequence, they are one of the major contributors to the high cost of government, and the intractable deficits of local governments. Local taxes are equally rigid; the poor have no money to pay taxes, and the new middle class has begun to have the political clout to oppose tax increases. However, these subsidies are widely seen as populist giveaways to buy political support, and while they clearly help people in the short term, their long term economic viability is in widely questioned. There are strong views that the better policy would be to put much of this money into programs to expand and enrich the economy, especially in the form of more powerful and coherent rural development programs.

If these perverse budget outpourings could be done away with or substantially mitigated, the budget could be stabilized and the government could finally free up some funds for higher and better purposes, most of which have been deliberately and horribly neglected in the name of economic development. India has never developed any national program of adequate social services. Health care reaches less than 20% of the population, and rural villages and urban slums can never afford any health care at all, much less any form of health insurance to pay for it. Elementary education is a national scandal. Few outside of government bureaucracies and SOEs can expect any form of old age assistance.

Another gap in government budgets has been public infrastructure – schools, hospitals, low cost housing, roads, bridges, airports, railways, sewage and water treatment facilities and almost everything else. Those facilities that exist are usually obsolete, overwhelmed and deteriorating for lack of maintenance and repair.

Another victim of deliberate government neglect has been India's natural resources and its environment. India is home to many of the world's most polluted cities. Environmental consciousness remains very low. Even when governments get around to passing regulations, they are largely ignored. And the whole pattern of the emerging problems of a new economy as seen in China are repeated in India. Billions of dollars each year are incurred in health costs because of air and water pollution, amounting to more than 4.5% of GDP.

Thus, almost every element of both national and state budgets show major and intractable problems. Each seems to require some form of miraculous political reformation, or some enormous injections of new funds – neither of which is likely to happen. In reality, budgets are full of ominous catastrophes seemingly about to happen. There are a series of staggering unmet obligations, unfunded mandates, unfulfilled promises, looming contingent liabilities and carefully concealed failures: a virtual shopping mall for corruption, waste and abuse of responsibility. In both India and China, the delegation of responsibilities to state/provinces and municipalities has not meant the creation of independent and counter-balancing authority, but rather the shifting of very expensive programs which the central government wants to abdicate. In India, like China, the government has all too often been guilty of approving expensive programs or projects in the budget without any real understanding of the problem they are supposed to solve, or what good they will do. In China, the Mao regime all but destroyed the capacity of local governments to make such needs assessments, or to do anything about massive waste and misallocation of funds ordered by the central government. It is hoped that, over time, the capacity in both governments to make better allocations of scarce funds will be possible.

THE INDIAN GOVERNMENT AND MONEY CONTROL

Many politicians do not believe the common sense view that "less debt is preferable to more debt." In India, the political urge toward populism and special interest politics causes them to push the budget and fiscal policy into deficit and debt. The Indian government now borrows 34% of its operating budget, and huge cost. This in turn creates a whole series of intractable problems which the politicians are not capable of handling. Most of the actors in government financial matters are playing for more resources, and there is little "market" for fiscal prudence. As a consequence, the deficit is now approaching 12% of GDP and 80% of growth is based on deficit government spending. In most cases, the budget is an "electoral" budget which drives the system to excess. As usual, inflation erodes the real impact of current debt. India needs balanced budget rules, deficit and debt ceilings, careful definitions of fiscal and monetary authority, especially at State and local government levels, transparency, and more understandable public explanations of financial matters.

An attempt was made to achieve some of this financial discipline with the passage of The Financial Reform and Budget Management Act of 2003 (FRPM) which mandates medium term targets for the size and deficit potential of the public budget, and the elimination of the current budget deficit by 2008 (not achieved). It does not deal with capital investments or the budgets of local governments. One of Indian government desires is the passage of such an act for each of the 28 States and 7 Union territories. Technically, it requires the Parliament to take whatever corrective laws are required during the budget season to meet the targets. The FRPM Act mandates greater budget transparency, but it provides no special enforcement powers, and as ever, the government muddles through by making neat but unreal budget assumptions and then providing long explanations after the fact as to why the targets could not possibly have been met. Or the Parliament can simply change the targets, and in the end, they can simply be ignored.

Government financial affairs always seem to center around the classic conflict: as States are given more power to control their own finances, the macro economists assert that they are out of control (i.e. "non cooperative sub national behavior"!), but the local governments enjoy their freedom from central government control, meddling and interference. Naturally, local governments want more money, but the central government is craftily avoiding just that. The States suffer from endless examples of unfunded mandates, and their revenue raising powers have never come close to the ability to finance even their formally defined obligations. The central government knows this perfectly well, and it is still reluctant to grant States more taxing power, and in fact, the centrist macroeconomists also argue for mandated limits on local government borrowing, which is the other main option to taxation as a means for local governments to get money.

Still, banks are required by law to hold State paper, and The National Small Savings Fund, a central government entity, is required to invest 100% of its net collections in State paper, and thus, it finances almost half of the State deficits. States also use various forms of SOEs such as power companies or transportation authorities as secondary borrowers, and much of this debt (as well as income) is off budget. In addition, the Finance Commission at the central government level has repeatedly bailed out States through loan buyback schemes and debt restructuring. Under the tax sharing system, 60% of central government tax revenues are shared, as are about 30% of the State generated tax revenues. In addition to shared taxes, the States benefit from a series of central government categorical grants, but they are rare, small, spastic, and often earmarked.

No Indian government is very good at generating revenue or cutting budget items. If any reductions are possible, the resulting savings are immediately re-spent, usually as capital investment projects. Heller and Rao argue for an "independent score keeper" organization to perform a combination of budget preparation, budget oversight, results evaluation and auditing to see to it that targets are met, and to provide a politics-free evaluation of the effectiveness of budgets. In effect, such a body would be a substitute for, and a counter force to, cowardly inefficient politics. **[15]**

Indian politics in the last 30 years has been based on the polarization of differences – of caste, religion, geography, economic status and anything else that can be used to push people into voting blocs. This divisiveness has succeeded so well that it represents a threat to rational political representation. Politicians do not really represent these group divisions, they merely mine them for votes.

This divisiveness has been created on the top of other strong national tides running in the country – nationalism, elitism, a yearning to escape poverty and helplessness, the desires for education and self improvement, and an overwhelming need for work and for stability. Indians seem able to cope with a democracy which is genuine but bizarre, wasteful and corrupt, but there is a constant and growing sense of outrage that this democracy seems doomed not only to be universally corrupt, but also unbelievable bumbling and incompetent. Brilliant policies and plans are endlessly announced only to be dissipated by astonishing ineptitude. Politicians seem totally preoccupied with slitting each others throats, and almost nobody seems interested in governing the country. This divisiveness has the secondary effect of damaging or destroying many of the old social balances of community and kinship that allowed people to live together for hundreds of years.

Two other tides are critical, but have not yet fully matured. The first is the serious (but ineffective) changed government policies with respect to the so-called Untouchables (dalits) in society. The Constitution has been amended to forbid any inequitable policies or actions against them, and in fact, new policies reserve certain advantages for them such as preferential hiring, education or land holding.

The second tide running is the creation of a new and far larger middle class, now estimated to exceed 200 million out of a total population of 1.2 billion. This is not the achievement of the government but of the private sector in India, often buttressed by foreign direct investment in the Indian economy. This new middle class possesses important new political power, but it is not yet realized and directed. When it is, it is not clear how it will relate to the power of the old elites.

APPENDIX A: MINISTRIES OF THE CENTRAL (UNION) GOVERNMENT

- Human Resource Development
- Information and Broadcasting
- Labour and Employment
- Law and Justice
- Mines
- Non-conventional Energy Sources
- Overseas Indian Affairs
- Panchayati (local council) Raj
- Parliamentary Affairs

- Personnel, Public Grievances and Pensions
- Petroleum and Natural Gas
- Power
- Railways
- Rural Development
- Agriculture
- Agriculture and Rural Industries
- Chemicals and Fertilizers
- Civil Aviation
- Coal
- Commerce and Industry
- Communications and Information Technology
- Company Affairs
- Consumer Affairs, Food, and Public Distribution
- Culture
- Defense
- Development of the North Eastern Region
- Environment and Forests
- External Affairs
- Finance
- Food Processing Industries
- Health and Family Welfare
- Heavy Industries and Public Enterprises
- Home Affairs
- Science and Technology
- Shipping, Road Transport and Highways
- Small Scale Industries
- Social Justice and Empowerment
- Statistics and Program Implementation
- Steel
- Textiles
- Tourism
- Tribal Affairs
- Urban Development, Employment and Poverty Alleviation
- Water Resources
- Youth Affairs and Sports CENTRAL AGENCIES

- Central Bureau of Investigation
- Central Vigilance Commission
- Comptroller and Auditor General of India
- Election Commission of India
- National Commission for Women
- National Commission on Population
- National Human Rights Commission
- Planning Commission
- Telecom Regulatory Authority of India
- Union Public Service Commission
- Department of Atomic Energy
- Department of Ocean Development
- Department of Space

APPENDIX B: INDIAN STATES AND UNION TERRITORIES

1. Andaman and Nicobar (UT)
2. Andhra Pradesh
3. Arunachal Pradesh
4. Assam
5. Bihar
6. Chandigarth (UT)
7. Chhattisgarh
8. Dadra and Nagar Haveli (UT)
9. Daman and Diu (UT)
10. Delhi (UT)
11. Goa
12. Gujarat
13. Haryana
14. Himachal Pradesh
15. Jammu and Kashmir
16. Jharkhand
17. Karnataka
18. Kerala
19. Lakshadweep (UT)

20. Madhya Pradesh
21. Maharashtra
22. Manipur
23. Meghalaya
24. Mizoram
25. Nagaland

APPENDIX C: A LISTING OF SOME OF ITS PRINCIPAL SOES:

- Air India
- Bharat Coking Coal Ltd.
- Bharat Dynamics Ltd.
- Bharat Elecronics Ltd.
- Bharat Earth Movers Ltd.
- Bharat Petroleum Corp.
- Bharat Heavy Electricals Ltd.
- Bharat Heavy Plate and Vessels Ltd.
- Biotech Consortium of India
- Broadcasting Corporation of India
- Broadcasting Engineering Consultants of India
- Cement Corporation of India
- Central Coalfields
- Central Electricity Authority
- Central Water Commission
- Chennai Petroleum Corp.
- Coal India Ltd.
- Commercial banks, most
- Computer Maintenance Corp.
- Container Corporation of India
- Cotton Corporation of India Ltd.
- Damodar Valley Corp.
- Dredging Corporation of India
- Electronic Corporation of India
- Engineering Projects (India) Ltd.
- Engineers India Ltd.
- Fertilizers and Chemicals Travancore Ltd.

- Ferro Scrap Ltd.
- Food Corporation of India
- Gas Authority of India Ltd.
- Goa Shipyard Ltd.
- Handicrafts and Handlooms Export Corp.
- Heavy Engineering Corp.
- Hindustan Aeronautics Ltd.
- Hindustan Copper Ltd.
- Hindustan Newsprint Ltd.
- Hindustan Organic Chemicals Ltd.
- Hindustan Paper Corp.
- Hindustan Petroleum Corp.
- Hindustan Zinc Ltd.
- Hospital Services Consultancy Corp.
- HTL Ltd.
- IBP Co. Ltd.
- Indian Airlines
- Indian Iron and Steel Co.
- Indian Investment Centre
- Indian Rare Earths Ltd.
- Indian Renewable Energy Development Agency
- Indian Telephone Industries
- Instrumentation Ltd., Palakkad
- Instrumentation Ltd., Kota
- Insurance, general
- IRCON International
- Kochi Refineries Ltd.
- Konkan Railway Corp
- Kudremukh Iron Ore Co.
- Life Insurance Corp. (LIC) of India
- LIC Housing Finance Ltd.
- Madras Fertilizers Ltd.
- Mahanadi Telephone Nigam Ltd.
- Maruthi Udyog Ltd.
- Goa Shipyard Ltd.
- Mineral Exploration Corp.

- MSTC Ltd.
- MMTC Ltd.
- National Aluminium Co. Ltd.
- National Bank of Agriculture and Rural Development
- National Book Trust of India
- National Buildings Construction Corp.
- National Centre for Software Technology
- National Fertilizers Ltd.
- National Insurance Co.
- National Seeds Corp. Ltd.
- National Textile Corp. Ltd.
- National Thermal Power Corp. Ltd.
- National Water Development Agency
- Northern Coalfields Ltd.
- Nuclear Power Corporation of India
- Oil and Natural Gas Corp.
- Oil India Ltd.
- Paradeep Phosphate Ltd.
- Pawan Hans Helicopters Ltd.
- Power Finance Corp.
- Pyrites, Phosphates and Chemical Ltd.
- Rail India Technical and Economic Services
- Reserve Bank of India
- Rural Electrification Corp. Ltd.
- Semiconductor Complex Ltd.
- Shipping Corp of India
- Singareni Collieries Co. Ltd.
- South Eastern Coalfields Ltd.
- Sponge Iron India Ltd.
- Steel Authority of India Ltd.
- Tehri Hydro Development Corp.
- Uranium Corp. of India
- Vizag Steel Plant
- Western Coalfields Ltd. [6]

CHAPTER II

China: Government from the Top Down

THE CHINESE GOVERNMENT STRUCTURE IS surely one of the most complicated of any government in the world, and one of the most authoritarian. It was allowed under Mao to burgeon out of control for decades, and it was used to promulgate communist theology, exert centrist control, enforce all kinds of extraordinary policies, provide employment for millions of Party members and faithful hangers-on, and only secondarily to deliver wholly inadequate public programs. The Chinese Communist Party (CCP) maintains a whole separate government-wide top to bottom structure of offices independent from the official bureaucracy and vested with almost total control over the bureaucracy at all levels down to villages. At the center is the National People's Congress (NPC), with its executive authority vested in a powerful Central Committee. The NPC elects China's President who in turn appoints the Premier, and these two head an elite and all powerful State Council.

Then there are the official ministries – currently 20 of them – which view themselves as "in charge" of their sectors of the economy and society. Most ministries then supervise a complex substructure of State Owned Enterprises (SOE) plus what are generally called Public Service Units (PSU) which are a large range of enterprises serving public purposes such as technical schools, hospitals, engineering organizations and many others. This array of institutions established at the national government level is usually repeated down through a hierarchy of provinces, counties, townships, municipalities and villages, with each lower level accountable to the one above it.

General reform of the economy of the People's Republic of China began in the mid 1980s as a reluctant retreat from the old style command and control economy toward a market based economy. Reform was driven by the growing recognition that state socialist economic policy was a failed experience, and would never produce the high levels of economic growth and development that would even keep up with population growth, much less permit any extensive improvement in China's economic strength or citizen quality of life. Inherent in the centrist state system was the widespread use of State Owned Enterprises (SOEs) which were instruments of the government, but supposedly free to function much like independent organizations capable of operating profitably in the realistic world. But SOEs as in India had proved failed experiences. Instead of generating revenue for government use, most had proved inefficient, and many operated at deficits that had to be underwritten by the government, using funds that could be better utilized elsewhere. SOEs carried larger overhead costs because they provided many social services to their employees such as housing, health care, pensions and elementary/secondary education, and these direct costs drained much of their profitability.

The collapse of the Soviet Union, largely through the failures of its command and control economy badly shook Chinese leadership, and helped the reform minded in the Party to overcome the inertia and resistance of the older leadership. The negotiations of the Chinese government to be accepted into the GATT and the WTO system made it clear that reform was a pre-condition of that acceptance. In addition, many potential foreign investors also made it clear that their willingness to invest in the Chinese economy rested on at least a minimum of reforms that would protect their investment commitments. Deng Xiaoping recognized that there were limits as to how much money could be squeezed out of the peasants, and saw foreign direct investment as a vital "shot in the arm" to precipitate a development surge.

CHINA'S LEGACY OF NEGLECT

In the period from 1985 to 1996, the Party and the central government pressed a process of devolution of power and control over many public programs to the provinces and municipalities but deliberately withheld the funds that would pay for these programs, telling the governors and city councils that they had to find their own sources of funds. They also transferred many of the national SOEs into the hands of provincial governors and municipal and township/county councils in addition to those already held, without the introduction of any real controls. Since these SOEs were often providers of certain social services, their transfer to local governments further expanded their roles. Decentralization ended up making everything worse, and the Chinese government has been forced to play "catch-up" with its own follies. An old guard clung to the view that centrist control should never be relinquished, and even the reformists were uncertain what the disaggregating of power would produce.

The failures of the socialist economy had left a huge population of unemployed and underemployed. There is an estimated 180 million people who cannot find work, or are in the informal economy, or are unauthorized workers in urban areas, or who are in temporary, part time or seasonal jobs who seek more permanent employment. In addition, 10-12% of official workers (20-25 million) are unemployed at any given time. [1] Most social programs are pitifully inadequate. Less than 16% of the rapidly aging population has any form of retirement insurance, and even when available, insurance provides only about 25% of need. Only about 14% have health insurance, and illness or accident can often drive people into bankruptcy. [2] Elementary/secondary education is now more fully available, but it still rests too greatly on heavy fees paid by parents. Most public infrastructure remains seriously inadequate, especially in rural and village areas. Economic development has caused explosive worsening of environmental hazards. China has 16 of the 20 most polluted cities in the world. [3].

There are thousands of areas of very high and often dangerous pollution such as runoffs from industries and irrigated fields, mine sites, burning of coal and wood, and heavy river and underground water pollution. Again, the political leadership faces a dilemma: China uses huge amounts of soft coal that is one of the main polluters of the atmosphere. But if coal use is reduced, the Chinese will have to buy more and more expensive oil and gas in an increasingly competitive world market. The burgeoning population, the demand for better and more varied diets, and the shortage of farm land has ended any hopeful policy of food self sufficiency and made China a large scale food importer.

Local governments face serious gaps in the social services safety net. There has been a necessary shift of social services from the SOEs to local governments. But in health care for example, 86% of care financing is still by the individual, and 56% of total health care costs are patient costs. There is little provision for public health and sanitation (available to less than 44% of the population), clean water is available for only 23% of the people, and the country is highly vulnerable to epidemics. [4] There are now 134 million elderly over 60 in China – the world's largest elderly population. [5]

The cumulative consequences of these long term failures demonstrate with great force the fact that highly centrist and centrally planned and controlled governance simply did not work very well. The CCP is thus being forced to draw back from its control of the economy whether it wants to or not. But the CCP and the central bureaucracies are not decentralizing two other factors of governance: central policy and political control, and central bureaucratic control by more subtle and indirect means. The Party and the government are undertaking more realistic and desirable policy and funding shifts, but while they brag about the 15-20% of the population they benefit, they are still over a billion people whose needs they cannot now conceivably satisfy.

Since about the mid-80s, one of the most significant and persistent patterns of reform has been to "rationalize" this huge, complicated and wasteful institutional architecture, and it is clear that, in structural terms, decentralization is winning out over the older yearning for central control. More than 200 subunits of government have been eliminated in the central ministries alone. The top down grip on even the most routine processes and procedures has been broken, and there is a new willingness to permit decentralization of operations.

In addition, a series of special task forces has been making serious assessments – often for the first time – of bureau operations, and thousands of them have proved to be unauthorized, improper, unneeded, obsolete, harmful, time consuming and thus easily terminated without adverse consequences. This in turn facilitated another major goal of reform: the downsizing of the bureaucracy. There had grown up a huge "redundancy factor" – that is, people on the payroll with no real jobs. Much of this redundancy was politically inspired as a form of patronage and reward for the faithful. By eliminating this redundancy, rationalizing the structure, cleaning up process waste, duplication and overlap of functions, at least 1.8 million people were removed from the roles with little impact on agency performance. **[6]** These reforms were accompanied by fundamental reforms in the major management systems of the government, discussed later in this article. It should also be noted that a similar program of reform was simultaneously carried out in the People's Liberation Army (PLA).

BUDGET AND FINANCE REFORMS

The extraordinary wild, chaotic, misguided and mismanaged governments of China's first 30 years were perfectly reflected in the financial systems that prevailed for the collection, allocation and spending of public money. Any level of government, and indeed many departments and bureaus were essentially free to invent their own sources of revenue and financial controls, and many were bizarre and incompetent. Concepts such as managerial efficiency or delegation of authority were suspect and totally abandoned. Excessive control was exercised under the State Plan, which was both a bureaucratic nightmare and the victim of the classic political motives of under funding, misallocation of funds, and centrist lack of reality. The State Plan was totally misdirected in terms of its long term objectives, and was ineffective in the short term as a budget planning system. By the mid 80s it was clear that it had to be abandoned.

The tax system was also completely chaotic. It overtaxed some elements of society and ignored others. It was underpowered and could not generate adequate total revenues. Neither the tax structure nor the budget allocation policy were capable of shifting revenues from stronger to weaker economic areas. Local governments were kept deprived of real local taxing power and had virtually no discretion over tax bases, rates of taxation or revenue targeting. Nor did governments develop really effective means of collecting taxes, especially from non-government organizations. Local tax rules were easily "interpreted" to favor friends and punish opposition. Few governments had any real capability to estimate revenues accurately and this produced many short-fall panics, chaotic reprogramming from year to year, and a persistent shortage of revenue even for the most critical of public purposes. Local officials were often guilty of inventing illegal taxes along with various fees and licenses to scrape up revenue wherever possible.

While the allocation of scarce resources is always difficult and contentious, it seems clear now that there were serious misallocations at every government level. Public spending was far too low a percentage of GDP. Too much was spent on the military and on the huge greatly overstaffed bureaucracy and Party structure. Even in the 1970's, and continuing until recently, there has been an overwhelming dominance of all forms of economic development, which seemed always to win out over demands for social services and public infrastructure. To its credit, the government is now at last spending much of its new found wealth on public facilities and urban improvement, but threats to the environment have multiplied and became more serious, but are deliberately neglected. Education, health, welfare and retirement benefits still remain seriously inadequate. But one major point must be emphasized. In the eyes of practiced bureaucrats, it seems clear that every single reform activity has been conceived, designed, and implemented in ways that have yielded the greatest power retention by the political leadership. In fact, many reforms have greatly strengthened central power.

REGULATORY REFORM

There has been an upsurge of government regulation – both legitimate and otherwise. The main emphasis has been to create or rewrite a body of regulations that enable the functioning of a market based economy, and facilitates rather than opposes the operation of private enterprises. Another purpose is to abandon pre-approvals of thousands of activities and shift to an "as needed" enforcement after the fact of new and more explicit regulations. But each new arena of regulation (e. g. environmental issues) seems magically to result in more power to the government and the use of regulation as the means to enforce the will of the government. When combined with "vertical administration" it gives each level of government powerful tools to control and interfere with the activities of subordinate governments and all forms of enterprises. Vertical administration means that the lower level of government reports to, and is supervised by the next higher level – villages to townships, townships to counties, counties to provinces, and provinces to the central national government. It all sounds so bureaucratic and innocuous that few recognize its power as a control mechanism. So, the rhetoric promises decentralization, but the reality is sustained control of whatever is critical to the government.

But the Indian approach seems to be inherently superior because it is bottom up instead of top down. Bottom up involves the energy and commitment of millions of people initiating economic activities, risking their own money, and making optimizing choices. China's leaders still think that optimization involves centrist direction and control by a self-chosen elite even when Chinese citizens favor the bottom up world and the resurgence of their ancient mercantile tradition. Chinese leaders fear individual initiative, and they will use every means to control or even prevent it whether it is political or economic development which conflicts with Party policy. They see the economies of the U. S. and Europe as messy, wasteful, duplicative and irrational. Further, their economic policy also requires top down control in order to produce what they regard as optimum results – not for the country but for the government. But in a sense, even where the general policy is to liberalize, this approach is still self limiting – and perhaps self destructive, if private enterprise is really allowed to compete successfully with state owned enterprises. For now, the government of China can and does fend off such competition. It still owns 2-3 thousand SOEs, but this number is deceiving because many SOEs are huge holding companies with hundreds of subsidiaries. The government still owns the commanding heights elements of the economy, including most of the banks. In addition, the government is a significant stockholder in other enterprises, and it does not hesitate to play the 900 pound gorilla.

In addition to such direct control, there are many secondary controls, including heavy government regulation, specific laws (e.g. who can offer stock on the stock exchange), the banking system, the tax/fee structure, and "selective" regulatory rewards and punishments. CCP approval is required for business plans, product line approvals, purchases of equipment or facilities, borrowing plans, and most other elements of SOE business plans. As compensation however, the government continues to have plenty of rewards it can dispense. In addition to the usual subsidies, the government can and does constrain competition, even to the point of creating government monopolies. It appears that, when China goes into the international markets after energy and raw materials, it limits this business activity as much as possible to state owned or controlled enterprises.

STATE OWNED ENTERPRISES: DECLINE AND RECOVERY

The state owned enterprise was almost universally adopted as the critical element of the expansion of state socialist governments that emerged after WW II. But in country after country, the success of the state socialist economic policies proved limited, and a discouraging number of SOEs proved to be failed instruments. But the political leadership that created them felt that it was politically vital to defend and protect them and they could not admit their failures. So governments went to extraordinary lengths to prop them up, subsidize them and conceal their difficulties. In China, at times, more than 50% of their 400,000 SOES were operating at a deficit and had to be subsidized with government funds that were desperately needed for other national priorities. In India, a similar pattern of SOE deficits burdens the government, and in fact the problems of SOEs plague most of the governments around the world that relied most heavily on their use.

Beginning in the early 80s in China and the late 80s in India both governments were finally forced to admit to themselves, that the SOEs system was simply not capable of producing an economy large and effective enough to meet the needs of either country, and both governments were being forced to abandon political philosophies that had been insisted upon with almost religious zeal for decades. The reluctant movement toward a market based economy forced the Chinese to abandon most of its Communist theology.

In theory, SOEs were expected to capture the income value of the economy and make it available to the government for the public good. In fact, governments subsidize SOEs is a whole series of ways: guaranteed loans, subsidized loans, loan forgiveness, special government lending institutions, subsidized resources (i.e. power, fuel, transport, raw materials, etc.), cross subsidization between SOEs, import protection, controlled access to markets, export subsidy, waived profits, monopoly advantage, controlled marketing advantages, preferences for supplies and materials, an overvalued exchange rate, artificially low prices for supplies and artificially high prices for outputs.

In order to protect their status, SOEs have been made virtually risk free: their deficits are covered by the government; their borrowing is virtually guaranteed; SOEs cannot "fail" in the private sector sense, and the government usually takes all of the heat for failure or incompetence. On the other hand, the government also forced many dysfunctions: unmanageable debt-equity ratios, sales at subsidized prices, labor redundancy, forced location of production, the required provision of social services, regulated pricing, excessive wage levels, mandated raw materials prices – in other words, a pattern of political interference in what were supposed to be business-like enterprises. "The empirical record seems to show that managers of public assets doctor their books, hoard goods, evade taxes, hide profits, and collude with other enterprises to delude or defraud the government. "They are poorly monitored, notoriously overstaffed, riddled with corruption, a big part of the patronage machine, chronic loss-makers, and financially sick in that their debt are often in excess of their real net worth." [7] In China and elsewhere around the world, SOEs relying on heavy duty political protection have turned arrogant and established an extraordinarily bad management reputation.

The whole SOE course of action often flies directly in the face of commonly understood concepts of industrial effectiveness. For example, monopolies in the hands of private entrepreneurs are seen as exploitive and overly powerful. Yet both the Indian and Chinese governments created

public monopolies which deliberately violate market control mechanisms. But they are defended because it is predicated that these enterprises will be supervised, audited and inspected by bureaucrats who will protect the public interest. The truth seems to be that, even in the best of circumstances, the overseers are not sufficiently trained or experienced, they tend to be underpaid and under motivated, they cannot sustain effective oversight over long periods of time, and they often are wrong in their strategies.

In both countries, their governments undertook a program for the reform of SOEs that was not just privatization but a far more complex program which the Chinese call <u>divestiture.</u> Under this concept, the government has a number of options from which it can choose:

1. It can convert SOEs into private corporations, with a corporate charter and a board of directors, and cut it loose from the government.

2. It can eliminate SOES through a process of consolidation and combination. The resulting enterprise can then either be retained or privatized. Many such combinations created single SOEs which were in fact huge holding companies with large numbers of subsidiaries. This made the numbers of retained SOES seem smaller without actually relinquishing government ownership control.

3. SOEs can be combined with private enterprises; these combinations can be either with domestic of foreign companies.

4. Many central government SOEs were simply transferred to local governments. Often these transfers were forced and involuntary, and the national government had a nasty tendency to "dump the losers" on the locals without any financial compensation or help. In China, local governments were able to resurrect a surprising number of these losers and make them relatively successful.

5. A very large number of smaller enterprises were simply terminated, or turned loose to sink or swim by themselves.

6. In many cases, privatized SOEs or those that were combined with private sector corporations were forced to accept a substantial percentage of government retained equity, and one or more government seats on their boards of directors.

7. In those SOEs that the government retained, a big effort has been made to upgrade their management performance and productivity, and the government will assist these SOEs to capture business around the world in places like Africa and S. E. Asia, using a tempting array of government rewards for foreign governments and companies.

8. The government continues to subsize its SOEs. A new means of such subsidy is to retain a monopoly philosophy. For example, where the Chinese government seeks to purchase or lease major foreign resources such as oil, timber or minerals, it seeks to limit this business to SOEs, and keep out private companies. In other cases, where the government contracts out some operation, it may make sure that the contract goes to another SOE.

But most significant, the great difference between the two countries is in their politics. Indian politics is a whirling, swirling, writhing mass of thousands of conflicting and overlapping interests, vigorously and loudly pushed. Most Indians see their governments as fabulously bumbling and incompetent, but at least it is not the hard, vicious tyranny imposed on the Chinese. India will continue to seethe. The question is whether, at some point, China will explode and precipitate its second revolution.

Both India and China, like Japan and S. Korea in the past, are feeling the pressures to spread the wealth more equitably. India will respond to that pressure; it is not clear that China will. Their whole system is predicated on the ability of the government to extract a huge percentage of national wealth to use for government purposes, and right now, the Chinese people accept this approach.

This extractive ability enables the government to spend very large sums on public infrastructure, and in limited ways, it has chosen to do so. But its top priority – often its only priority – is the infrastructure vital to its program of economic development. The roads and railroads that get built or upgraded are primarily those that serve business enterprises. Airports and seaports are improved because they facilitate international trading. Enormous mountains of coal are burned, despite the pollution, to provide power for new factories. Much of the burden of providing housing has disappeared from the Socialist agenda of the central government and has become the problem of local governments. The Chinese government has little or no interest in the public infrastructure needs of the rural countryside or the burgeoning ring of dark factories and pitiful slums that surround the shining towers of the new urban wealthy.

REFORM OF GOVERNMENT ROLES AND RESPONSIBILITIES

Governments are changing their roles by simply abdicating elements of these roles, expecting that either individuals or private interests will assume the burden. This is not necessarily wrong or inappropriate, since it may move the government and the economy in directions long practiced successfully in other countries. Examples are power generation, fuels development and distribution, airport operation, hospitals, and education.

Both governments have begun to retrench government monopolies which have distorted markets, and served as money pumps for political corruption. Neither country has fully abandoned their SOEs, but both have purged the worst of their "losers" and have attempted to make those retained by the government more efficient and less subsidized.

Neither government is willing to relinquish ownership of the key elements of the national banking system, but both have driven their banks to the point of collapse, and then been forced to bail them out at hideous cost. In China, they went through a series of policy panics. The government outsmarted itself by forcing a high proportion of SOE debt and subsidy costs out of the government budget and into the lending portfolios of state banks. The resulting burden of bad loans and bad politics left banks with huge numbers of toxic debts, many of which could not be collected in the face of SOE political patronage and protection. This problem was so severe that banks were forced to the brink of collapse the government had to re-assume much of this debt by creating four asset management companies to take it over those toxic loans from the banks.

In China, there have been massive efforts to reform the government itself, and some of this initiative is slowly percolating in India.

To quote Yang, "Contrary to prevailing predictions, China has made substantial progress in improving the institutional framework for economic governance. To anyone concerned about the welfare of the Chinese people or about the rise of China for regional and world affairs, the significance such institutional development is obvious. A sound institutional infrastructure is vitally important for sustained economic development. The rationalization of government administration has been a political act, and there is a mutual interdependence between the organs of the government and elements of the economy. At first, it was the government and the CCP that liberated the economy.

Now the economy is liberating the government and provided the justification for change." [8]

FAILURES IN SOCIAL SERVICES

Other major policy decisions that affect the public budget are in the arena of social services, and in India and China, the policy problems have been very much the same. Both are extraordinary political anomalies. What are governments for if not to provide the vital citizen necessities of health care, basic education, help for the disadvantaged and the assurance of care for the elderly? This should have been especially true in officially Socialist countries like India and China, where both governments demanded the authority to control social services "from the cradle to the grave". Yet both of them failed catastrophically in the delivery of these vital social services, and both did it deliberately.

To a large extent, the provision of social services was initially largely made a responsibility of SOEs. But SOEs provided employment, and thus social services only to around 20% of the workforce, and finally both governments were forced to admit that, even if SOEs had been more successful, they provided no means to reach the other 80% of the workforce. When this was recognized, both governments should have set out to develop genuine social services for the whole population, but neither did so. Both officially delegated responsibility for social programs to local governments, knowing that almost none of them had either the funds or the service delivery capabilities to undertake such enormous burdens. Later chapters summarize in more detail the disastrous consequences stemming from this policy.

ENVIRONMENTAL THEATS AND COSTS

In a similar vein, neglect of the threats to the environment are moving toward a whole series of potential disasters, and again the governments in both countries have blinded themselves to the threats. As with its social services, both governments have placed primary responsibility for environmental protection with local governments even where it is glaringly obvious that problems such as river pollution, or air pollution of desertification are nationwide in their nature.

Economic development in China means breakneck urbanization, endless construction, heavy concentration on manufacturing, greatly expanded coal fired electrical power generation, with pollutants and heavy metals dumped into the air, and nasty chemicals dumped into the water. The government now has large sums of money that it can deploy, but environmental problems continue to be low priority. As in India, the national government has avoided responsibility by delegating responsibility to local governments, but these jurisdictions are still very poor and seriously disorganized after the Maoist neglect. The CCP likes to point out that it is "spending more than $10 billion on environmental concerns", which is truly a pitiful trivial sum. China's environmental problems stem as much from its corrupt and indifferent political system as from Beijing's single minded concentration on economic growth. Local officials and enterprise leaders routinely – and with impunity – ignore environmental laws and regulations, illegally reallocate environmental protection funds or simply steal them. **[10]**

In case after case, huge environmental problems have been documented, but this simply highlights the real issue: <u>nobody in China seems capable or willing to deal with the enormity of these problems.</u> Instead, the government continues to issue bland political promises, Five Year Plans, Thirty Year Plans, and new laws and regulations, and to criticize local governments because they have not yet "solved" the problems. These plans and pronouncements are political cover for the fact that governments choose to provide only pitifully inadequate funding. All of this is deliberate. The CCP fully recognizes the heart of their dilemma: environmental problems are enormously costly, and they are heavy potential counter demands against the dominant policy of spending on economic development which is at the heart of the CCP's survival strategy. Local governments feel that they have been unfairly stuck with these problems with absolutely no help from anybody else. The SOEs were never involved. The private sector doesn't want the added expense or the responsibility. The whole manufacturing sector of the economy is still highly inefficient. Industrial plants have never been asked to be water efficient, and in fact, the government has often provided free or subsidized water to favored SOEs. The unit cost of water is 15 times higher than in developed countries, and 25 times higher than in Japan, and higher even than in India and Pakistan. Chinese factories use ten times more water than most developed countries to produce the same products, and Chinese irrigation uses twice as much. By contrast, the growth in the U. S. economy has been achieved without increasing overall water use.

One gets the increasing sense that environmental problems in total are mission impossible. Past sins are so grievous that they have put China in a massive hole. It would take the bulk of national resources to cure these past sins, much less improve the current situation. The CCP is simultaneously urging local governments to clean up the world, but at the same it continues to pressing forward at the maximum possible speed on economic development, creating hundreds of thousands of new pollution sources. The development of the 562 new coal powered plants is a classic case in point. It shows that environmentalism is one of the problems that can safely be handled by lip service and "correct" political rhetoric. But the economics of environmental losses may finally force the Party to change its policy. Even if this does happen, the situation remains the same – the gap is so enormous that it can't possibly be closed in the short run. So China will suffer for decades. Meanwhile, quietly, China has become the largest recipient of World Bank loans for environmental work, and the World Bank officially supports the huge Three Gorges Dam project despite its environmental threats. Political leaders have learned to say the right things and lots of laws and regulations have been issued, but funds are scarce, and enterprises still bribe officials to look the other way. Environmental laws are seldom really enforced, and everybody knows it. There is a famous old Chinese saying: "The mountains are high and the Emperor is far away."

There are four critical policies that create heavy drains on government budgets – special interest rewards, tax avoidance and lack of enforcement, SOE deficits, and the high cost of populist subsidies. If these outpourings could be done away with or substantially mitigated, very significant funds could be saved and redirected to far better national priorities. On the other hand, three other policy issues – a severe shortage of public infrastructure, inadequate social services across the board, and a lack of effective environmental protections –represent staggering unmet obligations, unfunded mandates, looming contingent liabilities and failed obligations to the public. Reality is that, even if the government were to reform each of these policies, it would have no hope of being able to finance such huge unmet demands.

But there are other reforms of the budget that may be more feasible. For one thing, both governments are attempting to emerge from a period where many expenses of the government were never really captured in the formal approved budget at all. These "off budget" expenses tend to be especially vulnerable to waste, confusion of objectives, and rampant corruption. In China especially, a serious reform has been undertaken to capture these off budget items and either kill them off or force them into a more effective accountability process.

Both governments have been guilty of approving expensive programs or projects in their budgets without any real understanding of what problem they are supposed to solve, or what good they really do, and many of these duds have been off budget. In China especially, the Mao regime all but destroyed the capacity of local governments to make such needs assessments, or to do anything about massive waste and misallocation of funds. Over the longer period of time, as the capacity for effective program evaluation grows, it is certain that much better allocations of scarce funds will be possible.

URGENT NEED FOR REFORM OF GOVERNMENT CONTRACTING

In both countries, their experience with SOEs taught them several important lessons which need to be brought to bear on government contracting. As SOEs are retrenched, both governments have expanded their use of third party contractors. In those SOEs that have been retained by the government, their own permanent staffs are being cut back in favor of having more work performed by contract, either with private companies or with other SOEs.

In the long run, the added flexibility and the ability to tap a broader range of skills can be very valuable, but the benefits can be realized only by highly sophisticated contract management by the contracting agencies. In China, this level of managerial skill is now increasingly being realized in the best of the SOEs that have been retained by the government, and in the growing private sector. In India, "management" seems still to be held in contempt within the government, but it is found at the very highest levels in the burgeoning private sector.

But the sins of the old SOEs were myriad, and they are simply being carried downward into the selection and supervision of government contracts. These supervising ministries themselves have long had notorious relationships between their own leadership and staffs of the SOEs they supervise. And the SOEs in turn have been not only corrupt but inefficient, incompetent, lazy and often arrogantly regarding themselves as "too important to fail."

Each year, the government may have thousands of contacts in force, but it suffers from inadequate resources to oversee these contracts, and in some cases, this shortage of oversight capability is deliberate, where corrupt politicians and officials want to keep oversight as ineffective as possible. [11] The single most effective curb against contract corruption continues to be the mandated use of competitive bidding. A carefully drafted law mandating competition can be used as the basis for defending agency contracting practices, and giving leverage to reformers and those officials in agencies who genuinely want fair and legal contracting to prevail.

But a legislative mandate for competition even if it is achieved, is far from enough. Much depends on the willingness and ability of public officials to implement such laws fairly and free of corruption. Each agency of government should be required to supplement the law with a carefully defined and published set of procedures for bid competition. All bidders should be made aware of these procedures, and bidders can and should police each other to make sure that the procedures are followed. The reputation of each bidding company can be tested by checking their performance on previous contracts and their financial and management ability to carry out the contract must be evaluated. The initial contractor selection process is critical because it is here that the likelihood of corruption will first manifest itself. If bad public officials and companies seize the contract at this point, it is likely that subsequent operations under the contract will be a constant problem. All contract bids should be subjected to a transparent evaluation process aimed at getting a realistic assessment of bidder capabilities. This evaluation should be open to review, at least for auditors and other bidders to examine. That way, if a selecting official makes a decision that runs counter to the technical evaluation, such an arbitrary selection can be more effectively challenged. In other words, sound, well developed methods for fair and honest supervision of contractors exists; in India and China these tools are seldom used.

Another significant protection is created when the government has the authority to debar bidders from future contract opportunities if there is evidence of collusion, factual misrepresentation or intent to conceal relevant information. Debarment is an administrative action, and it puts the burden on the alleged offender to upset the decision either by law suit or by appealing for help from political allies who may regard it as dangerous to interfere. Even informally, any rumors or partial evidence of improper bidder practices can be made known to other contracting organizations in both government and the private sector.

Another important way for public officials to protect their position is for the government agency itself to prepare its own estimates of the expected costs for all significant elements of the intended contract. Such estimates should be available at the time of the contract competition so that the government officials have a basis for judging the costs proposed by bidders. This is especially valuable if there is the likelihood that few bids will be received, or that there may be bid rigging collusion among bidders. Substantial variances from the government estimate should be suspect. If the bids are too low, it may signal that the bidder is trying to "buy in" to the contract. If the bids are too high, it may signal that bidders think they can soak the government. It is doubtful that many Indian contract overseers have the skill to make these in-house estimates, or the will to use them.

The need for government officials to have their own independent capability to evaluate costs is even more critical during the life of the contract because the potential for cheating is so high. Every single activity under the contract can be manipulated, and where internal corruption is far advanced, those who control contractor supervision spend their time dodging protective measures. In most cases, political officials are not controlled by the mechanisms applied to the career staff. Many ministers or agency heads have broad and unchecked authority under agency enabling statutes. They may make arbitrary decisions based entirely on their own judgment, and on political factors not considered in the staff technical evaluation.

To return to the main theme then, one of the greatest determinants of the public budget in both China and India is represented by the balance sheets of their SOEs. In the past, the balance has been negative. There were periods in both countries where more than 50% of all SOEs were operating at deficits and had to be propped up at great expense by the government. Both China and India have undertaken major retrenchments of their huge array of SOEs to eliminate the losers and improve the management of those retained, but the results to this point are very hard to assess. It would appear that, over time, it is likely that SOEs will slowly shift from lost makers to profit makers as they were originally intended to be. As this happens, the pressure on the public budgets will decrease and money may be freed up for allocation to other priorities. But the cost of government contracting will grow significantly. This is not inherently bad if contracts are skillfully managed. If they are not, then the losses through contract pathologies can be a significant drain on the budget.

The cumulative consequences of these long term failures demonstrate with great force the fact that highly centrist and centrally planned and controlled governance simply did not work very well. The CCP is thus being forced to decentralize at least government operations whether it wants to or not

CONSTRUCTION REFORMS

Of the many reforms that the Chinese government has instituted, none has been more necessary than in the arena of construction, land use and land leasing, and letting of contracts for purchase of goods and services. In 1998, less than 20% of public projects used public bidding, and even fewer were really competitive. Construction and land use abuses made up a large percentage of all cases of corruption. Funding for public projects were caught up in a vast spider web of conflicting political and bureaucratic infighting in the complex network of intergovernmental relations. Much of the contracting was between activities owned by the government ministries themselves, or controlled though each ministry's SOEs, and all were engaged in conniving and "gaming" both officially and under the table. There was too much power, too little supervision, and an open invitation to corruption and pathological maneuvers. The Law on Government Procurement was finally enacted in June, 2002, but the enactment of a paper law is not the same as enforcement. This whole system of reform has subsequently been extended to mineral rights exploration, extraction, transfers of mining interests, export licenses, and other allocations of public goods.

Results at the central government level under the new systems are very impressive. In 1998, cases of various corrupt practices resulted in 3.1 billion yuan recoveries. By 2000, this figure was 65.3 billion, and by 2001, it rose to over 150 billion. While these numbers show "accomplishment", they also show how enormously wide- spread and sloppy the whole field of contracting had been.

CHAPTER III

Economic Development in India

IN THE EARLY 18TH CENTURY, India was the leading manufacturing country in the world. It had 22% of the world's GDP and 25% of the world's global trade in textiles. In general, it had a highly sophisticated market and credit structure and a skilled and wealthy commercial class. It actually had an agricultural productivity equal to the best in the world. So why did India not develop a modern industrial economy? India fell significantly behind Western Europe in technology, institutions and ideas. British rule in India for more than 150 years was seldom concerned with the country's development except in its relationship to the British home economy. Then, after Independence in 1947, the government under the direction of Jawaharlal Nehru adopted the philosophies of State Socialism based on the example of the Soviet Union, modified by the philosophies of Fabian economics out of Great Britain. But then over the next forty five years, these socialist policies had the consequence of stultifying economic development.

In the modern era, India's economy has expanded and broadened in absolute terms, but declined in comparison with the rest of the world. Part of the economy is 21st Century. Much is 19th Century, trying for the 20th. Most is still mired in the rural poverty of the last several hundred years. The old apparatus still persists: wealthy merchants and landowners, traditional merchants and traders, middle men, brokers, factors and jobbers, kinship alliances, caste inhibitions, ancient alliances, secret cartels, money lenders, crooks, thugs and venal officials. Side by side with the ultra modern information technology corporations are old style merchants dealing in coal and salt, textiles, tea, indigo, brass ware, timber and opium. India's banking system is shifting from State owned banks to private sector banks, but in the villages, money is still borrowed from money lenders and large landlords, often at ruinous rates of interest. The modern economic world is slowly creeping into the countryside, but often inhibited by the archaic interests it is seeking to replace. The British Raj tended to favor European interests and allies among the Indian Brahmin elite, and the early Nehru regime, while enunciating broader policies was still a continuation of elitism under the rubric of State Socialism.

Even now, India has two separate parallel economies, the State sector and the private sector. Nehru's regime strongly favored the State sector and emphasized the following economic policies:

1. The notion of the superiority of the State as owner and controller of at least the "commanding heights" of the national economy in the form of State Owned Enterprises (SOE; often called Public Sector Undertakings), and as the vigilant watchdogs over a suspect private sector.

2. A deep suspicion of an open market economy which led to an intense, deeply detailed regulation of non-state economic elements.

3. A bias toward government provision of heavy industry, believing that the private sector did not have the capability, and that heavy industry would generate a large number of new jobs for India's unemployed and underemployed workforce. During Indira Gandhi's regime, (1965-mid 80s) she starved the industry of new investment money, would not finance new technology, made many industry decisions political (e. g. plant locations), and enforced distorting pricing and distribution policies. Taxes were heavy, and the industry was not able to generate self financing that they could keep. [1]

4. Heavy mandating of an elaborate import substitution philosophy where both SOEs and private enterprises were to be protected from foreign competition.

5. Discouragement of foreign investment – because private investors were not trusted and were seen as trying to steal India's nationalist identity.

6. General discouragement of exporting because it was thought to deprive Indian citizens of access to scarce commodities.

7. The allocation of social services responsibilities to the States, and the complete abdication of any serious role for the national government, except of course policy control, planning and "direction" – but little money.

8. The agriculture sector was to be ignored except for some land reform and some investment in irrigation projects. The whole sector was seen as more or less hopeless, and it was felt that any available money was better spent on building huge steel mills, which, in the end proved to be highly inefficient and non-competitive in international terms. The government repeatedly stated it policy intent to solve the problems of rural/village areas, but instead squandered money on low value but politically popular subsidies.

Nehru was the ultimate elitist. He was absolutely convinced that the country would be better off run by a small group of highly educated elitists. He thought democracy was a good thing because it would affirm the position of his elite, but he thought competition was wasteful, and central planning by these leaders was the only acceptable course. The Industrial Policy Resolution of 1956 reserved 17 industries exclusively for public ownership, including iron and steel, mining, machine tool manufacture, and heavy electrical machinery manufacture. In effect, Nehru was trying to develop both Socialism and capitalism as a mixed two level economy: but this mixed economy failed to deliver expanded wealth, seriously increased employment, or even social justice. In fact, the economy suffered from government directed skewing of investment often in wrong directions, and from political rent seeking and deliberate rip offs of government ministries. Government directed "policy loans" by banks severely constrained the freedom of action of central banks, and thus their ability to mitigate inflation.

These policies were kept in force until 1991, and vestiges still remain, leaving a lot of government ministries with little real influence. Meanwhile in places like Japan, S. Korea and even in China, shifts had been successfully made to open up the economy and encourage the private sector.

One could argue that the most real and most valuable accomplishment of the early Nehru years was a relatively stable representative democracy – even though it has been controlled by a limited elite that chose to neglect the needs of the poor. In India, public social programs do not aid the poor because few such programs exist. The heavy concentration on political needs and demands took precedence even over realistic economics, which is to say that the state socialist agenda often made little economic sense. The elitist regime also depended heavily on favoritism, patronage, genteel corruption and enormous self delusion. [2]

The great world tide of State Socialism originating after WW II peaked in the 70's and has been receding since. Even before the collapse of the USSR in the early 80s, the Chinese had, within two or three years after Mao's death in 1976, begun the slow, cautious rethinking and eventual abandonment of the apparatus of centrist state control – but not the basic theology. By 1985, the Chinese were well on their way to the full jettisoning of communism in all but name.

For India, the comparable date was 1991, and 1991 might well go down in posterity as one of the most important dates in Indian history. To quote Nilikani, "India's particular nemesis has been oil price rise which sent the economy reeling toward bankruptcy time after time. In 1991 yet another oil price rise triggered a crisis. It was one that transformed our attitudes toward India's entrepreneurs."

India was staring into an abyss by the beginning of the 1990s – thanks to reckless government borrowings, our foreign debt had more than tripled since 1981 to $ 64.4 billion. Then came the Gulf War and high oil prices, which sucked out our foreign reserves to the extent that India had enough money for just ten days of imports, and had to mortgage its gold for an emergency loan. With the Indian economy on the ropes, the finance minister, Manmohan Singh introduced a reform agenda explicitly meant to bring the private sector fully into the economy. With this 1991 policy the baton for growth passed from the government to 'the human spirit of creativity, adventure and enterprise.' "The new policy released the private sector from industrial licensing and controls on capital. Financial reforms eased up on access to credit for businesses by removing controls on interest rates." [3]

A whole series of reforms were initiated. Import tariffs were reduced; the "wealth tax" on stock investments and "money came out of the cupboards and into the stock market" [4] Tax rates fell and bank borrowing became friendlier for small entrepreneurs, and as a result, new businesses were started and existing businesses were expanded and this triggered a rapid growth in tax revenues. Many of these reforms have met stout resistance from vested interests including many in the government itself, and progress has often been slow and halting. But nevertheless, the tides of change are running strongly, and cannot now be reversed.

INDIAN STATE OWNED ENTERPRISES

The Indian central government owns 246 enterprises employing 1.6 million people and producing 8.3% of national GDP. [5] These enterprises are the creation of the Nehru state socialist regime. Initially, most of them were major enterprises representing the "commanding heights" of the economy concept, but somewhere along the line, the state acquired many enterprises that had no public policy value at all (artificial limbs producers, condom manufacturers, retail stores, etc.).

In the liberalization policy reforms initiated in 1991, various methods for divestiture were initiated, and there has been a long drawn out process of privatization, disinvestment, devolution and outright elimination going on. Of special interest is the fact that as many 98 out of the 246 SOEs were operating at a deficit. That number is now down to 53 (2008). The most spectacular recent case is Air India which lost $1.3 billion in 2009, and which is about to be expensively bailed out. But India has always had a dual system with a strong private sector, and over the years, the state has reduced the elements of the economy reserved for government control. As they have done so, the private sector has entered, and in many cases, has proved superior performers to the SOEs, taking business away from them. So state ownership has entered a period of decline; further privatization seems to make more and more sense. So far, the government seems only to be proposing the sell-off of around 10% of the equity of some profitable SOEs.

Like the Chinese, the Indian government **says** it is divesting itself of many of its SOEs, but like the Chinese, much of it is smoke and mirrors. The official Indian policy seems to be to maintain support for "public enterprises that are essential for the operation of the industrial economy" which essentially means whatever the government says it means, and often this means more or larger SOEs. [6] The priority areas for growth of public enterprises are:

- Essential infrastructure goods and services
- Exploration and exploitation of oil and mineral resources
- Technology development
- Building manufacturing capability in areas that are crucial to the long term development of the economy and where the public sector investment is inadequate.
- Products involving "strategic considerations", i. e. the military.

Ideally, divestiture should be based on reason and not politics, and any reduction in the SOE base should involve things like reducing and rationalizing industries that are obsolete or of low value added, releasing to the private sector small and non-strategic enterprises where there is little justification for the government to own; cutting loose inefficient and unproductive enterprises, those that have no public or social value or public purpose, or avoiding SOEs in sectors where the private sector has developed sufficient expertise and resources. But the government shows a strong tendency simply to sell off some of the SOE equity to generate money to cut the current budget deficit, and it then wants to hold on to the rest. As recently as 1995, none had been eliminated from government control. It is unclear what would be done with a SOE that is a heavy and congenital loser, but has some strategic or social value. Nor is it really clear what the policy is now with respect to State monopolies, since they represent critical elements of State control and political payoff.

Nehru's state owned companies were being managed by civil servants who had no training in running commercial enterprises. [7] Their subsequent losses were defended by Nehru, saying "their job was not to make a profit but to meet social objectives. Many of these SOEs had essentially been seized over the owner's objections without adequate compensation. Nehru was a strong believer in the socialist concepts of central planning and control through a massive complex array of policies and controls reaching far beyond SOE ownership. Much of the private sector leadership supported Nehru in large part because they benefited greatly from the import substitution policies of the time, and from the heavy government subsidies available for selected segments of the economy. In addition, government policy kept foreign companies out of whole segments of the economy such as banking, insurance, power, energy, aviation. This led them to accept heavy state control of prices, dividends, foreign trade, foreign exchange, import control, export control, and the license Raj. In short, business men are in part to blame for the 50 years of economic stagnation from which India suffered. Nehru and others thought of themselves as unusually rational and farsighted. In retrospect, they were almost always terribly wrongheaded. Mistakes were made in a far too expansive and incompetent public sector, emphasis on import substitution rather than export development, concentration on heavy industry and neglect of services and consumer needs, preoccupation with labor intensive activities and a failure to understand the concepts of productivity and cost effectiveness. All of this was reiterated again in 1955 when Nehru committed the nation to "the establishment of a socialist pattern of society where the principal means of production are under social ownership and control." Huge amounts of money were ploughed into the expansion of the steel industry, much of it from the Soviet Union, but also from Germany and G. Britain. In the Indian socialist concept, this was the ideal action: to produce a huge state controlled, capital intensive steel plant which provided jobs, and which was intended to produce "wealth" but need not produce profit. The only problem is that the Indian government had no idea of what the world competition was doing, and they had to share a shrinking market with other formidable competitors. At the same time, the government could not be bothered with agriculture, even though many improvements would have been fairly cheap. The U.S. offered aid for agriculture, and was bitterly criticized for it as a subversive attempt to "keep India poor".

FAILINGS OF THE LICENSE RAJ

As an adjunct of these flawed policies, the License Raj was created, beginning with the Industries Development and Regulation Act of 1951. The word Raj is Hindi and means "rule" or "ruler". British rule in India became commonly known as the "British Raj", and the phrase morphed over into Indian rule after independence and was applied to the vast hordes of major and minor public officials employed to oversee the functioning of the economy, and eventually almost everything else. The essence of the license mentality was that everything – absolutely everything – in the creation, operation, financing, location, marketing and even the death of enterprises had to be controlled through the granting of licensing or approvals before the fact. No business could be started – or in some cases even terminated – without a license from the government. Loans could not be applied for, parts could not be ordered, equipment could not be purchased, trucks could not cross borders, prices could not be set, markets could not be selected, and on and on, unless and until actions had been licensed by some element of the government. Whole special regimes of licensing and taxation applied to all goods to be imported into, or exported out of India. The value of the currency was controlled, as were the prices of thousands of goods and services.

This need to control everything became an extraordinary manifestation of the whole concept of centrist Socialist control. The commitment to state socialism was accompanied by the growth of this License Raj, and later, the Regulation Raj. There is such a thing as the "regulatory mind" – and in India this meant the love of regulation for its own sake, the love of regulation as an endless source of minor bureaucratic power, and regulation as the vehicle for bribery, preferment and the ability to favor one's friends and punish one's enemies. Every element of economic policy, and much of social policy became the subject of broad, vague laws, and vast oceans of regulation, layer upon tedious layer. Legitimate regulations became dysfunctional because they were driven down into absurd levels of detailed prohibition. There were multiple regulations dealing with the same activities promulgated by multiple ministries and commissions. Each regulation required excruciating piles of paperwork, much of which was pointless and useless. Many regulatory decisions were passed through the hands of countless interagency committees, working groups, review procedures and endless questioning. Many decisions had to be passed at a glacial pace up a tortured chain of command with further reams of paper up to the top for decision. Most governments are paperwork mills, but few could equal the Indian bureaucracy for the absurdness of its outrageous overkill.

The Industries Development and Regulation Act of 1951 sought to:

1. Create the approved pattern of official or permitted investment
2. Prevent private monopolies or concentrations of wealth (while permitting government monopolies and concentrations of ownership and control)
3. Maintain regional balances thru the allocation of industry location
4. Protect the interests of small-scale producers and encourage the entry of new entrepreneurs
5. Encourage optimum scale of plants.
6. Encourage the use of advanced technology.

The problems that emerged were not so much with this set of intentions but with how they were administered. According to one observer "The state controlled economy encouraged corruption as much as inefficiency, and the bureaucrats and politicians parceled out its large and varied booty of big public projects, defense contracts, bribes from businessmen, jobs, foreign trips, telephone connections, etc., a serious steady internal plundering of the over centralized State's resources that, in the early nineties would expose India to the drastic forced therapies of the IMF and the World Bank. India learned that the state does not work on behalf of the people. It works on behalf of itself – the politicians, bureaucrats and the interests that directly support them. The state became a combination of special interests responsible to no one. The class with money and influence was tiny and came entirely from the upper castes. It had monopolized power and privilege and the few scarce facilities for education, health and infrastructure. The rest of the population was left out in the cold. Nehru's "noble vision" was self delusion and led to serious failure." [8]

According to Gunnar Myrdal "Indian attitudes include poor work discipline, contempt for manual work, lack of punctuality, alertness and discipline; low aptitude for cooperation, theological and theoretical impediments to reality, low standards of efficiency and integrity in public administration, and a rigid and debilitating social structure of prejudice and inequality.[9] Low-level functionaries took months in the futile micro review of an application, and then sent it up the administrative chain to the headquarters of a ministry for final approval. The ministry then again spent several months reviewing the same data, then sent the application to an inter- ministerial licensing committee of senior bureaucrats who were equally ignorant of entrepreneurial realities, who operated by ad hoc rules and the absence of any sense of relative priority. Even after ministerial approval, the investor had to seek approval for the import of machinery for the factory. If foreign partners were involved there was another whole apparatus for an "inter ministerial foreign affairs agreements committee". If a bank loan was involved a whole new separate evaluation had to be conducted, despite the facts that the banks were state owned. And the final insult was the fact that politicians often allied themselves with criminals as bag men and enforcers. Some of these known criminals, with hundreds of futile police charges against them, bought their own way into top political positions in legislatures and ministries.

In many cases, the government set and controlled production goals for whole industries and granted licenses to companies for their share of these goals. Violations of these production limits were severely punished. The endless delays in clearing applications discouraged the truly efficient in favor of wily producers who concentrated on the manipulation of the system. Licensing was a monumental disaster. It was anticompetitive by its nature, and it raised costs, created delays, was arrogant and arbitrary, and the end really achieved little positive contribution except jobs for bureaucrats."

In 1985-86 Rajiv Gandhi introduced further changes which spoke to productivity, cost reduction and improved quality, reflecting dissatisfaction with the performance of the SOEs. But for most of the political denizens, it was like he was speaking in an unknown language. There were promises to dismantle the regulatory system, and there was some retrenchment of the License Raj, but mainly for public sector enterprises. Official rhetoric still talks about "the struggle for social and economic justice, an end to poverty and unemployment and the building of a modern prosperous and forward looking socialist state."

The License Raj has proved skilled at survival, and it has gradually evolved into what is being called the Regulation Raj. The distinction between the License Raj and the Regulation Raj is essentially that the License Raj demanded approval before the fact, and the License Raj relinquished such detailed pre-approvals in favor of general regulations that permitted after-the-fact inspection with authority to demand many forms of corrective action, accompanied by enforcement capability. Thus, the reform of the License Raj was not often in the range of their authority, but only in the manner in which this authority was applied. The motivations of government leadership since the watershed days of reform initiative in 1991 has been genuinely to reduce the adverse impact of both licensing and regulation, but actual reform has been slow and spastic. However, most of industrial licensing has been scrapped, a whole messy world of import/export controls has been reduced and rationalized, and in recent years, foreign direct investment has actually been encouraged instead of being implacably resisted. Controls over the distribution of goods and services are far less intrusive and time consuming, and movement of goods across State borders (plus accompanying fees) has been officially discouraged. A large number of minor price controls have been abandoned, and the government has even reduced the requirements to sell goods to state monopoly purchasing organizations. While the government has reduced the number of protected industries where only the government can operate, large segments of the economy are still under protection, and regulations abound that protect these enterprises against private involvement.

But the protection and subsidy of SOEs is still predominant, labor protection laws against which businessmen protest are still almost untouched, and there is the constant worry that the Regulation Raj is becoming the License Raj reborn.

THE NEW INDIAN ECONOMY

India is a "rags to riches" story since the abandonment of the failed socialist economy. Nehru Socialism failed to generate many jobs, just as state socialism failed in China and earlier, in the USSR. In the new India, bottom up entrepreneurship is now really the big job generator. The power of the old bureaucracy and socialist politicians has waned, and power has shifted to a new class of private entrepreneurs, usually aided and abetted by foreign investors and companies. Bangalore, previously known mainly for its military cantonment, is the modern center of IT in India with companies like IBM, Texas Instruments, Group Bull, Motorola, Sun Microsystems and scores of new Indian firms like Infosys, all of which are rich and influential. There is a high degree of movement of top people from their Indian bases to the headquarters or other technical facilities of these companies. Some of the top people in Silicon Valley are Indian. In India, education has shifted from sending the children of the wealthy to England, to sending (the smart ones) to a new technical institute in India. In 1947, India's wealth resided with the landed gentry. After Independence, most of the wealth resided with the socialist government, in the senior civil service and the top SOEs. Now, most of the wealth is moving toward a new generation of private sector entrepreneurs.

Recent economic success stems from the initiation of economic reform and modernization beginning in 1991, and it has created a New Middle Class born out of the limited tide of economic liberalization, and has now become a potent source of political support for continued liberalization. Urban India has more than 300 million residents, and yet only about 10% of them really pay income taxes. Today, the real strength in the Indian economy lies with the emerging services sector which is contributing more than half of the national income. It is the fastest growing sector, with an average annual growth rate of 8 % in the 1990s. [10] It is emerging to be very much like its counterparts in other more developed countries.

Therefore it is a "developed country" pattern with higher value added, more white collar employment, lots of upward mobility, multinational in composition, requiring a lot of education, and setting new levels of integration with other corporations, the government and in the globalized economy. Like other developed countries, the workforce is developing at two levels: the primary permanent staff with high salaries and benefits, and a second level of contract employees or contractor employees that can be obtained more cheaply and pared down more quickly.

The National Council of Economic Research has published an interesting report (1996) [11] which sought to characterize levels of the whole population as follows:

Very rich = 6 million (1 million households)
The consumer class = 150 million
Climbers = 275 million
Aspirants (poor) = 275 million
Destitute = 210 million

Only the very rich and some proportion of the consumer class are seen as willing and able to spend to buy the more expensive consumer goods. The rest of the new middle class, from clerks to executives are more prudent, but all want to be seen as separate and distinct from the poor, those in the informal economy, and even from most of the consumers and climbers. Thus, the "new middle class" is seen as a cultural creation as well as an economic one. Those in the informal economy now more frequently make their money serving the middle class.

Both caste and gender prejudices have been carried over into the New Middle Class, but in moderated and mutated forms. But it is still true that if your family is upper caste and you are male, you have a head start. It is no longer true that if your father is a senior civil servant, this secures you an advantage. Where do the smartest kids want to work? In private sector jobs with top international corporations; the Indian Administrative Service and SOEs are now uncool.

When India has finally succeeded in inventing first class education, it has not been to recreate Oxford or Cambridge; it has been to recreate MIT or Caltech or the Harvard Business School, through The Indian Institutes of Technology, the Indian Institutes of Management, and the Indian Institutes of Information Technology. [12] Education in India also increasingly means the substitution of an array of technical, managerial and "how to do it" training organizations for the flawed elementary/secondary education system–both public and private.

So what has changed? Well, the centrist elite are losing out, and most of the negative policies they created are being repudiated, redirected, or quietly allowed to expire. The anti-business bias is in retreat; in fact, the government now loves private sector money, including money for the development of public infrastructure. While China retains its "commanding heights" policy, India is much more inclined to let the government's state owned enterprises compete, and let competition take its course.

The growth of the new social services economy has been mostly private; in some cases like banking, manufacturing or construction, where it competes with the public sector, it is winning, and producing a decline in these public sector enterprises. Some SOEs such as airlines have or will be converted to private corporations – maybe even the Indian Railroad? A good example is that of banking. Studies have found that "public sector banks are more likely to lend to firms with directors who have political ties, and are less likely to collect on these loans. Politicians manipulate the allocation of public credit to achieve political/electoral goals through lending booms just prior to elections, and targeting of credit to swing states. The marginal political loan is even less likely to be repaid". [13] The banking sector is a critical arena for the retrenchment of staff to cut costs and make public banks competitive. While a strong unionized staff has prevented wide scale retrenchment, such external competitive pressures have led to a freeze on recruitment and the development of voluntary retirement programs. There has been no substantial recruitment in public banks since 1986. The powerful All India Bank Employees Association has not only fought bank employment retrenchment; it has fought (along with most other unions) the whole policy of economic liberalization." [14] Thus, public banks, frozen in place by their unions, are losing out to private banks, but the unions won't admit it. Voluntary retirement schemes to reduce employment simply highlights the visible decline of public banks. As one commenter put it "you walk into any public sector bank and there are people all over just doing nothing. They are being paid but they're actually not contributing anything." One can anticipate a somewhat similar pattern in many other parts of the economy.

Across the board, this contrast with public services is highly disturbing. New social services sectors of the economy (e.g. retailing, insurance, some education, transportation, distribution, power) are up to the standards of developed countries. Meanwhile public services, especially elementary/secondary education, health care, retirement and urban services are almost medieval in their obsolescent state. Also, many forms of industry such as textiles, clothing, shoes, and printing have either declined in market value or have been overtaken by competitors. But again, these trends are natural and follow the pattern of other developed countries.

Nehru had earlier seriously harmed India's huge textile industry, primarily because nobody in the government seemed to understand the functioning of an economic system. In order to provide more employment, the government supported the construction of big new textile production mills. But this had the effect of driving small local household based production out of existence. But then it restricted production of the new mills, taxed them highly, and in true Soviet style forced them to sell at prices below cost to provide cheap cloth for the poor. The net effect was to position the whole industry at the low end of the scale with very little value added. At no time did the government ever seem to understand the nature of market demand. Planners were driven by what India could produce, and not by what people would actually buy. So, unlike other developing countries, especially S. Korea and China, capital tended to be forced into low value low efficiency investments.

Indira Gandhi who succeeded Jawaharlal Nehru, and served as Prime Minister from 1966 to 1977 and then again from 1980 to 1984, emerged as something of a populist dictator a la Hugo Chavez. With respect to the government for example, she tampered with appointments in the civil service and the courts, dismissed "troublesome" chief ministers and some in the next level, and generally replaced them with absolute loyalists. This tampering was extreme in the court system which was already a famous mess. She also meddled where she could in local and regional appointments. Her general policy was populist, supposedly to "help the poor" – but in essence it was the traditional posture of buying voter loyalty in order to hold on to power. She was the one who nationalized the banks. She channeled money to supportive interest groups, misdirected contracts, encouraged radical labor activism, alienated private investors, encouraged the license Raj, rewarded her followers and punished her enemies when doling out government largesse. The tragedy was that, after inflating the hopes and expectations of the poor, she was unable to deliver.

India was facing a crisis of the decline of its public infrastructure largely through age and neglect, and this neglect clearly hurt industrial growth. Gandhi did nothing about this. In effect, she reverted to some of the worst elements of state socialist centrism, but mostly to capture money to distribute as patronage. Thru the period of her regime, new waves of populist politics threw up an ugly kind of "anti" politicians as well as a lot of genuine opposition. During the last two decades, the Bharitiya Janata Party emerged as a right wing religious, nationalist party, taking advantage of the ethnic and class clashes that Indira loved.

This also influenced the general government policy of economic development to create jobs – heavy industry was preferred because it created lots of jobs; automation was resisted because it eliminated jobs and angered the unions. The government never quite understood that job creation was really from the bottom up, and could not be created by government fiat from the top down. Now, India sees its trade strategy as high tech, with a large service sector element. China wants its private sector, and many SOEs, to be related to manufacturing, and its SOEs to be heavy in the commanding heights sectors, especially in the acquisition of foreign energy, where SOEs continue to be heavily favored and subsidized. China's government will give money to "bribe" African dictators, instead of spending it on domestic needs. Both China and India love developing their economies with foreign money and resources. In general, trade in India is privately financed; in China it is government financed. In India, imports are now mostly user driven, and not by socialist theory. In China, imports are still carefully modulated and controlled where necessary by the government.

THE PUBLIC BUDGET AND ECONOMIC DEVELOPMENT

Each year, as in the U. S. and elsewhere, the release of the new proposed Indian national government budget is a source of endless excitement and entertainment. The Indian budget for 2010-11 promised a mind boggling array of major reforms. But year after year, the Union budget continues in heavy deficit, and there was a substantial increase last year and another 36% increase this year, on top of a big stimulus package, and the government has not yet solved the "off-budget" problem where many sources of income are in channels outside of the official budget. [15]

The new budget proposed to raise money to offset a huge anticipated deficit by selling off shares in Indian SOEs under a policy laboriously labeled "disinvestment". This is accompanied by the usual pledge to reduce the size, or at least the deficit characteristics of the overall Union budget, and to reduce borrowing to meet the revenue gap. India now finances 34% of what it spends by borrowing. Part of this hopeful pledge is the usual promise to reform the budgets of India's 28 independent states.

The budget also proposed – yet again – to reduce the extremely costly public subsidies of food, fuel, power, fertilizers, insecticides, irrigation costs and several others. "The Congress Party that was returned to power is said to be more stable, less hysterical and more confident than its predecessors, but it is still imbued with socialist motivations and very undecided about more serious reforms. They might tend to argue, for example, that the "cure" for the fertilizer subsidy is not to eliminate it but to make it more "efficient". One very good idea that might be tried is to stop paying the subsidy to the manufacturers and distributors and pay it directly to the farmers." [16] There are some relatively modest proposals to further ease restrictions on foreign direct investment, and to make minor changes in restrictive labor laws and regulations. Also there will be a continuation of efforts to get control over income and expenditures that are now "off budget" and usually out of control. India has been executing a program of 100% write-offs of loans made to small farmers, and 25% write-offs for larger farms, and additional funds are provided for this popular program.

Of greatest interest are proposals for the introduction of a new universal Goods and Services Tax (GST) to replace an undisciplined mess of hundreds of national and local VAT and excise taxes. Presently Indian States can tax goods but not services. The central government taxes services plus excise duties on goods at the point of manufacture, but not further downstream. The GST would allow both levels of government to tax both goods and services at each link in the value chain, probably at a flat rate of 7% for the States and 5% for the Union government. The GST would also eliminate complex rules which result in a tax on taxes. It would also eliminate the infamous central sales tax which is set by the national government and collected by the States, but it creates border controls between States that cause "ruinous delays."

But in the last analysis, the great, fundamental implacable problem is the same: has any breed or combination of politicians got the guts to face up to adverse political/special interest politics and make any decisions for real change? Can the Indian budget really ever be cut?

THE FINANCIAL SYSTEM

In the 1950s and 1960s the principal instrument for controlling the commanding heights of the economy was investment in the capital of key industries (justified by the contention that the private sector could not generate enough capital). Today the State has other instruments of intervention, particularly fiscal and monetary instruments. The State commands the bulk of the nation's savings. Banks and financial institutions are under State control. In addition, the whole insurance industry, which has huge resources, is State owned and controlled.

It was not until the policy revolution of 1991 [17] that the government really began a concerted effort to reform the economy. As in China, the first and continuing step was the painful and often embarrassing process of abandoning what had been the holy theology of State Socialism. Most business decisions can now be made for strictly business reasons and not as elements of centrally dictated public policy. Most requirements for prior approval of expansions or changes of product lines are out. Only certain key industries are still substantially limited, including security, strategic concerns, hazardous chemicals, overriding environmental consequences, or "elitist" consumption. Cities under 1 million population are exempted. At the same time, foreign investors are now allowed to hold more than 51% of the equity of an Indian enterprise. For the first time, the government began to dump its long term policy of import substitution and fumble around with export promotion. In general, the Indian government is highly resistant to foreign investment in its banking system, which is still mostly nationalized, with government banks holding about 70% of banking system assets. Foreign banks hold 8% and 22% is held by Indian domestic private banks. Foreign investors can also set up "non-bank financial companies" which offer retail loans but do not take deposits.

Within the constraints of national ownership, the Indian government has undertaken a number of significant reforms. And indeed, even the concept of government ownership of banks has been quietly relaxed to the point that there are a growing number of new private banks appearing. India has devalued the Rupee, removed most currency controls and acted to increase the availability of capital while trying to reduce interest rates. Over a period of time, some success has been achieved in working off bad loans, but often at the cost of government subsidy. Increasingly, the government has drawn back from its unquestioning subsidy of state owned enterprises and sought to make them more financially self sufficient, and now, almost 80% of bank loans are made to the private sector. The portfolio of banking operations has been expanding in terms of the kinds and range of customers, more lending to the private sector, expanded home mortgage services, more loans for education, and small consumer loans for such things as home appliances.

Indian savings patterns are changing. The financial crisis drove some people back to banks. Since the 1990s the savings rate had risen steadily from an average of 23% to an estimated high of 35% in 2007. The household sector continues to account for some 70% of savings, but in the last five years, the growing profitability of Indian firms has led to a surge in corporate savings. There has also been some increase in public sector savings. One of the most compelling reasons for private savings is the fact that only 10% of India's working population is covered by a retirement scheme, and health insurance coverage is very low. So personal savings are vital to meet these future contingencies and also for major expenditures like home purchasing, children's education and autos and major home appliances. Many Indians still have a tendency to hang on to non- productive assets like jewelry. For the first time, the government has opened up the government's monopolies in insurance and mutual funds to private participation, and this has begun to attract some of that jewelry.

THE STATE BANK OF INDIA

The State Bank of India is a very large multi-faceted financial institution which is government owned, and it typifies what the government is trying to do to upgrade the performance of its owned enterprises. SBI, over the last few years has developed a whole range of subsidiaries to provide investment counseling in capital market and securities, to sell life insurance, to operate a credit card system, and to serve as commodities factors. It now provides pension funds, general insurance, (financial) custodial services, private equity, mobile banking, point of sale, merchant acquisition, advisory services, and structured products. It has ambitious plans to extend banking services to 100,000 villages and rural areas. The State Bank of India is not the central bank: that is the Reserve Bank of India. Other state owned banks are the Indian Bank, the Oriental Bank of Commerce, and UCO bank. But the competition is growing more serious. The speed of private sector investment in mutual funds has been remarkable since the government first permitted private participation in the industry in 1993. Also, by the end of March of 2008, private insurers had taken a combined market share of 36-40% of the life and non-life insurance markets respectively. It should be noted that the number of Indians in the working age group (15-64) will rise from 63% in 2006 to 68% in 2026, and increasingly, this portion of the population is able to enter the middle class and they will earn more money, but also want to borrow more.

THE TAX SYSTEM AND THE VALUE ADDED TAX

India's tax system is a stupendous mess and it desperately needs total rethinking and reform. The system is deeply inequitable and universally mistrusted to the point that beating the system is seen as justified and widely admired. The system is riddled with special interest giveaways and preferment. Only about 2% of Indian citizens or enterprises really pay income taxes; all of the rest have some form of escape mechanism. State owned enterprises not only escape most taxes, but are deeply subsidized. Even private enterprises are politically defined as "contributing to the public good" which somehow seems to justify tax exempt status. Almost all poor people and those in the informal economy escape.

Local governments particularly have been so poor and burdened with so many official responsibilities that they have spent 50 years scrambling to lay hands on any possible source of income. Thousands of minor, marginal and often dysfunctional taxes, fees, user charges, service charges, sales taxes, movement taxes and many other impositions got invented and erratically enforced. In an effort to clean up this mess, the government earlier installed a form of Value Added Tax (VAT) which was mandated at the national level but administered by the States. The current VAT is defined as an indirect tax on the exchange value at every stage of the production of goods. Because it is administered by India's 28 States, it varies in nature and effectiveness from place to place. In general, it has allowed the rationalization of many of the confusing and conflicting older taxes and fees. It is largely self administered and easy to collect, and seems to be less vulnerable to corruption, or so the government hopes. Recently, the national government has proposed laws to create a new Goods and Services Tax (GST) which would replace the VAT and the centrally administered sales tax. This further reform is highly desirable and it would have the further advantage of increasing the income of the central government. It would eliminate the use of cesses, dividend double taxation, and the current "fringe benefit" tax which hurts private sector firms. [18]

Like most other countries, the Customs Service in India is sloppy, irrational and "leaks" badly. For questionable State Socialist reasons, heavy taxes have been used to constrain both imports and exports. In addition, a second and equally irrational barrier exists in the form of elaborate tariffs, limitations and fees. If the usual rapacity of Customs officers is added, it seems vital that the government attack this whole mess as vigorously as possible.

Like the U. S. and other nations, the tax laws and tax administration is an absolute bazaar of government/special interest connivance. The whole system is riddled with obscure provisions that are escape hatches for the politically connected, and rewards for the politicians that enact this bonanza. The whole system is a cesspool crying out for draining, but the political system is more the villain that the rescuer. Governments at all levels have expanded sources like fees, licenses, rents or fees on business operations where the income is "off budget" and capable of magically disappearing. These maneuvers are so substantial that it would profit governments greatly if these off budget sources could be captured and forced into the normal tax collection regime. In the process, many of the fees and charges would probably be found to be legally questionable.

Business interests in India constantly lobby for reductions in corporate income taxes, along with reductions in dozens of petty fees and charges. But perhaps the most feasible next step in tax reform would be to make more equal the tax burdens applied to state owned enterprises and those in the private sector, because increasingly the Indian economy now permits broader fields of competition and a greater willingness by a less Socialist government to recognize the values of this competition.

TRADE AND FOREIGN DIRECT INVESTMENT

The major trade policies that were established in the first years after independence centered on the need to protect Indian domestic producers of goods and services from foreign competition so that they could develop and expand to meet domestic needs. If this was not feasible, then it was felt that the government should step in and meet these needs through state owned enterprises. This led to an unwarranted expansion of the SOE base beyond the needs as defined by Socialist policy and into small enterprises that could not conceivably have any policy impact. This led in turn to a whole elaborate complex of regulation and control of almost all elements of the economy, in part justified by a strong belief that the private sector could not be trusted to act beyond greed and in the public interest. The government failed to accept that a more vigorous and productive and varied economy was in itself in the public interest.

In simplistic terms, the government, exactly like the Chinese, did not believe in a self modulating economy, but only in a centrally directed one. They also seemed to think that only the public sector could understand or produce economic virtue.

Import substitution centers on some extensive analysis of what the public, business, and other economic actors needed and wanted, and an assessment of whether these needs are being met, or could be met by domestic Indian providers. To the extent that these needs were being met by foreign providers, import substitution policy committed the government to seal off such foreign sources and somehow to generate domestic sources to fill the gaps. If local companies could develop these capabilities themselves, this was tolerable, but the government seemed to take a dim view of this prospect, and seemed to prefer pushing into these gaps itself. This took dozens of courses of action from import limitations to subsidized bank loans. In the last analysis, the government was actively interested in the widespread creation of state owned enterprises (SOE), not only to fill gaps but to expand the economy in ways that the government wanted to control.

Thus, concepts of protectionism and the "nurturing" of domestic industry seemed inevitably to lead to a heavy commitment by the government to block off penetration of the Indian market by foreigners. Even today, when the Indian government seeks to negotiate trade agreements with China or other countries, small Indian businesses lobby to block such efforts for fear of the competition. It is easy to see some part of this attitude as a reflection of the rejection of the British regime and the successful fight for independence. But the logic of import substitution also supported and justified the structure of centrist control which permeated the whole State Socialist philosophy. The political and bureaucratic structure absolutely loved the whole thing; it all seemed to fit together with the caste based sense of natural and historical superiority, and the God given right to rule.

Both trade and industry were dominated for almost 45 years by this elitist certainty.

Foreign Direct Investment (FDI) is defined as an investment involving a domestic enterprise and one or more foreign partners, where the domestic enterprise is controlling. There are many forms of foreign investment: the purchase of equity in the stock market; either minority or majority ownership equity in Indian enterprises; partnerships with Indian firms; operating units of foreign owned firms; sole ownership in Indian enterprises, or the newest of relationships – public/private partnerships with public bodies such as build-operate-transfer schemes, build-sell, build-transfer-manage contracts. In general, the Socialist view appeared to be initially to prevent FDI "penetration". Then the policy seemed to mutate toward "as little as possible as seldom as possible." Then, after the epochal changes of 1991, the whole philosophy changed to one of encouragement of foreign investment. Why? President Rao and Finance Minister Singh had come to understand that urgently needed development capital could come from three general sources: first from the revenues acquired by governments; second from resources that could be assembled by private sources; and third from the funds that foreign investors could be induced to provide.

Here again, State Socialism seemed out of joint with economic reality because it saw the government in conflict and competition with the private sector to capture a finite amount of capital. And the harder the government worked to win this competition through laws and policies and regulations, the more it reduced the capacity of the private sector to expand the economy. Even if the public and private sector were in competition, it began to be more clearly understood that foreign investment was a vital third source of capital – a hugely attractive add-on to what was available domestically. And how wonderful it would be to use the money of foreigners to enhance the Indian economy! Why didn't we think of this before?

Today, FDI has been dramatically opened up, but the country remains among the most protectionist in the world, and the private sector is still prohibited by the Indian government in arms and ammunition, atomic energy, coal/lignite, rail transport and most minerals mining, including diamonds, and insurance up to a limit of 49% of ownership. FDI capital investment is permitted in other sectors of the economy but only up to defined limits of equity ownership ranging from 26% to 100%, and all of these investments plus many others require the approval of the government, which is in reality, absolute control. Exports had been minor: cotton, tea, jute, cocoa, rice, mango pulp, etc. It is very weak in exports to other parts of Asia, and to Africa and Central America. Its exports to the U. S. and Europe have declined moderately in the last few years. And still, the proportion of total trade to GDP has risen from about 15% in 1990 to more than 45% today. The salvation seems to be the decline of the role of SOEs and the far more effective track record of Indian private enterprise, and the shift toward high technology and other higher value added goods.

INDUSTRY AND MANUFACTURING

The bedrock of Indian industrial policy was established under the Nehru government through the very important Industrial Policy Resolution of 1956. The policies of these early years also spoke vividly of the lack of trust in the private sector, and the fear of monopolies. This led to the Monopolies and Restrictive Trade Practices Act of 1970.

The Industrial Policy Resolution of 1956 boldly defined whole sectors of the Indian economy that were thenceforth off limits to the private sector and were reserved to the public sector. These included: arms, ammunition, aircraft, warships, and other military hardware; atomic energy and any minerals related to atomic energy, coal and lignite, mining of iron ore, manganese, chrome, gypsum, sulphur, gold, diamonds, copper, lead, zinc, tin, molybdenum and wolfram, plus railway transport, insurance and most of banking.

Further, private sector involvement was permitted in other industries, but only under compulsory licensing by the national government, which amounted to total control where the government thought it necessary. These sectors included petroleum and distillates, alcoholic beverages, sugar, animal fats and oils, tobacco, asbestos, plywood, veneers, particle board, hides and skins, motor cars, paper and news print, electronic aerospace and defense equipment, industrial explosives, drugs and pharmaceuticals, white goods, and entertainment electronics. Price controls were enforced on steel, cement, drugs, nonferrous metals, chemicals, fertilizers, coal, autos, oil, tires, cotton textiles, food grains, bread, butter, vegetable oils, tobacco, and most imports of any kind. Licensing was not required for small scale industry, but it too had a further list of requirements and reservations.

This is an industrial policy and does not deal with the service sectors of the economy, small scale industry (SSI), and the informal economy. An amendment was enacted in 1973 which identified high priority industries where investment by large private industry and foreign investment was permitted. In 1977, another amendment emphasized decentralization and the reservation of a large number of products for small scale industries. In 1980, policies promised competition promotion, technological upgrading and modernization, all intended to draw back from an increasingly ineffective public sector. In addition, foreign investment was for the first time encouraged for the whole economy and not just a limited number of priority industries. Management in the private sector is seeking to be more high tech and automated, and this is a direct challenge to the government policies that seek to back industries that employ masses of workers. But this in turn has had two serious consequences: first, it is seriously harming India's traditional cottage industries; and second, it is threatening the unions and their political allies who are being forced into slow retreat.

As an example, an article by the Communist Party of India (CPI) [19] bemoans the fate of the state owned Steel Authority of India (SAIL) because market liberalization had led to the growth of private steel companies (Mittal Steel, Jindals, Essa, Tata, et. al.) and the subsequent decline of SAIL. Production is down to 34% of the market, and almost 15% of its equity has been sold off to the private sector (and the banks). Import duties have been brought down to 5%, excise duties on domestic production have been increased, and the cost advantage has been shifting to imported steels. Only one third of domestic steel production is used domestically and the rest is exported. The CPI further bemoans the reduction of employment in Indian steel plants in the name of "competition", but this simply suggests that state enterprises must have been overstaffed to begin with. Similarly, it opposes the use of contractors, mostly because many of them are not unionized. It also points out that its heavy political campaigning has prevented some privatizations. The CPI also points out the bad safety record throughout the industry including SAIL.

The Industrial Policy Resolution of 1956 created the justification for a public sector in oil and gas. The government owns the Oil and Natural

Gas Commission, the Indian Oil Corp., and Oil India Ltd. In 1984, the Gas Authority of India Ltd. was set up to handle transportation and distribution of gas. In 1964, the state Indian Refineries Ltd. was allowed to merge with the Indian Oil Co. Ltd to form the private Indian Oil Corp. Ltd. But of the 18 oil refineries in India today, 17 are public.

However, by the end of the 80s, the petroleum sector was clearly seen as inadequate, meeting only about 35% of domestic need, and it thus joined other sectors urgently requiring economic liberalization. Finally, in 1997, the government enacted the New Exploration Policy to give the private sector equal access to the right to explore for oil. State owned firms are at least as active as the Chinese in foreign countries, having stakes in oil and gas fields in Russia, Sudan, Iraq, Libya, Egypt, Qatar, Ivory Coast, Australia, Vietnam, and Myanmar.

ENERGY AND ELECTRICAL POWER

In the Socialist world created by Prime Minister Nehru after Independence, one of the critical elements needed to establish government control over the economy was the nation's electricity system. Its three elements – power generation, power transmission grids and the final distribution to customers – were all placed under government ownership or direct control, with the expected profits to be captured by either the national government or State governments.

Power generation was controlled by the 28 States in what amounted to a vertically integrated monopoly controlled through a State Electricity Board created by national law and overseen by a Central Electricity Authority which was expected to formulate national policy. But the national role was vastly enlarged in 1975 through the creation of a National Thermal Power Corporation, a National Hydroelectric Power Corporation, and a National Nuclear Power Corporation, and it was intended that these enterprises would become major power generators more directly under the control of the national government. Today, almost two thirds of the generation capacity in India is owned and operated by the states, and central generating companies supply about 25% of total capacity

The pattern for power transmission and distribution involved control by the States through their State Electricity Boards which were authorized to let contracts or to grant licenses to others to transmit or distribute power. But as with power generation, the national government decided to assert its authority more directly in 1989 by creating the Power Grid Corporation of India which was given general authority over all transmission systems in the country, and specifically to control interstate transmission of electricity and the development of a national power grid. It was not until 1998 that power transmission could be treated as separate from generation, and at that time it was also opened up for private sector participation.

Thus, fairly early on, it was recognized that the usual approach by government through state owned enterprises (often called public sector undertakings in India) had once again proved a flawed concept leading to a wholly inadequate electrical capability for the country. Funds for the expansion and improvement of power generation capacity have never been adequate. As the population increased greatly, especially in cities, generation capacity fell farther and farther behind demand. To quote Panagarya: "The State Electricity Boards and their successor transmission and distribution companies suffer from the usual inefficiencies of government-run operations. They are overstaffed, and their technical operations are highly inefficient." [20] Plant load factors remain low, 15 to 20% of the electricity is lost in transmission, and losses to commercial customers are intolerable. This includes lack of meters, faulty meters, unread meters, under billing or no billing at all, non-payment of bills often through plain old bribery, and widespread power theft. Political leadership at both the national and state levels gives away electricity to farmers and poor people, thus destroying any hope of profitable operations. As a consequence, State Electricity Boards are financial disasters, incurring congenital losses each year, and having to bail themselves out by running up huge debts to their suppliers and to railroads, then resorting to expensive loans or soliciting bail- out subsidies from various government entities. Out of total electricity generated, only 55% is actually billed, and just 41% is regularly paid for. Current retail prices represent less than 75% of actual costs. Rural power is highly subsidized, with prices set to recover less than 20% of unit costs. While the government claims that 86% of villages are electrified, the fact that a power line reaches a village does not mean that most residents have power. In fact, in 1991, only about 30% of homes were really supplied.

This record of incompetence was not only embarrassing, but it was clearly having a strong negative impact on the improvement of the Indian economy, so finally, in 2003 the national government passed a new Electricity Act of 2003 that mandates a number of important changes which the government seems actually to want to implement. Other new laws were passed: a National Electricity Policy, Tariff Policy and Rural Electrification Policy, all in 2005. The vertical monopolies of State Electricity Boards have been broken up to be replaced by state transmission units, power generation companies, and distribution enterprises under license. An independent regulatory agency has public utility type powers to grant licenses to operate and to set tariff rates and is defined as "independent" meaning more or less free of political capture. For example, a law was passed in 2006 which mandated universal metering, which appears to have cut off a large number of political favors.

While most of the whole structure has been opened in some way to the private sector, starting as early as 1991, the past history of State Board financial weakness seems to have given the private sector pause, and their involvement is very slow. Private sector distribution interest is inhibited by the tendency of the political leadership to give away electricity to farmers and to set subsidy tariff rates for poor residential areas or favored commercial customers. State owned generation companies are often asked to sell power to distributors at "discount" rates. The result is that much of the time, power companies cannot even recover their costs, which in turn leads to inability to keep up with demand, poor service, lack of maintenance and losses to companies who are driven to generate their own power. It is hoped that the growing willingness of governments to abandon some of their bad politics and flawed regulation will permit much more serious and professional management: full universal metering, proper billing, vigorous bill collection, full cost recovery, reduction of power theft and abandonment of the culture of corruption and bribery. The electricity system has proved to be another example of the failures of state socialism, but it has not yet managed any significant shift to a more market based system. If the financial position can be rectified, private interests will be more willing to get into the market, and they cannot help but be more effective than governments have been. As the financial health of the sector increases, funds may well become available for a real program of rural electrification.

India has huge reserves of coal, but little of it is anthracite for use by industry, most of which must be imported, but soft coal is widely used for power generation, meeting 55% of national needs, and this is not likely to change in the foreseeable future. Coal is domestic and cheap; oil must be imported and is expensive. The government is pressing for more use of Liquid Natural Gas (LNG) but it is not clear why. India has limited natural gas supplies and LNG must be imported by tanker or pipeline at considerable expense. Oil is used to produce about 1/3 third of power needs, another third by natural gas, and most of the rest is traditional fuels like wood, or new renewable sources. Remarkably, only 1% of energy needs are met by atomic power, and the government is trying, over stout resistance, to enhance nuclear power generation.

TRANSPORT

India is also improving other elements of its physical infrastructure. Just 2% of India's roads are highways, even though most freight and nearly all passenger traffic are carried by road. Rutted highways, old airports, decaying ports and chronic electricity shortages weaken nearly every aspect of India's economy. (Prime Minister) Singh told Parliament in 2008 that India would have to raise infrastructure and related expenditures from 4% to 9% of GDP by 2012. [21]

India's road net is one of the most extensive in the world, and much progress has been made but only in the last few years. It now has more than two million miles of roads, but 80% are rural roads of which 27% are single lane and 59% are two lane. Half of the villages still lack access to all weather roads, and few cities and towns possess adequate vehicle safety and traffic control. It is still likely that once you leave one of the few modern 21st century highways, you will end up on an ancient dirt road competing with ox carts and wandering cattle. The road system is almost entirely government, with a division of responsibilities just like the U. S. where all roads except national highways (42,000 miles) are the responsibility of the states.

Roads are without doubt the most important element of the national transportation system, carrying 80% of passenger traffic and about 65% of freight traffic. The creation of the National Highways Authority in

1968 was crucial, along with a full array of laws: the Road Transport Corporations Act of 1950, the National Highways Act of 1956, and the Motor Vehicle Act of 1968. Large subsidies continue – free customs movement, tax exemptions and "holidays", and a dedicated tax on fuels to finance construction and maintenance. At the same time, the government is desperate to find ways to cut the financial burden of road way expansion and maintenance, and in the early 2000s, a major shift in policy occurred where the government, while maintaining its ownership, began increasingly to shift from government operations to contracting out construction and maintenance to the private sector. Where there is no possibility for recovering costs through user charges, the government will simply let contracts for construction and maintenance. But a more popular approach has become BOT contracting, where the government grants a concession to a private company to "build- operate-transfer" projects with enough earning potential to cover all or part of these costs. The concession agreement may allow the private contractor to collect tolls or charge fees to cover all or part of the project's costs, with the government covering any shortfalls by a lump sum payment, or an annual fee or annuity. The government in turn has created a Central Road Fund getting its income from a national gas tax, but it may also come up with the money out of general revenues, or by borrowing.

One major success is The Golden Quadrilateral, a multi-billion dollar superhighway linking New Delhi, Kolkata, Chennai, and Mumbai – a distance of 3,600 miles. This project was initiated by Najiv Gandhi in the mid 80s, and while experiencing the usual problems with land acquisition, cost overruns, political meddling and even violence, it was essentially completed by 2006. Highways are clogged with traffic, and drivers still have to deal with bicycles, camel carts and herds of goats.

Another success can be claimed with the opening of the first 11 mile stretch of the New Delhi Metro, and huge subway system which ultimately is expected to have over 200 stations. It is notable that the construction of the system has been by one of the new public-private partnerships, deliberately set up as a corporation designed to be free from government interference.

One element of the transport picture is especially bright. Asia is the home to nearly 80% of the world's 315 million motorcycles, and 45 million of these are in India, second only to China's 100 million. This market is seen as having a lot of growth potential and India has three of the world's largest 2 wheel vehicle manufacturers: Honda, Kawasaki (partnered with local firm Bajaj), and a local firm, TVS, which recently terminated a partnership with Suzuki.

THE WORKFORCE

India currently has a population of over 800 million who are potential workers, with about 610 million of these people in the 15- 60 age range. The actual workforce however is measured at about 500 million, and it is expected to grow by 15-20 million each year, and an estimated 30% of all gross additions to the world's workforce will be added in India. The number will be greater in part because more and more Indian women are seeking to enter the workforce. At any given time, there are over 40 million who are temporarily unemployed.

The Indian government has invented what are absolutely the most outrageous official designations of its workforce. It defines the "organized sector" of the workforce as that 7% of workers who work for governments and SOEs, and is heavily unionized. The rest, in a masterpiece of Socialist elitist arrogance are referred to as the "unorganized sector" - which means 372 million workers, or 93% of the workforce! And that 7% of unionized workers are the protected and subsidized darlings of the political elite. When the government promises to improve the lot of Indian workers, it really only means that 7%. Most labor and management laws on the books are written to convey some benefit to that 7%. In a strange and very "Indian" way, the countless benefits bestowed on the 7% seem somehow to "justify" the position of the government in ignoring the 93%. Is the government attentive to the needs of Indian workers? Of course! But according to India's employers association "the central government imposes over 55 labor laws and the States another 150 or more. The most notorious of these is the Industrial Disputes Act which requires any establishment employing more than 100 workers to ask the State's permission before firing anyone.

Who are the 93%? Most of them - 70% - are employed in agriculture as farmers, sharecroppers, farm workers, or in related occupations. Others work for private sector companies in everything from manufacturing to services. Others are in the informal economy of semi-legal workers in urban areas. Despite the prejudices and preferment of government policy, the "unorganized sector" is the real Indian workforce. It contains 95% of all jobs and despite the numbers of very poor and underemployed it contains, it generates more than 50% of the GDP. The reforms stemming from the watershed decisions of 1991 did not face up to this dilemma, but they set in motion a wide range of economic policy shifts, every one of which is now whittling away at the traditional positions of the "organized sector". Note also that child labor laws were passed in 1986, but child labor is still currently estimated at 44 million – mostly in agriculture and small village crafts and family businesses.

Importantly, the government has drawn back from its unquestioning favoritism of SOEs and it is permitting greater private sector penetration into previously walled off SOE territory. As SOEs have diminished, so have the numbers of "official" workers. Public sector employment has been decreasing in banks, insurance enterprises, the railroads, and even in the military weapons systems industrial establishments. The competition between public and private sectors is being won by the private sector, and the most attractive jobs for young professionals are no longer the Indian Administrative Service or the declining SOEs.

In general, manufacturing in India is declining, and in the past it has been the top priority – almost the only priority – of the government's economic development policy. Most of the new jobs are being created in the private sector, and especially from the bottom up in the small scale industries and in the informal economy which not only does not need government preferment, but actively resists both unionization and government oversight. Unions have had a great deal of difficulty unionizing the private sector, largely because of their absolutely hideous record in governments and the SOEs. In fact, about 87% of manufacturing employment is in very small enterprises.

The nature of the informal economy is changing. It is becoming more stable and wider ranging, and it is most often the first home for young workers entering the workforce. It is open to lower castes who want to shake off the stigmas of caste so embedded in rural/village life. It is also often the first home for women who also want to break the old barriers and establish new opportunities for themselves. Even the elitist government is slowly waking up to the values of the informal economy – which it has succeeded in ignoring for more than 50 years – but as yet, efforts to "assist" the informal economy are spastic and marginal. In fact, new laws and regulations to help, turn out to be mostly regulatory and controlling (e. g. mandatory worker registration, workplace standards, wage standards, mandatory disputes resolution, and many more). Meanwhile, the promised funds for assistance, or the expansions of social services have largely failed to materialize and a large part of the incomes of people in the informal economy is in the form of non- money bartering, trades, and exchanges, hopefully out of sight of the government.

The trends of modern management around the world have been toward more automation, and this acts to reduce the numbers of workers in both factories and offices. Unions everywhere have long resisted these tides, but they have largely been losing ground.

Public sector SOEs must either learn to adapt these innovations or they will find themselves losing out, and many will go out of business. The faster the rate of change, the more they tend to fall behind. But their allies are fast becoming their enemies. Unions implacably oppose any innovation that might cause the loss of jobs; and politicians, who typically fail to finance technology or even simple repair or maintenance, are confronted with big demands for money which they don't have, and haven't got the courage to go out and get.

The service sectors of the economy are rapidly expanding – from the bottom up, and no thanks to the government. As import substitution barriers have been abandoned and withered, consumers are now seeing a world class range of consumer goods, and they are enriching their lives with a range of better and cheaper foreign goods and services.

Even the politics of India represents an attack on the old elitist labor alliances. Much political power has shifted from the national Congress and BJP parties into the hands of new and more powerful regional and local parties and leaders who draw their support from various elements of that 93% of the unorganized workforce which the government has so ignored.

The failure of the government to address the needs of the informal economy is a source of growing resentment against this indifference. People don't necessarily want to be in the informal economy. Most have been driven there out of necessity, given the inadequacies of the formal economy. But they are often the victims of corrupt (mostly local government) officials, vicious local police, rapacious public officials, greedy merchants, extortionist land owners, and endless numbers of racketeers. Many of these problems could be mitigated by honest and supportive government, but these are rare outcomes.

For many years, the government has been working on bills to provide assistance to the unorganized sector. Half of this proposed legislation was regulatory and unwanted, and most of the "financial help" stuff has never materialized, even though the government did finally, in 2008, make provisions for social services programs for unorganized workers. The only real part of these proposals that has passed is the Unorganized Workers Social Security Act. A National Fund to propose ways to improve this sector was never enacted. In a typical utterance of political nonsense, a 2008 policy statement was issued in which the government solemnly promised that it would cut government jobs by 30% in five years (exactly the same promise was made in 1997 after which government employment rose), and that 50 million jobs will be created nationally in the next five years!

THE INFORMAL ECONOMY

According to De Soto, the informal economy is defined as "the refuge of individuals who find that the costs of abiding by existing laws in the pursuit of legitimate economic objectives exceed the benefits. It is essential that the state remember that before it can distribute the nation's wealth, the must *produce* wealth. And that in order to produce wealth it is necessary that the state's actions not obstruct the actions of its citizens, who, after all, know better than anyone what they want and what they have to do. The state must restore it its citizens the right to take on productive tasks, a right that it has been usurping and obstructing. The state must limit itself to functioning in those necessary areas in which private industry cannot function. This does not mean that the state will wither away and die." **[22]**

The underground economy is broader and includes illegal activities such as drugs, prostitution, illegal betting and smuggling. The informal economy is not confined to poor countries, and in fact every country has a substantial informal sector in its economy. However, the size and variety of the informal economy is directly related to the capacity of a national economy to generate enough economic strength to support its people. When the formal economy is too weak, people often have no option but to enter the informal economy as a means of survival. One of the pathologies of many governments is that they fail to recognize this reality, and view the informal economy as a form of crime, often called a "black market" existing only to avoid taxes and escape regulations. In truth, in many countries the informal economy is saving the country from economic collapse. In India, the informal economy along with some elements of the underground economy, are estimated to make up 30% of the

GDP. The government can and does use laws and police enforcement to suppress the informal economy (i. e. "slum clearance") even when it knows that it provides employment and income that the state has failed to provide.

There are no barriers to entry into the informal economy. Anybody capable of performing a service or providing a good can enter. The most likely types of work in the informal economy are casual laborers, construction workers, and personal services providers such as servants, janitors, trash collectors, porters, messengers, errand runners, delivery people, child care providers, street vendors, and even panhandlers. In addition, if some capital is available, other people may be able to become small retailers or customer service providers. One of the most frequent such service is transportation in urban areas where networks of jitney cars and minivans supplement scarce and inadequate public transportation. Small scale manufacturing is widespread, including the fine arts of making cheap copies of Gucci handbags and Omega watches. Many crafts are represented, including carpenters, plumbers, masons, electricians, tailors, and auto mechanics, and many of these entrepreneurs are capable of working in both the formal and informal economies at the same time, depending on what work is available.

The informal economy has many obvious downsides. First, while the activities are all legal in the formal sense, they are illegal when they escape the tax collection system and avoid most government regulation. Their small scale of operations often prevents them from economies of scale and mostly they must refrain from some management practices like advertising or internet linkages that can be traced. In many cases, bribing the police, or to buying off inspectors are added costs of doing business. Property ownership is also dangerous, and thus the protection of physical facilities is difficult. Informal operators may be the victims of thieves and protection rackets since it is difficult to appeal for police protection. There is seldom any real job security, work may be uncertain, income and wages are often unstable and fluctuating since most informal activities are highly competitive, with too many workers seeking too few jobs. Few work benefits such as health care or unemployment compensation are possible. But surprisingly, wages in the informal sector often compare favorably with those in the formal economy, where the excess of workers also keeps wages down.

In many countries, it is often the only starting point for young people who do not have the education or skills to enter more formal businesses. Many entrepreneurs are women who might be barred from prejudiced formal businesses, and who would have little chance of becoming owners or managers of their own formal enterprises.

Nor is the informal economy the home of crooks and rip-off artists. In most instances, there is a surprising degree of organization and self discipline. Almost like the guilds of old, members of groups such as street vendors or transport providers create coordination groups to allocate locations, prevent rip-offs, set price ranges, and even organize the business of bribing police and other officials.

Most people in the informal economy are really seeking to upgrade themselves and enter the formal economy if possible. It is irrational to live in the shadows, and on the edge of survival, and with some help, many informal businesses could make even greater contributions to the economy by being allowed to go formal. For example, women have demonstrated, in the face of much local prejudice, that they can run successful businesses, and it would be an easy jump for even the murkiest of governments to work out low cost loans for women to do just that in the formal framework. Much of the evolution of the economies of developing countries is not from massive state owned enterprises, but from the bottom up – from small entrepreneurs with the drive and ability to take care of themselves.

And yet this society is not basically vicious or criminal, nor is it negative and chaotic. Slum areas can and do transform themselves into neighborhoods and communities. But they have found from experience the world over that they can expect very little from governments except oppression and neglect. Therefore, slum areas, especially in India organize themselves to provide their own schools, medical aid stations, taxi services, water connections, sewer connections, food services and almost everything else. Many slum dwellers live in shacks made of sheet metal and cardboard, with little or no water or sanitation connections. Often there are slum landlords who own (or pretend to own) the land, and who extract money from slum dwellers by any means fair and foul. Remember, there are an estimated 170 million slum dwellers in urban India. Land has become a controlling urban asset, and the perversions of its use favor special interest politics between developers and public officials. Also, a lot of land seems to be owned by Mafia-like gangs who own it for speculation and "leverage." The tendency is for land to be made increasingly scarce through regulation and misallocation, and slum dwellers are forced either farther out from the city center, or onto the streets and alleys. According to Nilekani, "The residents of the Dharavi slum in Bombay are among the most disadvantaged communities in the world in terms of their access to education, capital or land. Many of them come to the city in search of work, and resorted to entrepreneurship when they failed to land a steady job. And most or their enterprises operate out of Dharavi, which has also become the hub for an estimated fifteen thousand single-room factories with an annual output of $1.47 billion. This teeming community of entrepreneurs includes recyclers, potters, furniture makers, private schools, cable operators, as well as beauty parlors, pubs, and businesses that provide water and electricity, and help kill the slum's rats. The people here are largely self-employed, and while many of them are successful, there are also many among these small entrepreneurs who have turned to businesses for want of steady work."

As these realities are finally recognized, it appears that the attitudes of governments are undergoing some change. It all starts with the essential issue – can the formal economy generate enough national wealth to maintain a reasonable standard of living for its citizens? If the answer is yes, and if the government in fact delivers on its commitments, the value of the informal economy is lessened, and it makes sense for the government to attempt to recapture lost revenues to help finance its social agenda. But if the answer is no, then it would be wiser for the government not only to tolerate the informal economy but to encourage it. In both India and China, socialist theology had insisted that the government would provide jobs and benefits for all, and thus an informal economy was considered a crime against the government which felt that it could not even admit that it existed. In reality the informal elements of the economy in China and India are vital for a huge number of people.

In other countries, the World Bank estimates that it employs from 1/3 to ½ of the total workforce. The informal economy exists in both rural and urban areas, but it tends to be largest and most significant in large urban conglomerates where it is closely linked to urban slums and ghettos. Indian has a staggering 180 million people who live in urban slums, and a very large percentage of these people make their living in the informal economy. China has an equally large "float" of 180 million workers who are in the informal economy, or in transient and part time work, or who are unemployed. If the families of these workers are included, China's slum population is undoubtedly larger than India's.

CHAPTER IV

Economic Development in China: From the Top Down

THE WHOLE WORLD HAS BECOME enchanted with the new wave of economic development in China, but there is a serious risk that this enchantment will cause observers to overlook the many negative factors that exist in the Chinese economy and society. In summary, this great wave of economic expansion and development is less great that it seems because it is offset by a whole series of negative factors:

1. Inflation has been high; in some years, it is almost equal to the level of GDP increase.

2. State Owned Enterprises (SOE) have long been a hidden drag on the economy. As the SOE divestiture program of the government advances, it reduces the drag, but it also creates a sag in government revenues and the government continues to spend funds to subsidize them.

3. SOEs, the People's Liberation Army and local governments have run up huge debts. In many cases, billions of yuan in book values have simply evaporated, but they may still be listed as assets. The national government has had to pour other billions of yuan to prop up the SOEs, but still, banks had to eat huge losses because the government shifted the burden of SOE budget deficits into bank loans, which are often never repaid. The creation of special asset management companies by the government then moved this

debt out of the banks and back into the government, and these companies have really yet to manage much except to write off more bad debt. Local governments are still heavily in debt, much of which will never be paid off.

4. Even the success of the economic development program has had its ironic negatives in the sense that it has caused the inflation of many prices, especially for energy, materials, transportation, imports of modern equipment, and even costs of skilled and semi-skilled labor.

5. The workforce is absolutely chaotic. It finally had to be admitted by the government that most SOEs were overstaffed for political reasons, with the redundancy factor running from 20 to 40%. So even while the government was urgently seeking to create new jobs, it has been forced to dump out millions of workers from their SOE "iron rice bowl" jobs. At the same time, there are an estimated 180 million workers who are in a work "twilight zone" or "float" – unemployed, underemployed, in temporary or transient jobs, or in the informal economy. There is no way that the Chinese economy could absorb these unskilled workers for decades to come; and meanwhile, they constitute an increasingly restless force in society.

6. Even the new economic enterprises are often working on the thinnest of margins of profitability. Many small businesses are very hard put to survive, and the slightest turndown among their customers could be fatal. There is some information about new office buildings that are half empty, or new high rise apartments that are not selling, or new shopping malls that are sparsely visited. Many elements of the economy are obsolete even when built, with archaic production techniques, and cheap construction that will deteriorate rapidly. Production is inefficient in the use of power, fuels, water, and raw materials – often using 2-3 times the quantities used by similar businesses in developed countries. Quality control, reliability, safety and durability are scarcely understood concepts and are seldom achieved. The whole industrial establishment is marked by an excessive number of very inefficient production units. Many new factories are merely taking business away from older ones.

7. The shift to a market economy reinvigorated the tax base and provided new sources of revenue, but it is still true that the tax base is too narrow, the capacity to collect taxes is very low, and the art of tax avoidance is widely admired and practiced. The government has written new and more productive tax laws, but they still can't quite manage to get their hands on the money.

8. Governments at all levels have ignored the economic consequences of their environmental disasters too long, and it is almost certain that, in the near future, this bill will come due, and it will become a big drain on the new wealth. The CCP knowingly escaped these problems by shifting them to local governments, even where it is obvious that most of the problems such as river pollution, acid rain, and poisonous air are country-wide in nature.

9. China has a shameful, embarrassing, outrageous, unhealthy and dangerous lack of every vital social service: health, education, welfare, old age protection, unemployment compensation, aid to the handicapped, and housing for the poor. The government has announced a whole series of policies and Five Year Plans full of useless incredible "solutions", but the country seems little better off because of any action of its governments than it was in 1990, except perhaps for higher education. If individuals are better off now, it is because more of them can now afford to buy vital social services for themselves. But the new middle class, and urban dwellers, and better off farmers and villagers see these gaps as government failures – and as unfunded mandates – and they will increasingly demand that these mandates be delivered. Thus, there are four or five mammoth and highly expensive obligations that will threaten to inundate the government's budget.

10. The state of working men and women is very bad. Millions of people have come to cities to look for work for the simple reason that nothing could be as bad as it has been in rural areas, where hundreds of millions have been living lives of grinding poverty, with no future and no hope for themselves or their children. The government has never been able to stem this tide, despite heavy handed efforts to do so, and this has created deep resentment among the migrants. Big cities like Shanghai and Chonquing are

huge sprawling complexes of shoddy unsafe factories, shanty towns, overcrowded slums, beggars in the streets crime, prostitution and corruption. Even those workers who have jobs in the "official" economy are working long hours in the worst possible working conditions, for extremely low wages. But even then, they will be making 3-4 times as much as they did growing rice on the farms. Those who are in the "unofficial" economy were forbidden to bring their families with them, and have no access to government provided housing, health care, food supplies, or education for themselves or their children. While the government has begun to deal with these people, the efforts to date are very puny. Many of the factory workers are women, and even despite the poor wages and working conditions, and the potential for sexual harassment, they still may feel that they have improved their lot compared to rural poverty. Recently, municipal governments and, reluctantly, the national government, have been forced to concede the necessity of extending social services even to this migrant population.

11. Finally – and forever – there is corruption, and this has more significance than just the theft of government funds. There seems to be a growing cynicism about the Party, that corruption within the CCP is not just about stealing but about trampling people's rights and the pathological retention of power.

If all of these negative factors are considered, the "miracle" of the Chinese economy is that it took off as well as it did. While this economic success is what is propping up the CCP, one should get beyond the political issue and recognize that the economic surge is doing a powerful lot of good for the country – and the people recognize and appreciate it.

FIRST: THE REFORM OF STATE OWNED ENTERPRISES

The dilemma of failing SOEs is very difficult to deal with, since the whole concept of SOEs was firmly imbedded in the intellectual and philosophical framework of state socialism itself. But the fall of the Soviet Union was recognized not only as the failure of the socialist economy but the failure of state socialism, and this lesson was not lost on the CCP, which for several years had already been seeking to restructure its own economy to avoid the same fate. State planning had skewed the economy toward heavy manufacturing, and there had been extensive neglect of other elements of the economy such as consumer products and social service needs, and more modern technology potentials. he heart of this restructuring was that the state was forced to withdraw from its almost exclusive reliance on SOEs, and, for the first time, turn to the creation and articulation of a genuine private sector, market based economy. SOEs had produced a reasonable base of manufacturing and some services like banking, but in total, they had never proved vigorous enough or capable enough to provide stable work for more than about 20% of the Chinese workforce.

Why did the SOEs so often prove to be a failed experience? Most critically, the basic concept itself proved to be flawed, in that SOEs had too little real independence and far too much political intervention. The political leadership had never really accepted its own philosophy. They could not accept the idea that SOEs would be free to accommodate to the realities of the market place. Instead they believed – and continue to believe in both China and India – that each SOE should be under the control of a politically driven government ministry, and that they should be directed in detail by the top down policies which dictated such vital decisions as what to produce, how to fix input and output prices, when money could be borrowed and for what, which suppliers had to be used, and almost every element of every SOE business plan. The level of political intervention was utterly stifling and debilitating, and often corrupt. Most SOEs were forced to hire workers they did not need and could not use, and it was estimated that, at one time, more than 30 million workers in SOEs were redundant. The state also mandated the existence of labor unions and "Workers Congresses" but their role, as seen by the government, is not to represent the workers, but to transmit government directives, and monitor worker activities. In addition, great numbers of workers were locked in by the government to low value work such as agriculture and cheap manufacturing. These workers were unskilled, and many were women who had almost no education, and no skills other than machine tending. The tradeoff, of course, has been that SOEs are generously protected and subsidized, and they are given huge business advantages both domestically and in foreign investment roles by government backing and financing.

At the peak, there were more than 400,000 SOEs (although this number includes many that were very small), but about half of them were operating at an actual deficit. In 1997, the state sector included not only most manufacturing, but also the whole banking system, 65% of the wholesale distribution system and 40% of the more than 14 million retail outlets. It included most schools, housing and local transportation. Many of these enterprises were operating at very low levels of performance, or on very slim margins of profit and in total they ran up heavy debts which state owned banks were forced to maintain, or even forgive.

Many SOEs were also famously inefficient, and hundreds of economic sectors had fallen victim to centrist planning mistakes, especially the fallacy of mandating increases in production almost to the exclusion of all else. As a consequence, these sectors contained a very large number of small inefficient and poorly managed local factories turning out poor quality goods that nobody really wanted.

The watershed over the fate of the SOEs occurred in 1998, when, after long debate within the ranks of the CCP, the order was issued to initiate the massive program of what is termed SOE divestiture. [3] The divestiture order applied to the People's Liberation Army and to government ministries and organizations reporting to some CCP offices. From an estimated major 75,000 SOES the goal is to keep only 2,000 to 3,000. About 80% of small SOEs have been divested, mostly to collectives or cooperatives.

It turned out that "divestiture" was not the same thing as "privatization". Many strategies for divestiture were developed. In many cases, the preferred approach of the government has been not to divest at all, but to attempt to upgrade the performance of the SOEs it wished to retain. This retention approach was particularly important in what can be called the "commanding heights" sectors of the economy – those sectors that drive or control many other sectors. Key examples are gas and oil and coal production, energy processing and distribution, production of iron, steel and other critical metals, food distribution, banking, public utilities, all forms of communications including the media, electronics production and the manufacture of all military weaponry. In many cases, whole sectors have been restructured through mergers and acquisitions, consolidations, combinations, and "thinning out". In other instances, the preferred strategy with retained SOEs has been to seek to partner them with solid private sector enterprises, either Chinese of foreign invested. The intent here has been fourfold: to get an input of fresh capital from the private sector partner; to tap into the private partner's technology base; to learn modern management; and to link with better sales and distribution networks.

While the total number of SOES retained by the central government is relatively small (around 2-3,000), many have actually been set up as vast holding companies with hundreds of subsidiaries. Holdings may be either horizontal and sector specific or vertical, from raw materials to sales. There are also some groups that are becoming conglomerates, ranging across many sectors. These groups are doing very well, and there appears to be strength coming from economies of scale. It is often one of these large enterprise groups that are used by the government to undertake massive business projects in Africa and the Far East.

In a very large number of instances, the central government in Beijing has divested itself of SOEs by transferring them to the provinces, townships and municipalities. Not surprisingly, a large number of these transferred SOEs were the "losers" in the central government portfolio, with poor management records and a long history of operating at a deficit. So while the central government was happily unburdening its books, local governments were forced to go into business, often using local tax money, to upgrade these losers. To the great surprise of many, these officials have often succeeded, and SOEs have been revitalized to the point that "Township/Village Enterprises (TVEs) have become a large and valuable contributor to the Chinese economy. [4]

But despite the typical meddling of oversight ministries, SOEs still have a miserable track record of bad management: asset stripping, declaring excessive dividends, poor quality control, lack of interest in safety of products or services (witness the spate of unsafe products exported to the

U. S.), and heavy indebtedness accompanied by efforts to use political pressure to avoid repayment.

Key personnel appointments remain largely under the control of the CCP, and Party loyalty still counts for more than ability. In a lot of cases, "sick" SOEs have been placed under the control of a new kind of government oversight agency, the Assets Supervision and Administration Commission, which is primarily responsible for working off the huge debts that the sick SOEs incurred. The government keeps insisting that eventually, all SOEs will be turning a profit and that all government subsidies will end.

Divestiture does not mean that most of the enterprises will end up as pure private sector organizations. China is now officially a "mixed economy", or "a market economy with Chinese characteristics". The State will remain in full control of defense industries, the 2-3,000 "strategic" SOEs, and sufficient equity position in hundreds of other entities to retain effective control. Strategic industries continue to include utilities, energy including oil and gas extraction and refining and coal mining, power generation, natural resources, transportation including railways and civil aviation, major infrastructure (e. g. ports, airports, etc.), steel, shipbuilding, petrochemicals, retail banking, telecommunications, newspapers and TV, publishing, machine tools, agricultural distribution, and certain projects that require very large scale investment such as the Three Gorges Dam.

The hope is that those sources outside of government including Chinese collectives, corporations and foreign investors can be induced to provide huge influxes of new capital. The negative factor is whether outside investors want to get into enterprises where the government is clearly retaining some degree of control. In fact, much of the "outside investor" money comes not from new investors, but from Chinese SOEs, asset management companies, or local governments. Many of these cross-shareholding investments are highly suspect, especially to foreign investors.

There are new provisions that allow foreign companies to invest in public infrastructure projects such as roads, bridges, IT projects, and sewage disposal systems. But these investments must be through some form of contracting, build-lease or mandated buy- backs, so that private sector companies have some means for earning a profit. These contract relationships are usually controlled by provincial government, but often through some SOE.

URBAN MIGRATION: THE IRRESISTIBLE FORCE

The Chinese government has implemented a series of industry-wide restructuring programs in basic industries such as textiles, coal, metallurgy, oil refining, sugar refining, power generation, cement, glass, alcoholic beverages. A main problem has been dealing with problems of excess capacity, partly from "irrational exuberance" during the huge build-up of the 80s. There are hundreds of thousands of new, small factories that have emerged, and they are mostly poor places to work and to live, resembling the industrial society like the worst of the early sweat shops found in Europe and America in the late 19th century. Many are physically repugnant – ugly, filthy, crowded, noisy, smelly, unsafe, and often dangerous. Most of the employees – 70% or more – are women; young girls really, fresh out of their villages and farms, thinking about the excitement and glamour of the cities and hoping to get good jobs. Instead, they get these miserable factories where they end up as mindless machine tenders. Most of them live in dreary barracks-like dormitories, 8 to 10 to a room, with little provision for their comfort or pleasure. In the city of Shenzen alone, there are estimated to be 4 million of these dorm dwellers. The work is long and brutal, averaging 13 hour days and 70 hour weeks, and if the company has a rush order, it could mean 7 days a week. The government has mandated an official maximum work week of 49 hours, but only a few "show" factories observe this rule to satisfy inspectors from their American or European buyers who have people at home pressing them. In many cases, a Chinese enterprise will have a compliant show factory for everybody to inspect, with the real and larger sweat shop factory across town.

Profit margins for these factories are razor thin and therefore the job of the managers is to hold down costs on everything all the time. The key is low wages. The factory work is usually rather simple, consisting of some form of processing or machine tending, and with 180 million potential workers in the urban "float", factory managers seldom need to authorize wage increases or pay bonuses.

There is an officially established minimum wage, but the majority of employers appear to feel free to ignore it, and if the government inspects, the assumption is that the inspector can be bought off.

For young people, there is little hope for a better life in these factories, but there are a few ladders to climb. First there is an almost unbelievable amount of job hopping. Workers are constantly looking for a better job, even if it is only a better factory. In the bad old days, the Communist regime officially controlled and usually denied movement of workers from one job to another, much less from one city to another. But people by the millions just busted through such controls and now trains and buses are full of searchers checking job prospects elsewhere.

For many, the real breakpoint – the great divide – is to move from the factory floor to an office. One way to do this is to seek education, and there are thousands of self help courses, books, and magazines on how to handle computers, other office equipment, office work situations and relationships, and "how to get ahead". But offices seem to have developed along some of the same corrosive paths that afflict factories. Office environments are under great pressure from too much work, too little money, time pressures, destructive competitiveness, ruthlessness and the usual forms of pettiness and office politics, which the Chinese seem to love.

Despite the corrosive work described above, young people from farms and villages continue to see migration as their hope and continue to migrate to the cities to force their way in the urban environment, which says a lot about what it is like back home. It used to be that urban migrants were looked down on as deserters from their families and homes. Now, to be a migrant is a source of pride. Young people see themselves as brave and bold. The old folks sit at home and criticize, and ask for money. It may be that many migrants will retreat to the farms when they can't get work, but they tend to return to the cities as soon as they can. Rapidly, these young people become less rural and more urban in attitude, and slowly they resolve conflicts with urban locals who, after all, may not be long off the farm themselves.

The cities in which these factories are located are huge messes, like being thrown into a cement mixer. Everything is in a constant state of flux, always changing, full of high risk, and maybe high potential. There are a couple of hundred cities in China today where one can be overwhelmed by noise, disruption, chaos, stress, traffic, bad driving, pollution, poisonous air, short tempers, crass materialism, corruption, gambling, prostitution, a scam artist in every hotel lobby and a hustler on every street corner. The police are corrupt and bullying and can still decide that migrants are "illegal". Bus and taxi drivers often stop their vehicles and force people to pay extra. But still they come.

LEGAL FRAMEWORK FOR ECONOMIC REFORM

The Chinese are developing new legal frameworks for domestic economic transactions; for foreign trade and investment both in the country and overseas; for administrative/regulatory decisions; and for the fair and equitable functioning of the legal system.

First, it must be understood that the legal system is not independent; all of its elements are seen as part of the overall government structure, subject to general administrative controls, and vulnerable to the usual political interventions. Reforms of the legal system are a reflection of the very low state from which it starts. As with so much else, the courts and prosecutors were the victims of Maoist populism, and the system was all but destroyed. Economic reform has also created many new forms of economic activity that was not even allowed under Mao. But it remains true that the legal system is almost entirely designed for the protection of the State and the control of the population, and it is not well designed for individual use. [8]

All private enterprises must be registered and approved by the government and operate under detailed and complex regulations. The Economic Contract Law (ECL) of 1981 was a first step that allowed agreements between "legal persons", and defined their rights and duties. "Duties" are best understood as duties to the government, at least as much as duties to the other parties to the contract or agreement. For many years, and still to some degree, a "hidden" element of a contract or any agreement is that it must conform to government policy and the State economic plan. Any contract with any enterprise that is partially owned or controlled by the government is likely to be slanted toward the interests of the government. Most regulations dealing with commercial activities contain provisions for extensive intervention by the government if it chooses to do so.

The General Principles of Civil Law (1986), and Revisions of the Economic Contract Law (1993) apply mostly to "horizontal" relationships, but they apply only to "extra-plan" contracts. Civil law deals with such things as land use, use of state-owned land or assets, rights to mineral resources, authorities of collectives, and rights in the operation of SOEs. Most of these laws are deliberately vague, general, and incomplete, and these gaps can be seen to be deliberate. There is some retreat from the compulsions of overall economic planning, but it remains a serious factor in the "plan" portion of the economy. The 1993 revision removed all references to the economic plan from the ECL, such as the one that had linked economic contracts to the fulfillment of the plan. Yet, as usual, a lot of real power lies in implementing regulations, and courts had often used the old law to overturn price terms stated in contracts for "unfairness" even though they had been freely negotiated.

Collectives, which are widely used forms of enterprise at local government levels, became attractive because the government views them as small local ventures which were outside of the economic plan, and thus less rigidly controlled. Thus, TVEs and other local enterprises often took the form of collectives, and local governments were often the owners or heavy investors. Many collective boards were combinations of public officials, officials from SOEs, or other local notables including officials of the CCP local office. This made it hard to distinguish the private from the public sector, and put a lot of influence on "influence". This overlap was addressed by a new TVE law in 1997[9] that tried to legislate a separation of government and private sector, and tried to pin down responsibility for such things as pollution control, land use, product assurance, and collection of taxes, fees and licenses.

Similarly, the disappointments with SOEs were initially met with a movement toward "corporatization", but still, the power and influence of the administrative state is far more important than the rights of the shareholders. Corporatization means mostly the right of an enterprise to issue stock, but it is not the same as privatization, and the government has deliberately held enough stock in most instances to control policy. Many SOEs became the victims of insider managers who stripped assets through fake subsidiaries, over- invoicing, cheap sales, and plain old fashioned stealing. There is a real competition in the government as to who controls equity related issues. The competitors are The People's Bank of China, the State Development and Planning Commission, the Ministry of Finance, the State Commission for Restructuring the Economy, the management of the two stock exchanges, and of course, the CCP itself.

The essential conflict remains: the demands for a true legal and policy basis for private enterprise, vs. the tendency to favor the government in all things. The Party-State retains enough power to regulate many activities very closely, and the mix of rules that facilitate market relationships is still offset by rules attempting to control what is perceived to be harmful (to the government) economic activity.

Many years have been invested in creating the legal framework for foreign direct investment (FDI) dealing with such matters as percentage of equity allowed in Chinese enterprises, technology transfer contracts, patent and trademark use and protection, foreign exchange, bank borrowing, import-export regulations, ownership protections, contract enforcement, labor relations, and so forth. All FDI investments must be approved by the Ministry of Foreign Trade and Economic Cooperation (MOFTEC). Local governments are still very hungry, and they often ignore national laws and regulations – which is probably a wise course, but must be very confusing to foreign investors. Many companies find that they enter into a contract or other agreement, only to find that it can be modified by unilateral government action. The real meaning of any regulation can be found only in its application, where local politics or bureaucratic horse-trading can modify the meaning, distort the nature of the deal, and require later compromises or the payment of bribes. While the central government has enacted laws that prohibit local laws that violate national laws, the "interpretation" of these laws is a local government art form. The Chinese are experts on selective regulation. It is always true that there will be conflict between FDI ventures and local enterprises that are in competition. In some cases, government ministries will issue secret internal regulations or policy positions which are then concealed from investors or the network of government-provided "asset valuation agencies" which distort real values in the government's favor.

The culture of management is also an issue. The Chinese seem to value subtle connivance, opaqueness, and elliptical thinking. Americans especially seem to value fixed and settled contract agreement, straightforwardness, truth between partners, and rejection of outside influence on the affairs of the enterprise. The Chinese partners regard the contract as a starting point that will evolve over time, rather than an end point. They regard as an asset their contacts, proper and improper, with government officials, regulating agencies and CCP officials. For the Chinese, bribes and other corrupt practices may be regarded as skillful "lubricants", while Americans tend to see them as dangerous and improper. The government's reform efforts are aimed at the unwarranted and illegal practices of the bureaucracy. They are deliberately and knowingly not aimed at the unwarranted and illegal practices of politicians. The Ministry of Supervision that is supposed to investigate violations of laws, regulations, and policies, and to investigate complaints against officials, is a creature of the political State Council, and any decisions on sanctions or punishments are subject to the approval of the local Party committees of which they are a part.

THE NEW ALTERNATIVE: ECONOMIC DEVELOPMENT FROM THE BOTTOM UP

In the face of grave doubts about the fate of the CCP "top down" pattern of economic development, there are three "bottom up" patterns that seem to fit more naturally into the mentality of the Chinese people. One is the emergence under great pressure, of entrepreneurship in the hands of local governments. Many local businesses have emerged which are upgraded versions of the state owned enterprises dumped on local governments by the national governments, or the remnants of enterprises previously run by Maoist collectives and communes, plus new ventures emerging from the private sector. These are generally called "township and village enterprises" (TVEs). These TVEs have been a powerful force for growth, but most of them are in the favored provinces in the south and on the coast. While employment in government run TVEs seems to have peaked, it has reached about 135 million (1996) or 28% of the rural workforce. At the same time, private employment in TVEs has tripled to about 15 million. Thus, the rural income profile has radically changed for the better in some areas. In general, these TVE and private enterprises and private ventures are more profitable than SOEs.

The second "bottom up" force is the kind of individual entrepreneurship unleashed in the informal economy. A distinction is usually made between the informal economy and the so called "underground" economy which is broader and includes illegal activities such as drug trafficking, prostitution, illegal betting and smuggling. The informal economy is not confined to poor countries, and in fact every country has a substantial informal sector in its economy. When the formal economy is too weak, as it has been in China, people often have no option but to enter the informal economy as a means of survival. One of the pathologies of many governments is that they fail to recognize this reality, and view the informal economy as a form of crime, often called a "black market" existing only to avoid taxes and escape regulations. The government can and does use laws and police enforcement to suppress the informal economy even when it knows that it provides employment and income that the state has failed to provide. In China, the informal economy has had a particularly vital significance. In an attempt to limit migration from rural to urban areas, the Chinese created a limited "official" workforce in cities, largely working in SOEs, and tried to prevent migrants in cities who were not eligible for this official status. But in addition to its migrants, Chinese cities attracted millions of people who settled into the informal economy.

As in India, there are no barriers to entry into an informal economy. Anybody capable of performing a service or providing a good can become a provider. The most likely types of work in the informal economy are casual laborers, construction workers, and personal services providers such as servants, janitors, trash collectors, porters, messengers, errand runners, delivery people, child care providers, street vendors, and even panhandlers. In addition, if some capital is available, other people may be able to become small retailers or customer service providers. Many crafts are represented, including carpenters, plumbers, masons, electricians, tailors, and auto mechanics, and many of these entrepreneurs are capable of working in both the formal and informal economies at the same time, depending on where work is available.

More recent examinations of informal economies reveal some startling facts. The World Bank has estimated that, in many less developed countries, the informal economy employs between one third and one half of the national labor force. Various studies estimate that, in 2000, the informal economies in developing countries were about 40% of their official gross domestic product. In Zimbabwe, the figure is around 70%, and it clearly reflects the terrible damage inflicted on what was once a prosperous country by the pathological policies of the dictator, Robert Mugabe. In other countries such as Turkey, Brazil, Egypt, and the new Russia, the figure ranges from 40 to 60%. Even in developed countries, the number averages about 18%, and there seems to be a direct correlation between the size of the informal economy and a country's total tax burden and the intrusiveness of its economic regulation. Thus, among rich countries Spain, Belgium, Italy and Greece have large informal economies and the United States, Canada, Switzerland and Great Britain have far lower levels.

As these realities are finally recognized, it appears that the attitudes of the Chinese government have been undergoing some change. It all starts with the essential issue – can the formal economy generate enough national wealth to maintain a reasonable standard of living for its citizens. If the answer is no, as it remains in China, then it would be wiser for the government not only to tolerate the informal economy but to encourage it. Much of the evolution of the economies of developing countries is not from massive state owned enterprises, but from the bottom up – from small entrepreneurs with the drive and ability to expand their informal businesses if allowed to do so.

The third "bottom up" pattern of economic development in China is the emergence of a more truly private sector, almost totally free of direct government involvement, and representing a new and formidable competitor in economic arenas formerly monopolized by SOEs. As the private sector has grown, there has been a not coincidental shrinkage of the market share of the official SOEs retained by the government and the People's Liberation Army (PLA). The CCP appears very muddled about what to do about this competition. It is very defensive about the SOEs that it has retained and promoted, and local governments have the same defensiveness about their SOEs and TVEs. Many of these enterprises are still marginal, running deficits, heavily in debt and needing lots of protection.

STILL: ECONOMIC DEVELOPMENT FROM THE TOP DOWN

The CCP, out of dire necessity, knows it must drastically change its economic strategies, and since 2005, CCP utterances have emphasized promoting domestic consumption, developing sectors of the economy other than manufacturing, promoting the emergence of an even stronger private sector, and continuing to expand the whole economy at a pace that the SOEs could never achieve. There are then collateral policy desires linked to these new strategies: higher enterprise productivity, creation of more jobs, reductions of expensive environmental problems, reducing overproduction in some sectors, and more equitable geographical balance of economic improvement. But at this point, the "SOE protection" policy still dominates. While the government no longer believes that it must <u>own</u> everything, it still believes that it must <u>control</u> everything, and it retains direct control of 2-3,000 SOEs. Many of the approximately 2- 3,000 major SOEs retained at the national level are really very large holding companies. The following are examples of the specific SOEs still retained by the government;

China National Petroleum Corp. Petro
China
Sinopec
CNDOC

China Telecom
China Mobile
China Unicom
Lanovo
TCL
Baiwen (retail)
D'Long (conglomerate)
People's Bank of China
Industrial and Commercial Bank
Agricultural Bank
Construction Bank
Chery (autos) and other auto companies
Dalain Machine Tool Company

While the government has largely eliminated its universal price controls, it still tends to manipulate prices in certain key sectors such as land and water resources, public utilities, coal and oil, and bank lending and interest rates. And still, the government resists making the kind of policy change that would have the most dramatic impact on expansion of domestic consumer spending: a shift of funds from economic development to the expanded provision of social services, especially heath care, primary education and welfare. If people could get more help from the government, they might stop putting money under the mattress. And this shift might also alleviate a problem defined in the report of the National People's Congress in 2006 which warned against "adverse effects of surplus production capacity in some industries which have begun to emerge. Prices for products of these industries dropped, and inventories grew, corporate profits shrank, and losses mounted, and potential financial risk has increased."

An important subset of the emergence of a true private sector is the effort of the Chinese government to attract what is called "Foreign Direct Investment" (FDI). The long term restrictions of the CCP for more than 40 years against private enterprise simply choked off huge potentials for capital formation, as did the sealing off of national borders against foreign investment. But these are both areas of previously sacred communist economic theology that proved disastrous and have had to be abandoned.

With respect to domestic Chinese capitalists, the government has had to create the legal base which permits the relative economic independence of private business operations, although it still clearly favors its own SOEs wherever possible. With respect to investment by foreigners however, the government has been more enthusiastic. It really loves the idea of foreign money and management fueling and driving the economy, with a high percentage of the profits from such ventures winding up in the hands of the Chinese government. As restrictions on FDI are reduced, FDI has increased. Foreign firms shifted from contract operations to ownerships/ partnerships with equity traction which shows intent toward longer term penetration of the Chinese domestic market.

Initially, this FDI took the form of the construction of inexpensive plants producing cheap goods for export, or the purchase of goods manufactured by Chinese enterprises, under contract, for export. In part, this "minimum exposure" seemed almost like a test run – not only of the business arrangements, but of the attitude of Chinese governments at all levels. It was not clear early on whether the new economic reforms were indeed going to win out over the older Communist/socialist resistance. Few businesses could afford to invest heavily in China if the government were to revert to its old habits of favoring SOEs, imposing usurious taxes and fees, and possibly making arbitrary reversals of policy.

Over the course of more than 20 years, the confidence of foreign investors has grown, led by business people from Hong Kong and, ironically, Taiwan. This is important to the Chinese government because their policy remains to reduce investment by SOEs (many of which lose money) and to shift the burden of investment to foreigners. Foreign investment in long term ownership is better than short term investment in contracted operations. Foreign investors don't like investing in SOEs because government political interference remains high, but they will link with them mainly where there is a large government subsidy element. SOEs continue to provide a large percentage of fixed asset investment using government funding or forced loans from State banks. As a result of this growing mutual confidence, China has become the second largest recipient of FDI – second only to the U. S. Investment peaked in the period 1992-1998, and then declined modestly thereafter. FDI has been providing about 13% of gross capital formation annually. A subset of FDI that has been growing is where foreigners have been allowed to acquire some equity ownership of Chinese enterprises, many of them TVEs. These enterprises are called "foreign invested enterprises" (FIEs), which by 2000, accounted for over 60% of exports in many products, mostly of consumer goods, and for 32% of all manufactured sales. **[13]**

Consider the major elements of economic development: land, capital, labor, technology, management, government policy. Land remains owned by the government, and its use under leases is carefully government controlled. Capital remains largely controlled thought state banks, and banking regulation. Private sector and FDI money is now officially sought, but also under careful government control. The SOE system has been used to control the deployment of labor – plus largely unsuccessful urbanization controls. Labor has escaped direct government control by mass migrations, and by entering the informal economy. Internal technology development is still rare, as is management skill, and the government hopes to "import" both by allowing foreign participation in Chinese enterprises. There remains little protection for technology or any intellectual property. Money is still largely controlled, or at least manipulated by the use of credit plans in banks that privately dictate who can obtain credit, and for what, and how much. This control has been gradually loosened, but the ability to tighten up again is almost instantaneous. There is some attempt to develop non bank lending sources, but this is still not much advanced. Private enterprises are far better at borrowing from foreign sources than are SOEs. New business laws have been developed for contracts, foreign investment, both in FDI and through joint ventures; patents, trademarks; copyrights; environmental protections; foreign trade; arbitration; court standing; rules of evidence; and bankruptcy.

PUBLIC SERVICE UNITS

Public Service Units (PSU) are a separate range of institutions serving public purposes, and separate and distinct from either formal organizations or state owned enterprises. Most were initially established by government agencies, and are defined "legal persons" capable of entering into business activities. In general, PSUs provide social services, while SOEs provide economic operations. Such services include major categories of public service delivery such as schools, universities, hospitals and clinics, research and engineering organizations, and so forth.

Today there are 1.3 million PSUs, employing more than 25 million people, or one third of the people working in the public sector. Almost all function under standard civil service rules and regulations but there are very vague or non-existent ground rules for their creation, supervision, support, and financing. Many were created haphazardly as a result of demands of the old Central Plan process, which is now extinct. There is a need for sectoral rationalization; there are too many units of low effectiveness, with narrow and often conflicting activities.

They are characterized by poor and confusing funding, and most are seen as lacking budget control internally and budget/financial discipline and external oversight. Despite the fact that they are mostly funded by governments, and often receive various subsidies, they are, like the governments that sponsor them, constantly scrambling for money. The cost of PSUs in total has been skyrocketing and has begun to seriously worry the government especially because of a large unfunded obligation for pensions, which must be financed out of the current budget. Total revenues to PSUs now account for two thirds of government spending. However, progress in finding alternative funding has been increasing; 20% of them are now self-financed and overall, perhaps 50% of their total revenues are now coming from alternative sources including fees from clients. But there is a lot of concern over the corrupt aspects of these relationships where the urge for money has led to illegal transactions and fees.

Many have a history of poor performance, both from their lack of funds and from a lack of skilled personnel. In general, the personnel are of good capability – there just aren't enough of them, and some have obsolete skills. But overall efficiency does not seem to be improving, despite more than 20 years of trying. There are efforts to experiment with more hiring latitude, including the substitution of personal service contracts for tenured employment, as well as more management flexibility in hiring, firing, and promotion, but their uncertain future makes them unattractive as places to work. In many cases, there are attempts to fold their work into standard government organizations, and in any event, bureaucratic oversight is pretty extensive. Still, they lack clear policy guidance, and many are seen as in business for themselves rather than as instruments of government policy. In other cases, there are attempts to separate them from their government oversight, in large part to relieve governments of the financial burden. One organizational alternative is to convert them to some form of "non-profit organizations", another one of those vague categories of organizations associated with the government – with no clear ground rules. The government still wants to own/control non profit organizations (NPOs), but will not require that they make a profit. NPOs should not be confused with NGOs such as exist elsewhere; they are not independent, and are allowed no status outside of their local role.

The government is certainly trying to push reforms in this huge arena of public service. There is a slow willingness to grant managers more latitude in operational terms, and some efforts at the national government level to provide more clear definition and policy guidance. But it is clear that policy is all that the PSUs can expect, and there is little indication that the government wants to increase its financial involvement. There are efforts under way to rationalize personnel practices and provide more real competitive opportunity to seek employment. In some cases, the work of PSUs can be "commercialized" and both PSUs and oversight agencies are urged to explore such opportunities. But this brings into conflict the issue of what constitutes necessary government functions.

CHAPTER V

Social Services in India and China

EDUCATION INDIAN STYLE

AFTER WW II, THE GREAT clash between the concepts of a largely private market based world, and a world of centrist socialism seemed to have been won by the forces of State Socialism in a variety of forms from the total absolute centrist dictatorship in the Soviet Union and China to more moderate versions such as those in Sweden, France, Italy or India.

The leadership in both China and India both believed that centrist authority and control was vital in managing their vast, chaotic countries, and both felt that this centrist control should be exercised by a small self chosen elite. In China, that elite took the form of a Chinese Communist Party (CCP) dictatorship under Mao Zedong, who could only see the world in terms of enormous revolutionary conflict filled with ominous "foreign imperialist" enemies, seeking to ally themselves with dark reactionary forces within the country.

In India, the elite were more benign and not as militant. Power was held as a matter of "right" by a combination of Socialist theorists and economists and high caste Brahmins who never doubted their own correctness. [1] This elitism led to a set of negative attitudes about the education of the masses, some of which still persist. First, starting with the period of British rule, education of any kind was simply not seen as a role of governments, except possibly at the lowest levels, and this attitude was shared by the British themselves and by the senior figures in Indian government and society.

This attitude manifested itself in the design of the national education system that emerged after independence. To begin with, India operates the biggest education system in the world with 740,000 schools, five million teachers and over 200 million children aged 6-14, 70% of whom live in rural/village areas. But the fundamental reality is that the government's indifference and neglect represents the single greatest failure of governance in modern day India. The political leadership at the national government level has been skilled at avoiding its responsibility, handing it off to local governments knowing full well that these governments were not able to handle it. The national government starved the system of funds, played destructive politics, tolerated bumbling incompetent school management, and vastly inferior performance in the classroom. Most positions of power and influence were held by upper caste Brahmins who strongly felt that even elementary education for "lower castes" was a waste; that education was a privilege to be reserved for certain elite groups; that even mid level castes needed only very basic education; that education for girls was outrageous; and that the possibility of lower castes learning to read sacred texts was sacrilegious.

One of the most significant policy decisions made by Nehru was to delegate responsibility for elementary and secondary education to India's 28 States and 7 Union territories. There is nothing really wrong with such a delegation, but the decision was largely based on some perverse motives. First, it appears that the national government was really signaling its complete indifference to primary education; the delegation to the States was with the full recognition that almost all were relatively poor and could ill afford, without central government help, the costs of educating what is now over 200 million children. It was also certain that this devolution of authority was bound to result in wide disparities in the quality of education. But the national government really did not care. A second motive exactly parallels the decisions made in China: by delegating responsibility for education and other vital social services, the central government avoided huge costs, which allowed it to concentrate available money on economic development.

The two giants of post-independence India – Gandhi and Nehru –opposed widespread formal education, but for different reasons. Gandhi felt that educating the people's children was a good thing, but that it should be confined to basic things such as crafts and practical skills for the boys and child rearing and household skills for girls. Nehru typified the elitist, class biased interpretation of the government's responsibilities for education, which meant that formal education would be largely reserved for a relatively small elite, mostly the sons (but not the daughters) of senior government officials, military officers, high caste Brahmins, and influential political figures. For this elite group, nothing was too good. Their elementary/secondary schools were first class, with handsome buildings and often amenities including swimming pools, tennis courts and cricket fields. Meanwhile, within walking distance were crowded slums where schools for the urban poor were conducted in rickety buildings lacking toilets, running water and even books and blackboards. The children of the elite were sent away at government expense to Great Britain and elsewhere for advanced degrees in economics, political science, science and engineering, and military training, all very much in the patterns employed by the British in the Victorian era and up to WW II. As with China and the Soviet Union, state socialism was the perfect justification for elite centrist control; the masses were to be led (or driven), and all they needed to know was to do as they were told. India's political leadership, including the Nehru and Gandhi family dynasties were high caste Brahmins, and they drew their political support largely from the higher caste large land owners, merchants and the military. This caste elitism was especially strong in rural/village areas where it was linked with the landed gentry, most of whom sought preferment for their own children, but were not about to pay for the education of the children of the poor. [2]

This Brahmin elitism was blended in with several other prejudices, the strongest of which was and is against the education of girls. It seems simply never to have occurred to the ruling elite that girls were capable of serious intellectual attainment, or that almost half of the talent base of children was being neglected. Despite repeated earnest and pompous policy utterances to the contrary, even in periods when India had a woman Prime Minister, it was still true that less than 1/3 of girls <u>ever</u> got into any kind of school.

India remains an absolutely incomprehensible puzzle of religious, cultural, regional, social, economic, and language differences, representing formidable barriers to acceptable progress in the reform – or even the creation – of an adequate education system. For example, classes may be taught and books provided in local languages rather than English or Hindi. This may satisfy some narrow cultural or political need, but it leaves children who are unable to connect with the greater world outside of their own region.

What has finally emerged from this pattern of neglect and indifference is a school system that has the following major components:

1. Public schools
2. Private schools: but publicly aided
3. Private schools: recognized, but not aided
4. Private schools: unrecognized.

The abdications of the Indian government are never clearer than in this arena of primary education. The government is famous for its skill at issuing pompous, overblown plans and policy pronouncements which never seem to be taken seriously, and lead to little action. Time after time, the central government has issued national "Plans" to achieve universal elementary (but not secondary) education. The first such scheme was issued at the time of the new Constitution in 1950. The Constitution did not mandate universal education but merely "urged" it. Initial Plans targeted the achievement of universal education by 1959! No clear and comprehensive government policy was even published until 1984, and again it was merely rhetoric. Another National Policy on Education was drafted in 1986, along with "Operation Blackboard" which was supposed to be an implementation plan. The National Policy was revised in 1992, again stating goals for free mandatory elementary education, but none of this had any real impact. In 1998, the National Council of Education Research and Training issued another "National Policy on Education" which appeared to make elementary and secondary education a shared responsibility between the national government and the States, but in fact officially got the national government out from under this responsibility except for "plans". Again, in 2000 the government issued its "Education for All" program, but it simply repeated the rhetoric of earlier pronouncements. In 2001, the government again emphasized its intent to "universalize primary education by 2007", and also supposedly mandated a hot lunch for every Indian school child, but 2007 has obviously come and gone and neither of these goals is even close to achievement, and almost nowhere in India is universal primary education a reality.

In 2005, the government again issued a directive requiring States to implement the "Right to Free Compulsory Education". Finally, as recently as 2009, a new law was enacted mandating compulsory, universal free education. But this civil rights approach is political rhetoric covering 60 years of hypocritical inaction. In India, elementary/secondary education is definitely not universal, certainly not free, and many doubt that much of it is even education. When this litany of political posturing and abdication is understood, one begins to recognize the profound failure of primary education in India. Consider that, of those children who reach the 5th grade, an unbelievable 1/3 of them are still unable to read or write. In rural areas, only about 5% of parents can even read their children's report cards. [3]

But here were the roles which the national government assigned itself:

1. To develop a national policy (supposedly compulsory, but largely ignored)
2. To provide consultation about education
3. To establish necessary commissions, committees and working groups
4. To stimulate and promote public debate and discussion

This is the perfect expression of the Indian education elite; highly sophisticated and intellectual, lots of discussion, but no money, no action, and little actual help. The national level of funding for primary/secondary education at all levels of government is just 3.9% of GDP, although some estimates are lower. Funds for secondary education are a disturbing .94%. These are very low by world standards even for poor developing countries. At least 25% of secondary schools are private, and all too many are really one room operations, and many are not very effective either.

LOCAL GOVERNMENT SHORTCOMINGS

Local governments deserve some sympathy because the national government has abdicated any responsibility and left local governments holding the bag, but in truth, elementary/secondary education is most logically a responsibility of local governments. They simply have had great difficulty bearing this burden, and they have not done it well. Primary education, for whatever reason, is perennially under funded. Despite the existence of 740,000 schools, there are constant complaints that they are too few and poorly distributed. The national government "promises" to raise the expenditure on primary education from the current 3.3% to 6%, but nobody at the local government levels expects the central government to come up with the money, and they have no idea how local funding can be generated, if at all. While the central government constantly "mandates" that primary education will be free, in fact, local governments get by only because they charge heavy fees and related expenses. Many rural/village families are so poor that they can't afford to pay for these fees, and the slum population in cities is more than 60 million and mostly extremely poor. [4]

The rise of private school education is a powerful reflection of the universal failure of pubic schools, which are so bad that even the poorest of parents give up on them and somehow find the money to send their children to the more expensive private schools. Even recognizing that India has been and remains a poor developing country, had there been the will, the funding for adequate schools could have been found. The national government need not have abdicated its responsibilities and dumped the full costs of elementary and secondary education on the States as huge unfunded mandates, and this includes the serious failure of the seven thousand vocational education institutions which are nearly all part of the public sector system.

Local governments must also cope with heavy cultural bias. Upper castes tend to think that it is perfectly acceptable for the children of the poor to work, and that it is equally acceptable for the privileged classes to design for themselves a rich and highly subsidized system of education. While child labor is now, finally, officially illegal, huge exceptions are allowed for work in agriculture, family households, restaurants, and so called cottage industries. In other cases, the laws mandating compulsory elementary and secondary education are simply ignored. This helps to explain why, despite such laws, almost 50% of all children are not in school. There is a big slippage between "student enrollment" and "student attendance."

Another serious problem relates to the power of teacher unions in India. The Indian Constitution provides for a special representation of teachers in the upper houses of Indian State legislatures. The unions take great advantage of this preferment and have exerted what seems to be an unwarranted degree of leverage on laws and policies. No local politician or school administrator can afford to cross these unions. If teachers want to be truant, their absence is "excused". Teacher strikes and agitations over pay, benefits and working conditions are intimidating and almost always successful. Many teachers are absent from classes, but can be found offering "special tutoring" after hours to their students – for an extra fee.

Finally, while political leaders in New Delhi call for reform, most of the forces in and around local governments and school systems oppose reform. The unions are implacably opposed to any reform anywhere in the whole miserable system, and their political sponsors enforce that opposition. Other local politicians sit on the sidelines, fearing conflict. School administrators oppose reform because they profit perversely from the present system which is notorious for its corruption and venality. Only local parents and concerned citizens support reform, but they are generally ignored.

"General condemnation of the school system refutes two generally accepted assessments of what is wrong. First, surveys of actual parent attitudes reflect widespread recognition of the need for education, even for girls, rather than indifference or opposition. Second, work is not a barrier;

most children may help with the crops at times, but they have plenty of time for education. [5] But a World Bank study states that, in 60 years there has been almost no change in the demographics of rich vs. poor, urban vs. rural, or minority vs. non-minority rates. According to Nussbaum, general opinions of Indian public education are that it is an unrelieved disaster. [6]

In short, local governments have been overwhelmed by the complex problems of primary education, and have not performed well. The usual reason is quite legitimately a shortage of money, but many places have succeeded in making more progress in the early stages of their economic development, and many ways to improve primary education stem not from lack of money, but from the grim failures of public management. The official and almost unanimous opinion of government leaders is that the problems of elementary education are financial. Almost every outside analysis disagrees with this view and sees it as a feeble excuse for government failure. A lot could be accomplished relatively cheaply by better management – and being smart!

THE HORRIBLE FAILURES OF SCHOOL ADMINISTRATION

There are about 740 thousand schools and five million teachers, and generally their reputation is unbelievably bad. Administration in public schools suffers from gross inefficiency, an intensely bureaucratic mind set, timidity, cowardice and corruption. There are too many administrators and two few actual teachers. Local politicians and school administrators have never been able to generate adequate funds for school systems. While the Constitution supposedly makes free education a right, poor families must pay fees that are a real drain on their resources. For the average agricultural laborer, sending two children to primary school would cost the equal of 2-3 months wages. And outrageously, a lot of the money that is provided is squandered, stolen or misappropriated. Teacher appointments are sold to the highest bidder without regard to qualifications. Politicians intercept funds destined for schools and reallocate them or cause them to disappear. Administrators supposedly hire contractors to make badly needed school repairs, but the work is never done and the money vanishes. Everybody knows what is going on, but nobody official seems to care.

Money for basic education actually began to increase in the mid 80s, but most of the money has gone for higher teacher salaries and benefits. Yet the numbers of teachers in classrooms has declined, classes are larger, and performance remains drastically bad. Today, almost 90% of school budgets go for teacher/administrator salaries and benefits, so that even if more money is provided it simply enriches the people who make the system so bad. And still, repeated surveys and opinion polls say the same thing: most classes are practically useless. And still, overall, 50% of children are not in school, and after more than 60 years of independence, only 17% of the current adult population has any secondary education. Whole large segments of student population are almost completely ignored including girls, members of the Scheduled Castes and Tribes, remote rural areas, and urban slums filled with "invisible" children A UNESCO index recently ranked India 102 out of 129 countries on the extent, gender balance, and quality of its primary education and adult literacy. [7]

Teachers have been known to collect their salaries and then pay some local substitute to show up in their place, so that they can be marked "present". The rate of teacher absenteeism and truancy is absolutely astounding. Repeated school samplings, even by school administrators themselves, have shown that, on any given day, as many as from 25% to 65% of the teachers were absent. This level of truancy, according to the UN, is the highest measured anywhere in the world. It is inconceivable how any school administration could be so pitifully incompetent as to allow this truancy to persist year after year. School inspectors, who cannot fail to know about these problems, are famous for their ability to solicit bribes. How is this appalling mismanagement even possible? Does no one ever check why teachers are truants? Are none of them ever held to account? Is anybody ever fired? Is there no management at all?

Administrators may lie about the numbers of children enrolled because some funds are based on the size of that number. But in reality, there is a big difference between "enrollment" and "attendance". Many children have really dropped out and are studying in some local private school, but remain illegally carried on public school roles. Administrators even managed to foul up the good idea of free lunches, which was introduced with much bragging in 1995, but allowed to wither. In most districts, cooked meals never happened, and even the substitute of food grain rations never materialized. As one official put it "a good example of how a well-intentioned program degenerates into a farce due to bureaucratic apathy and corruption."

In an article in India Today [8] another government phony policy was lambasted. Operation Blackboard (1986) officially abolished single teacher schools. But in a recent survey, 12% of all primary schools still had a single teacher appointed. In another 21%, more than one teacher had been appointed, but only one was present and teaching. Thus, 1/3 of schools effectively were still one teacher, and 80% of all schools are just for primary grades. Nor is there much teaching actually going on in the majority of schools. The favored technique seems to be rote learning, achieved by student copying of written or blackboard material. But the survey team found "notebook after notebook filled with meaningless scribble." Schools are often like detention centers with beatings by teachers common.

More forms of incompetence can be found in course content. [9] Classes are often judged to be so simplistic and obsolete that they are all but useless. More than 70% of students live in India's 680,000 villages, and many children cannot even reach a school. Books are old, poorly written or non-existent, and many are in regional languages of limited usefulness. They are supposedly selected by professional standards groups, but they are widely regarded as inferior: dull, inaccurate, obsolete, full of mistakes and of no practical value. Even where better texts are available, often the money to buy them is not. Teachers lack subject matter knowledge, and are weak on teaching technique. In a survey in one State, only 30% of children ages 6-14 could read textual material easily, nor could they do basic simple arithmetic. According to Panagaria, "only 6.6% of students in the first grade can read at level one (short paragraphs with small sentences and simple words). 8.3% of second grade students can read at level 2 ("story" text with some long sentences, still simple words). At the 5th grade level, just 53% can read at level 2 and a further 28.1% can read at level 1. But this means that 19% of students really cannot read at all! If it is recognized that level one is still seen as illiteracy, then 47.1% of children in the 5th grade are functional illiterates. In fact, surveys, even those conducted by school administrations, show that, **in primary schools, 40 million children can't even recognize or explain the alphabet, and 30 million students at the 5th grade level cannot read. [10]**

In sum, the elementary/secondary school system is a national disgrace, and has been forever. The elite leadership of the country badly underestimated the number of reasonably educated people needed to run a modern economy, so for 60 years they felt that basic education could be safely ignored. While illiteracy has been greatly reduced, somehow it seems never to have sunk in that to be "literate" is not the same as to be educated. India's new laws still aim merely at universal **primary** education, and still, most children can't make it through the 5th grade. Even less is being done for secondary education, which is the portal to higher education. While India targets for education through the 8th grade, most of the developed world is thinking in terms of master's degrees. Other developing countries, many in the Far East like Indonesia, Malaysia, Thailand, Vietnam and the Philippines have achieved universal primary education, and China is very close.

The first and most valuable substitute for lousy public schools is private schools, and they have been taking students away from public schools in large numbers. But less than 30% of rural students have access to private schools, even if their parents have the money. In general, private schools pay their teachers much less (maybe 1/5), but their teacher/student ratios are smaller, and absenteeism is much less. When unannounced visits are conducted, 70% of teachers in private schools were teaching, compared to 38% in public schools. "On average, students in unrecognized private schools scored 72% higher than their counterparts in government schools in mathematics, 83% higher in Hindi, and 246% higher in English. Students in recognized private schools did even better. Private schools tend to replace public schools in rural and poor urban areas. In richer city areas, public schools are better, and private schools usually can't compete financially.

A lot of hope for an educational resurrection is being placed on two tides running in the country. The first is the obvious high degree of success that has followed the retreat of the government from state socialist economics and the license Raj. The political leadership is finally realizing that the surge of economic expansion demands a far broader base of young people educated at least through 12 grades. One of the real success patterns for the government has been that they have produced some really outstanding enhancements in higher education. India is no longer trying to duplicate Oxford or Cambridge, or even the London School of Economics. Instead, they want to replicate MIT or Cal Tech, or the Imperial Institute in London. The twelve Indian Institutes of Technology, the seven Institutes of Management, the four Institutes of Information Technology and the Institute of Science produce outstanding graduates, and these institutions were initiated and nurtured by the government. Clearly, the national government, while ignoring primary education, wants to be seen as the patron of higher education.

The second hopeful tide that is running is that, as the private sector becomes more broadly based, sophisticated and technological, it tends to do two things: to pressure governments at all levels to reform education; and to provide their own support for education. Education in India now often means private sources providing a broad range of technical and managerial training, and a lot of "how to do it" training programs for everything from computers and office management to motivational sales programs. In many cases, parents have filled the gap toward eligibility for university with years of private tutoring, often by the same teachers in the public school system who can't be bothered to show up for their regular jobs. India's new middle class is well educated and is expected to force change on the laggard government. Both caste and gender prejudices have been carried over into the new private sector world, where high caste males have an edge, but these prejudices are much weaker there. The Indian Administrative Service and the state owned enterprises are no longer the favored path to success. Where do the smartest kids want to work? In private sector jobs with large international corporations.

INDIAN HIGHER EDUCATION

According to Nilekani, "At first, Indian universities were designed to create a small pool of aristocratic, English educated people who were destined for the civil service and state owned enterprises. The education was based on the classics of English, Greek, Latin, Euro-centric history, and the ratification of the mores of the ruling class. There was very little interest in training people to think; there was an undesirable emphasis on conformity which led to crammers and "swotting". Indian universities were intended to be free of politics, but a landmark decision in 1990 established caste reservations and quotas in universities and in government. This precipitated a highly politicized clash about the role of universities and sensitized whole new types of politicians to university issues so that now political intervention ranges across all university activities. Two key questions are being debated: first, to what extent should universities be expected to reflect or even represent the agenda of the government? And second, what is the top priority: social justice as defined by the government or merit and independence of choice?" [11]

India in 2006 had 17,625 colleges and 335 universities, with 10.5 million students, but all of these numbers are misleading. India has many outstanding universities and colleges – but the great bulk of institutions are inferior and poorly regarded. India produces many brilliant students, they are the product of a limited number or really high quality institutions, and the great bulk of degrees from all other schools are of little value. (Apparently, most colleges are the sub elements of universities, and few are free standing institutions.). Essentially, the market ignores the vast majority of the graduates that the system produces. It knows that students who are in the top quarter of the class can excel. But the degree has very little value for the bottom half of the students. [12]

The controlling body in the country is the University Grants Commission (UGC) established formally by law in 1956, and exercising almost total control over all schools of higher education. But in the early 50s, India had just 578 colleges and 28 universities, with perhaps 200,000 students. At that time, a single central control commission may have made good sense, but the system is now so huge that centrist control is wrong. If a school is not approved by the UGC, it can't grant a degree; this includes the prestigious Indian Institutes of Technology, Management, and Information Technology, and many other very competent management institutes of other kinds. The UGC is seen as unable to keep up with rapid changes in subject matter or innovations in teaching, especially in IT. It is also seen as bureaucratically slow paced. Therefore, the quality of education in far too many schools is seen as "rapidly deteriorating", with high teacher and student absenteeism. Students never know whether the professor will bother to show up; faculty never know how many students will attend.

"There are currently 150,000 Indian students studying in the United States, Canada, the UK and Australia, spending close to $2 billion. In comparison, the entire annual expense of the central and state governments on higher education in India in 2003-04 was $3.7 billion. This is a damning statement about the perceived value found in Indian classrooms.

The government continues to want all universities to be State institutions, and recently it adopted the "centers of excellence" idea to upgrade a limited number of universities – while ignoring the rest. In other words, by concentrating on a few schools, the government could claim success and avoid facing up to a serious reexamination of the whole higher education system.

The UGC can "deem" some private schools to be universities for the purpose of granting degrees, but it seldom does so, and it regulates private universities as stringently as it does public. No school of any kind had autonomy until the passage of the National Education Policy (NEP) in 1986 and revised in 1991. At that time 8 were granted autonomy. By 2006, there were still only 214 autonomous colleges, as part of 47 universities. The UGC was also supposed to exercise a "quality control" function, but it was not until 1994 that an accreditation body, The National Assessment and Accreditation Council (NAAC) was established. By 2005, it had accredited only 105 universities and 2311 colleges. But the UGC decided that accreditation would have no value for funding priorities, salaries, or other recognitions, so it is essentially meaningless.

The single most important positive feature of the higher education sector in recent years has been the rapid growth of private colleges and non degree postsecondary educational institutions. More universities are also being chartered by States and even municipalities. These schools are divided between "aided" and "unaided". The aided schools receive financial aid from governments, but this makes them subject to regulatory control. The unaided schools are completely independent, and they now attract more than 30% of all students, and it is argued that in fact, India really has de facto privatization. The children of the new middle class now have the money to vote with their feet and they have been moving away from government schools to private schools, especially in science, engineering, business and the other skills of the new economy. But a big fear is that these private schools have, to date, been too often developed by people who are after the fast buck. Two thirds of them have been evaluated as below par, and one third cannot achieve accreditation. Meanwhile, more than 150,000 students still study abroad.

The whole issue of privatization of universities is still serious. Political leadership continues staunchly to defend socialist ideals for public education, but the emergence of private universities/colleges is very much a reflection of the failure of this socialist policy. India has yet to figure out how to match the record of the US, where there are top quality schools in both the public and the private sector. India needs a major change in philosophy; it must finally shed the vestiges of its socialist past and embrace the concept that private institutions are a good thing and that the government should encourage them by liberating them. The Chinese second revolution has involved the abandonment of many policies that were considered sacred theology under the Communists. Why can't India make the same kind of change? The answer seems to be the implacable resistance of vested interests. Political leadership continues staunchly to defend socialist ideals. But no Indian university can be found in the top 400 of the world. One study found that 75% of graduates were unemployable for the work for which they were supposedly trained, and there is a related serious failure of the seven thousand vocational education institutions, which are nearly all part of the public sector system.

Money need not be such a fatal problem. While it will take lots of time, private universities in the US and elsewhere have augmented their revenues beyond what governments provide by higher fees, the development of large endowments, and the proceeds of research and contracting. Nor is it necessary that all 348 universities and 12,296 colleges survive. If they are of low quality, they should go under, and the students moved to augment the attendance and revenues of the survivors. Other income might come from charitable contributions, grants from industry, sales of publications, or rents. In fact, public universities in India are suffering from the same syndrome that influences universities elsewhere: governments have proven politically unreliable sources of long term funding. They demand control, but won't pay the tab. So even public institutions need to find ways to augment income.

EDUCATION CHINESE STYLE

The inability to provide adequate education for China's children is one of the greatest failures of the Chinese Communist Party (CCP).

China has 235 million school children – one fourth of the world's total. They have about 13 million primary and secondary school teachers, and it is estimated that 10 million of them need far better training. Universities were badly battered in the Mao years, and little was done in the period up to the late 90s; in other words, a whole generation of 20 years was lost. It is not surprising that there is a huge gap between the numbers of well educated people needed in the new economy, and the numbers that are being produced. But at least, this is one gap that the Chinese government is seriously attempting to fill. [13]

The CCP attempted to make primary education universal in the 60s, but delivery rested on Maoist communes and brigades (now townships and villages) which were incompetent. [5] These "people run" schools operated outside of the regular government structure and used untrained villagers as teachers in obviously inadequate facilities. In many villages, schools can't be used during rainy weather. Many have dirt floors, outdoor rest rooms, no running water (except thru leaky roofs), and not even blackboards. In rural areas many of the schools are still financed voluntarily by villagers. Further, much instruction has been rote memorization and recital, and much of the substance was really communist political propaganda aimed at brainwashing students. Adults as well were subjected to mandatory training sessions aimed at "ideological remolding". There were many students and academics starting in the 60s who advocated change in the education system, but who accepted the communist/socialist state. No student "democracy" movement ever seems to have had much impact, and many students bought into the Cultural Revolution. In fact, students were one of the mainstays of the revolution, often against their elders and professors, and most of the notorious Red Guards were students. The Education Revolution of 1968-76 sent many students to the countryside to do manual labor, and many schools were simply closed down. Student populations were supposed to be egalitarian rather than the brightest and the best. So were teachers, and the policy was "open door" schooling rather than selectivity. Mao expressed his contempt for teachers who had "for years done nothing useful". **[14]**

There are only very weak government motivations for social services delivery, provision of public infrastructure, the principles of public administration responsibility, the notion of individual rights and freedoms, or even the need for "truth". Much of the policy has also been driven by the shortage of funds and the fact that social services and public infrastructure runs a poor second to economic development. Thus the retreat from the State Socialist "cradle to grave" commitment has been driven by necessity but has often been readily abandoned to avoid the costs and commitments. In most cases, social services were shoved down onto local governments and their expenditures as a percentage of the total has risen steadily and now only about 5% of social services funds are provided by the national government, and this has changed little in the last thirty years. Total expenditures on education and health remain less then 3% of the national GDP. Of local government expenditures for social services, 77% are at the municipal and township level. Much of the provincial and county level expenditures are in fact merely fund transfers to lower government, often in the form of categorical grants, which are partly political whitewash and part bribes or favoritism.

As the economy strengthens, more and more teachers are bailing out and looking for better jobs elsewhere. Repeated government promises over 20 years to improve the system have not been kept. In a UNESCO study in 1995, the Chinese system was ranked 119th out of 130 countries in terms of per capita expenditure (at less than 2.8% of GDP), and 103rd out of 130 countries in number of university graduates per 100,000 people. [15] Only 2% of students attend universities, compared to over 50% in the U. S. There has been significant growth of private schools – driven not by national policy but by parents who see official schools as bad news.

Until the '80s, much elementary/secondary education was provided through SOEs, but in the late '80s this responsibility shifted to local governments, which finance schools largely by charging lots of relatively high fees. The whole system is marginal at best, and despite rhetoric to the contrary, it is not getting better very fast. This is a Maoist legacy, but even after more than 20 subsequent years of "reform" the education system is still in very bad shape. During the Cultural Revolution of 1966-76, schooling in much of the country was suspended; universities were shut down, some for as long as five years. A whole generation of Chinese received little or no education. In 1982, half of the population, or 520 million people were still illiterate. While this number has commendably shrunk in the last 20 years, simple literacy, meaning a minimum ability of Chinese children to read and write, does not even begin to prepare them to match education levels in the rest of the world. Faculty salaries were miserable; prestige of teachers was very low; existing schools were often converted barns and were ill maintained, dirty, and lacking even basic equipment like blackboards. Despite the fact that there are 515,000 schools, damaged school systems could not meet the pace of demand for classrooms and only 60% of children finished elementary school.

Local governments tried to obtain financing by charging high school fees, and special taxes on farmers, enterprises and collectives; by the mid 90s, about half of all school costs were off budget. But too much of the fees justified to parents to finance schools simply disappeared, or were diverted to cover other expenses such as bureaucratic perks. At the same time, local governments grabbed authority for school systems away from provinces and counties, including allocation of funds, setting of teacher salaries, and personnel decisions. Ideas for reform abound, but one must constantly be reminded of the "drop in the bucket" dimensions of proposed solutions, which are constantly being announced by some government agency or CCP "Plan".

There are 2236 higher education institutions with 20 million students, but a lot of these institutions are Party schools, available only to Party members, and largely devoted to political indoctrination. The government is deliberately selecting a limited number (maybe 100) for elevation into first class institutions, which concedes that many university level institutions are inferior, and that the new "top 100" are not really expected to educate that many people. But in fact, this is not really that different than the situation in the U. S. In typical CCP fashion, a set of "key institutions" are being created at all educational levels: 7,000 primary schools, 5,200 middle schools and 96 universities. They have been declared to be "centers of excellence" and draw the bulk of state funding, but they are really used to provide education for the children of the elite and have become an excuse and justification for ignoring the pitiful quality of most other schools. Entrance to most schools beyond the elementary is by competitive examination, a system that has grown increasingly perverse. Despite Tiananmen Square, the situation in higher education has gotten even worse. Protests against Chang Kai-shek in the 40's pointed out that his regime had cut education spending to only 3.6% of GDP, but in 1992, that number, under CCP rule, had shrunk to about 2%.

The government has set a target of 9 years of education for all children by 2000 and likes to take credit for the "rectification" of education, but in fact, it has achieved little or nothing, leaving the problem to local governments as a huge unfunded mandate. The education system has been heavily skewed toward the practical arts, and vocational and technical education, and political indoctrination, and this is now supposed to be shifted toward broader general education with more emphasis on technology.

Perversely, children born outside of the "one child" policy are excluded from state schools, as are the children of rural residents who are unauthorized urban residents. The whole education philosophy seems to be to teach adherence to established mores, stability, conformity and obedience to authority. It does not allow diversity or encourage independent thinking. One amazing fact is that 200 million Chinese students are studying English. Children start as early as the fourth grade, and over 2 million college students take a compulsory College English Test. The private fee-paying schools that have been established are widely seen as "aristocracy" schools for the children of the elite. Many of the schools in rural/village areas are private institutions because that is the only approach that works. But villagers complain that local politicians steal, misappropriate or squander their funds. Efforts are under way to replace the ill trained and uneducated teachers, but there simply are not nearly enough adequately capable people available to meet the needs since salaries are so low, and better jobs exist in governments or the Party, or in the "new economy" businesses.

Because local governments are either too poor, or they are spending their money on economic development, many universities have had to seek other sources of funding. Some went into business, forming collectives in the areas of retail sales, consulting and computers. In some cases, universities seek support from SOEs and private businesses. Many institutions were part of the complex substructure of ministries, such as a "Construction Materials College" or an "Urban Design College", and these relationships, always weak, are being terminated and folded into stronger and more balanced universities. The Ministry of Education has cut the number of university disciplines by more than half to 300, and has begun to merge universities into bigger units.

Reforms in higher education are now gathering some momentum, largely because the CCP now realizes the wide gap in both numbers and skills, between supply and demand, and also, the CCP is deliberately out to gain political credibility as the "creator" of new higher education capabilities Universities are finally being allowed to widen their academic horizons and offer a more relevant range of courses, and graduates were no longer assigned compulsorily to jobs by the state authorities. The first MBA program was introduced in China in 1990, and MBAs are now the rage. In 2002 more than 5 million students who had finished secondary school took college entrance exams. More than 50% were successful, compared to only 2.4% 20 years earlier. Restrictions on foreign study were relaxed (but not removed). Fewer students who study abroad stay there; it is increasingly desirable to find a future at home. But the "stay away" number is still about 150,000 out of 600,000.

The conflict between education and indoctrination continues. Big money is spent to provide hundreds of indoctrination schools and training centers reserved for the Party elite. Teachers are at risk and must not allow what happens in the class room to appear to question standard doctrine. Truth is less important than "correctness", as defined in communist theology.

[7] Official policy statements are still saturated with this doctrine. Students are supposed to emerge as both "red and expert". The official line actually states that students will be allowed to study only for the sake of learning to continue the revolution, and the leaders of the Party have continuously pounded home the great need for mastering "correct political orientation" as the goal of education. [16] Deng's speeches were full of references to "loyalty to the Socialist Motherland", or "building revolutionary order and discipline" or "protection of the proletarian cause, Marxism- Leninism, and Mao Zedong Thought" Elementary/secondary education must remain the responsibility of local governments, primarily at the village, township and county level, but with better transportation now available, it should be possible for these jurisdictions to "rationalize" the physical facilities of school into fewer but more productive numbers of schools. The policy of family self- sufficiency is a desirable one, but the governments must recognize that a large percentage of parents have serious trouble paying very high education fees, and they must assume more of the cost of the school physical plant and teacher salary and benefit costs so that exorbitant fees can be eliminated. The government should encourage, and not try to prevent, the development of private schools, but nobody really thinks that these private schools will ever be the answer for the great bulk of China's 235 million school children. It would be a great advantage if governments sponsored and mandated specific taxes dedicated to elementary and secondary education; but local jurisdictions only rarely seem to take such a step on their own. There is a concerted effort to upgrade the skills and competence of teachers and administrators, but the political leadership must overcome their normal urge to play cheapskates and learn to pay teachers much more attractive salaries, so that they don't all leave for better paying jobs elsewhere. But the percentage of funding from other than government budgets has grown to over 46%.

At the university level, concentration on a limited number of "key" schools probably foretells the abandonment of hundreds of lesser institutions. Millions will struggle to obtain a higher education, but current reforms are still designed to provide preferential treatment for the ruling elite, which are now extended to include the new middle class.

If one accepts the premise that one of the most important responsibilities of governments is to provide an adequate level of social services for its people, then both China and India have failed that responsibility in the arena of primary education, and these failures are enormous, and to a large degree deliberate.

Both countries placed main responsibility for primary education at the state/province level, knowing that most local governments were desperately poor. Both central governments were fully aware of the fact that primary education would be seriously under funded and neither has ever done anything about it.

In both countries, the numbers of schools is seriously inadequate, the physical plant for many is terrible to the point that children lack toilets and even running water in some cases. Almost always, schools lack modern accurate books and other teaching aids. Often they even lack paper, pens, blackboards and even desks.

In both countries, teachers are largely undereducated, poorly trained, and poorly motivated. In India, the rate of teacher truancy is terrible – said to be the worst in the world. On any given day, 40% or more of the teaching staff are absent, and classes, if held, are often by substitutes or office staff. In India, the reputation of state run schools is so bad that a high proportion of education is in the hands of private providers.

India has teachers unions that are highly politicized and exert powerful political leverage on politicians. Few school administrators are willing to challenge the unions over teacher truancy of poor performance. In China, teachers unions are under the control of the central government and are used to enforce teacher doctrinal conformity, and the government never hesitates to exert control over course content. India specializes in plans and policy statements, but not actual education.

Motivation for better education is in part a function of the level of education of the general population. In China, functional literacy now exceeds 90%; in India, it is about 60%. One third of India's adult population remains illiterate; only 17% have completed secondary education, but of low quality. China is headed for full secondary education, while India, 60 years after independence is still trying to get children through 8 grades. Only half of Indian children ever enter school. Of those, another 50% will drop out after the 5th grade. And in India especially, it seems pitiful to recognize that many fail to understand that "literacy" does not mean "education".

In both cases, the central governments remain responsible for higher education, but both still believe in educating a small elite. Both governments place top priority on economic development, and both have come to realize the importance of a big expansion of the numbers of well educated people in reaching economic goals. Both are driven no so much by good government policy, but by growing pressure from their new "Middle Class" of younger people, from the growing private sector, and even by state owned enterprises which have awakened to the fact that they cannot compete with a staff of poorly educated clerks and machine tenders. India has spent a lot of money and effort to create a series of highly respected Institutes of Technology and Institutes of Management. China is doing much the same thing, but it has also spent much of its education money on special schools and training centers for their politicians to reeducate them in the theology of Marxist/Leninist/Mao Zedong Thought.

Finally, in China, all instruction is in Mandarin, with some latitude for local language "add-ons". In India, three languages are authorized: English, Hindi, and many local languages. Thus, many Indian children suffer the added disadvantage of an education in a language that provides very poor access to the outside world.

HEALTH CARE

HEALTH CARE INDIAN STYLE

It is truly alarming to read in various tourist guides about the health threats that a tourist may face in India. Travelers are usually advised to get vaccination and immunizations for typhoid, polio, tetanus, infectious hepatitis and malaria. Also recommended are preventions against tuberculosis, meningitis, diphtheria, encephalitis, rabies, small pox, cholera and yellow fever. There are also constant admonitions about infections from food and water, insects, diarrhea, salmonella, cholera, dengue fever, and intestinal worms. Such warnings point out that most Indian cities have poisonous air and water. And then there is HIV/AIDS. In other words, India is among the most dangerous places in the world for individual health.

The Indian government has deliberately neglected the national provision of health care in favor of other priorities. Only 0.9% of GDP (2006) and 1.3% of the national government budget, or about 17% of total health care costs were spent by governments on health care, less than almost any other country. In rural India, there are 2,000 people for each doctor, but 70 million Indians cannot afford to see a doctor or buy medicine, and many go bankrupt trying to pay for medical emergencies. This failure puts a strain on people's health, and illnesses and diseases flourish. India has seen the rapid growth of HIV/AIDS, a return of polio and tuberculosis, and increases in heart diseases, diabetes and congenital obstructive pulmonary disease (COPD). Less than 17% of the funds for health care come from the government, compared to 36% in China and 45% in the United States. The medical needs of women have long been neglected, and the medical profession seems not to understand the vital influence of women as care givers and the protectors of the health of children and the elderly. Even the advent of modern technology such as ultrasound seems to have contributed to the ancient practice of disposing of girl babies.

According to Panagaria, "--- a close examination of the public sector since the early 1950s shows that the government of India is largely incapable of delivering critical social services to the public. Despite continuous assertions of commitment to serve the poor -----the government has simply failed to deliver services adequately to the poor, or even to the rich." [17] Or as Dreze and Sen put it, "Much of the mismatch between resources and achievements is due to the poor functioning of the public health care system, especially in rural areas. In some States, this system is little more than a collection of deserted primary health centers, filthy dispensaries, unmotivated doctors, and chaotic hospitals. Ground level implementation is simply no there." [18] There has been a pattern of less government support and more out-of-pocket medical expenses for the poor, especially the rural poor in India and China." Instead, "more expensive private care – or fee-for- service care at public facilities – is rising in place of inadequate publicly funded systems." [19]

The number of doctors and health care in general has not even kept up with population growth, much less, increasing their availability. Local health care facilities at levels below the county are seldom more than first aid stations. Furthermore, what service they provide is curative, and they are not capable of pressing any preventative medicine program or public education program. Further, the family planning program is so hated that it often sours the reputation of many of these primary health care centers. The perceived failures of the public health care system has led to the emergence of private sector health care capabilities. Doctors and nurses and technical facilities make more money linking to the private sector; patients are so put off by the horrible reputation of public facilities that they are willing to cough up the money to go private. Better health is linked to increased wealth. Using a poverty line measure of U. S. $1.08 per day, out-of-pocket health expenditures increased the poverty rate in China to 16.2% from 13.7%, and in India to 34.8% from 31.1%."

Although the overall expenditure on social services appears to be increasing in real terms, States are accounting for a decreasing share of the total, while the national government's share is increasing slowly and reluctantly. Many individuals do not seek physician care or hospitalization when needed since they cannot afford this care.

"In China and India, both countries have experienced a significant shift from government funded health care to privately funded health care. In China, this is mainly due to the transition from a centrally planned provision to a more market oriented economy. Government spending decreased from 30% of GDP in 1978 to 10% in 1996, and government health care spending fell to about the same degree. In India, government spending has been between 20-25% for the last two decades, but debt payments and pension liabilities have eroded the government's ability to fund adequate health care. China has maintained public ownership over most health facilities, making public provision of care the dominant mode for the majority of services, while "legitimizing" profit- seeking behavior at public facilities through a set of perverse incentives. In contrast, India has followed a policy of benign neglect, and allowed entrance into and expansion of private sector to fill the gaps, with little central government involvement, ever for effective regulation or enforcement." [20]

In China, as the government reduced its financial inputs, it still enforced a number of price controls which perversely reduced the charges for medical procedures below costs. This has forced hospitals and to a lesser extent, doctors to seek other sources of funding, and it has turned most hospitals and township health centers into somewhat shady profit seeking enterprises. In India, the government pays for most of the care in public facilities, and as in China, it forces costs to be kept very low. In both countries, everybody is going private; the difference is that in India, this is legal and now officially encouraged, while in China it is extensively illegal and officially ignored. In both countries, providers are well known for systematically overprescribing drugs and tests because this is where they make their money. Counterfeit drugs are very prevalent in China, especially in rural areas, and nobody knows what harm they cause. In India, it has been shown that even licensed doctors generally provide poor quality service. Smaller hospitals in India lack even basic medical equipment and trained personnel. The public sector continues to be marked by inefficiency, shortages, absentee personnel and bumbling administrations.

India has introduced the National Rural Health Mission – another phony which promises to "increase Indian government spending on health to 2% of GDP." This is merely self-serving; spending is currently around 1% of GDP and seems well stuck at that level. In addition, the Indian government, in 2003, introduced yet another insurance scheme which is supposed to be heavily subsidized by the central government budget to aid the poor. But little money has been forthcoming, and few people have signed up for the voluntary program – they are too smart. There are many community based programs often run by trust hospitals or NGOs, and much of the money is from grants, donations or patient fees. But such programs at best reach 30-35 million people, fail to reach the real poor, and are considered bad bargains – too much money for too little treatment.

Here are some current health care statistics that offer further assessment of the state of Indian health: [21]

- Couples are having fewer children: 1993 =3.4; 1999 = 2.9
- More than 1/3 of married Indian women have chronic energy deficiency; more than 50% of them are anemic.
- 45% of children under 3 are severely and chronically malnourished. Protein-energy malnutrition is twice as high in India than in Sub-Saharan Africa.
- Only 42% of small children have gotten all of their immunizations. 15% have received none.
- Only 31% of the rural population has access to drinkable water, and less than 1% possess full basic sanitation.
- Death from infectious diseases was about the same in 2001 as it was in 1947.
- 27% of the rural population are below the official poverty line, as well as 24% of urban residents.

In sum, India's record is among the very worst in the world. The poor face high unemployment, relatively high food prices, failure to benefit from food subsidies, diseases like diarrhea, lack of noon meals, in Indian schools, lack of basic education in general, and poor agricultural management."

"India's social services were used relatively little by the poor. Access has been limited in housing, social security and social welfare services because these services were inadequate relative to needs and because services have been usurped by the non-poor. The quality of services is very low. There is weak management, ineffective targeting, and inflexible service delivery systems. The bureaucracy is inadequate to handle the case load or reach out to the poor." [22]

A measure of the government's failure is that the private sector today provides as much as 80% of outpatient care in both rural and urban areas. Private care is not that good; but often it is the only option. According to a World Bank report (2001), the total number of private hospitals rose from 3,000 in 1981 to 10,300 in 1995, and the number of beds from 133,000 to 225,000. But these numbers are refuted by other independent studies that suggest that 67,000 private hospitals are in operation which would be more than 90% of the hospitals in the country. But both public and private care is poorly financed, and the better doctors, nurses and technicians tend to gravitate to the richer cities, the better hospitals, or private practice. An exception is the Family Planning Program which Sanjay Gandhi initiated in 1981. It is relatively well financed and heavily supported on both economic and social theory, but it is very expensive and sucked most of the very limited funding right out of government budgets. It is widely hated, largely because, as in China, in its initial phases it was a "punishment" program relying heavily on forced abortions and sterilizations, along with fines and other penalties. Belatedly, the government has moved toward more education and less punishment, but the bad memories blight the program, and indeed all of public health care. And note that, despite these programs, the population of India has grown from less than 500 million in 1965 to 1.1 billion now, and the population of China has risen from about 580 million at the time of Communist assumption of power in 1949 to 1.3 billion today.

The state of public hospitals is essentially a disgrace. Even the report of the official National Commission on Macroeconomics and Health (2002) stated:

"For the outdoor medical facilities in existence, funding is generally insufficient; the presence of medical and paramedical personnel is often much less than that required by prescribed norms; the availability of consumables is frequently negligible; the equipment in many public hospitals is often obsolescent and unusable; and the buildings are in a dilapidated state. For the indoor treatment facilities, again, the equipment is often obsolescent; the availability of drugs is minimal; the capacity of the facilities is grossly inadequate, which leads to overcrowding, and consequently to a steep deterioration in the quality of services. As a result of such inadequate public health facilities, it has been estimated that less than 20% of the population seeks Outpatient Department services, and less than 45% of those who seek indoor treatment avail themselves of such service in public hospitals. This is despite the fact that most of these patients do not have the means to make out of pocket payments for private health services except at the cost of other essential expenditures for items such as basic nutrition." Overall, public care is now around 25% of the total. [23]

Indian governments at all levels have neglected the most basic needs for public sanitation, the importance of preventative medicine, and the values of educating the public on a wide range of health and life style threats and opportunities. All of these are relatively inexpensive and can be fairly rapidly implemented. While the performance of individual States varies widely, the overall picture appears to be a health care system that is basically incompetent. The heart of the system is its people, and those in India are overworked, underpaid, under trained, poorly motivated and under performing. So much of the limited available money goes to cover salaries and benefits of the staffs that far too little is left for actual patient treatment. And a discouraging number of doctors neglect their official duties and spend their time seeing private patients. Independent surveys have found that, on any given day, as many of 40% of doctors are absent and not available. Often, fees are charged when care is supposed to be free, and huge quantities of medications are bought by hospitals and sold to the general public. As with so many public programs in India, effective management cannot be expected and institutional reputations are that of slow, indifferent, petty paper shuffling bureaucracies.

The Indian Constitution assigns responsibility for health care to the states, which provide 75-90% of public health care funds. The rest is from the national government, but it is parceled out through a series of categorical payments, or is reserved for emergency situations. The central government role seems to be primarily in planning and priority setting, and as a back stop for surges of communicable diseases such as HIV/AIDS or malaria. As usual, the central governments main approach was to shove health care down further into the hands of local governments by "decentralizing" the program to the District level of government, and to encourage more participation by Panchayati Raj (i.e. town and village councils). At the same time It also seeks to expand the responsibilities of heath care units to include other complex concerns such as leprosy, blindness, obesity, and AIDS. But the principal contribution of the national bureaucracy seems to be hundreds of boards, commissions, committees, subcommittees, advisory councils, coordination committees, institutes, programs, schemes, councils, consultancies, task forces, working groups, planning groups, and of course hundreds of government offices and officials. Despite all the bureaucratic superstructure, actual health care is getting worse. As cities grow, funds increase very slowly while the problems grow very fast. There are huge new risks from cars and trucks, new diseases, bad air and polluted water, and sanitation failures. And India along with China are the two heaviest smoker countries in the world.

There was simply no vestige of a coherent national health care plan until 1982, and it was primarily an empty policy utterance with little reality behind it. The latest health care plan is called the National Common Minimum Program", and it promised the increase of government funding from the current 0.9% of GDP to the range of 2 to 3% by 2005, which of course never happened. The political hypocrisy of the time promised the goal "to provide accessible, accountable, effective and reliable **primary** health care, especially to the poor and vulnerable sectors of the population. The newest utterance is a National Rural Health Mission: 2005- 2012, in which the government (once again) promises to raise public expenditure to the 3% range, but again, it sounds like smoke and mirrors.

There is rising hope in some circles that India's growing economic wealth will somehow translate magically into a more effective health care system, but there is no such automatic connection. There is a critical need not just for those fancy "national plan", but for a realistic pattern of actual implementation and for thousands of communities to develop strong service delivery capabilities. Stronger organizations could do much to enhance public health, even without a lot more money. But to upgrade the more expensive components such as better hospitals and more and better trained doctors and nurses is the work of generations.

STRUCTURE OF THE HEALTH CARE SYSTEM

The health care system is designed to function at three levels. The lowest is the Sub-Center which provides very basic services intended to serve a population of about 5,000. The standard staff usually consists of one male health worker and one woman who is a Nurse/Midwife. The main responsibility of these centers is maternal/child health care, family planning, family welfare, nutrition, immunizations, diarrhea control, communicable disease control, health evaluation, and health education. The central government finances the physical plant, but the States cover personnel costs. There are 1,450,272 sub-centers (2007), but a large number are not much more than pill dispensaries.

The next level up is the Primary Health Center, which is the first point of service with a trained Medical Officer. The main roles are for preventative treatment and diagnosis. The Medical Officer is assisted by a staff of about 14, and it services and takes referrals from half a dozen Sub-Centers. Each Center has 4-6 beds, and is supposedly to serve a population of 30,000. There are 22,370 such Centers, maintained and funded by the States, trying to serve India's 550,000 villages and 740 million rural residents. These Centers are expected to enforce the hated Family Planning Program. The sad fact seems to be that both of these basic centers are often marginally competent and heavily overworked.

The next level up is the Community Health Center, and this is the first level at which a full range professional capability is found. Each has at least four surgeon/physicians and a gynecologist and a pediatrician, with further staffing of about 20 other staff. Each will have at least an X-ray machine, a technical laboratory, and other basic equipment. Eash is supposed to serve as the place of reference for four Primary Health Centers, and it is the point of diagnosis for patients whose illnesses will need more sophisticated treatment. There are over 4,000 of these Centers, all maintained and funded by the States.

India has about 10,200 hospitals with more than 800,000 beds, but if this seems like a lot, one must remember the 1.2 billion people. Also, some estimates are that there are far less than the official numbers. There are supposed to be about 4,000 public hospitals, perhaps 2,000 maintained by charitable organizations, and the rest are private, but many in the last two categories are very small "mom and pop" facilities.

The deeply disturbing fact seems to be that all facilities except a few really excellent hospitals are marginal at best, and are wholly inadequate to meet the real demands for health care. Child immunization rates against communicable diseases like measles and tetanus are seriously low, at less than 60%, and India now has more HIV/AIDS infections than any country in the world with 5.7 million victims. The government's attitude is horribly typical. In 2005-06, the government budgeted $103 million, and the government bragged that this number will rise to $138 million in 2006-07. Its antiviral program reached about 15,000 in 2005, and hoped to help about 35,000 in 2006 – out of a population of 5.7 million victims! Private donors like the Gates Foundation and the Clinton Foundation actually commit three times as much money as the Indian central government. The U. S. government furnished

$26 million in 2006, and the World Bank provided $84 million.

Public health facilities are also seriously lacking. Almost 70% of residences lack adequate sanitation facilities, and 15% of the population does not even have regular access to drinkable water. Rapidly expanding urbanization is creating huge new problems including highly dangerous driving conditions which produce the largest number of road deaths of any country in the world. India now also has more heart related deaths than any other country. Like Chinese cities, Indian cities have their new shining towers, but are mostly full of filth and dirt, with garbage dumped into the streets, mountains of trash, open sewers, contaminated ground and underground water, deadly air quality, and hopelessly inadequate regulatory protections of foods, drugs, and chemicals. An estimated one million Indians die each year just from tobacco related diseases.

HEALTH CARE REFORMS

There needs to be a thorough wringing out of the respective roles of the central government and local governments at all levels, and the roles played by the private sector. The central government roles should deal with epidemics, provide health care education, aid the truly poor, and as advocates of basic nutrition, national vaccination programs, public health sanitation, catastrophic health crises.

One proposal often advanced would be a compulsory annuity system which has automatic enrollment. This assumes that the government would never be able to afford to pay the full national costs of a single payer government system and this means that some part of the cost must be borne by the users. This seems especially true given the continued huge informal sector of the economy, and the agricultural sector where people are largely self employed. For the very poor, there are two proposals. First is the idea that they can be paid a negative income tax specifically for the purpose of purchasing health insurance. The second is the traditional provision of health care as a charitable obligation of the state. Another idea could be to make part of any pension a set-aside just for health care. But in any event, India needs a massive expansion and revitalization of basic health services in rural/village areas. The need is daunting – how to deal adequately with the needs of 1.1 billion people.

The central government as usual has been slow to react, and most programs are still run thru public facilities which are known dummies. By 2006, just 28.6 million people had enrolled, which is truly pitiful. Obviously, the government needs to marshal all of the health care resources of the country to fight what is clearly labeled as a major national crisis. But it seems incapable of mounting such an effort, either politically or bureaucratically. World organizations and NGOs are offering help, but the government just bumbles along. [24]

Panagariya repeatedly makes the valid argument that, while the government may have an obligation to assist the poor to obtain health care, they need not do it through a public service delivery system. This is a compelling argument, given the 65 year failure of the government to do anything competent. What seems right for India is a decentralized part public/part private system with funds going to the patients and not to the bureaucracy. The need for patient flexibility and choice is very heavily tied to geography and reality. Until the public system is reformed, the private provision will continue to be the better choice, but with most of the money going to private providers, the politicians may never have the guts to face up to the unions and reform the public system. Vouchers or cash payments are possible, but both are subject to corruption. But nearly 65% of India's poor get into debt and 24 percent fall below the poverty line at least temporarily, because of medical costs. Only 6% of Indians have health insurance. Free public hospitals are not an option as two out of five doctors are absent, and there is a 50% chance of receiving the wrong treatment. Preventative medicine seems to be invisible. India joins China as the two largest populations of smokers in the world. About 1 million Indians die each year from tobacco-related diseases. Government policies aimed at "food security" and self-sufficiency have caused regulations against food imports, and stunted family nutrition.

Finally, the State has initiated a new program called "RSBY", a visionary national health insurance scheme which provides support for workers in the <u>unorganized sector </u>(93% of the workforce), but only for those living below the official poverty line. US $620 in patient health benefits are provided, at a premium of just $12.40, which the government will pay for abjectly poor people. A patient can choose from almost 1,000 private or government hospitals. States can choose from 18 public or private insurance companies. Insurers have an incentive to recruit poor patients because they earn premiums by doing so. Because patients can avoid bad hospitals, the system should become not only more competitive, but of higher quality.

A key element of the plan is that each insured will be issued a "smart card" with a photo and finger prints for each member of the family. The card will make cashless and paperless transactions for 725 pre-agreed medical procedures. The card will contain a value of $620, and it makes automatic reductions for each medical expenditure with no pre-approvals or bureaucratic involvement and the money goes directly to patients, thus reducing the chances for fraud and corruption.

"Given that the health care employees are employed and paid by the state governments, and that they cannot easily be fired despite shirking their duties, no amount of resources can make a dent in the rate of absenteeism. The solution to this problem, which constitutes the key to reforming the public health care system, is not more money, but the delegation of full authority to hire and fire to the relevant local administrations. Unfortunately, given the political clout of the health workers, the government lacks the courage to make this key change."

Another highly feasible approach would be the adoption of vouchers for health care (also education and food supplements), but as with education, the concept of a voucher system is stoutly opposed by doctors, hospital administrators, health care unions, and sellers of medicines.

In general, the health care system suffers from:

- Lack of management skills, and a heavy handed bureaucracy.
- Low salaries and the fact that still, too much of the available funding is consumed by salaries and overhead and not for patient treatment.
- Lack of overall public funding forcing excessive reliance on personal and non-government sources of funding.
- Lack of accountability; employees are paid by the state and cannot be supervised by local authorities
- Doctors who often neglect public duties and run private practices half of the time. On any given day, 40% of doctors are absent from public hospitals and treatment centers.
- Fees are charged, even when treatment is supposed to be free, and there are serious benefit disparities where 20% of the patients get 10% of funding; but the top 20% get 30% of available funds.
- Too much of the available funding is consumed by salaries and overhead, not for patient treatment. Still, health care people are seen as chronically underpaid. **[26]**

Some hospitals accept residents right out of high school, where education was probably marginal. There appears to be an assumption that there are a whole range of medical practices which can be handled by marginally trained doctors. The hospital complex seems to be overdone in some places and all but non- existent in others. For example, there are too many hospitals in urban areas and they are overstaffed – for 1,600 beds the hospitals employ around 700 "doctors" full time and 300 of them are supposedly surgeons. Beds and services are both tiered – cheap to expensive. Costs are often very low, and this is a function of the fact that few people have insurance and have to pay cash up front. Quality of care varies throughout India and is an especially big concern in villages and major urban slums.

The article also states that "more than 300 million Indians out of a population of 1.2 billion still live on less than $1 per day. But in a Tweeter comment, somebody else states "456 million Indians (42% of the total Indian population) now live under the global poverty line of $1.25 per day." If 300 million live in "abject poverty", and another 456 million live in "poverty", this is about 45% of the entire national population! If the supposed 300 million in the "new middle class" are subtracted, then an additional 264 million people are "near poor" or close to it. And many of those who are supposedly in the touted "new middle class" are in the lower reaches of that class. [27]

Thus, the macroeconomists and the India enthusiasts brag that the new Indian middle class is as large as the entire population of the U. S. But these numbers fail to state that those living in poverty in India are 2.5 times the population of the U. S.

It is also argued that nutrition is an important element of health, and that nutrition has declined during the 90's because of the very large and embarrassing and expensive accumulation of grains which the government has bought and stored in warehouses in the last 10 years. Also per capita energy and protein intake has declined very sharply during the 1990s and the percentage of the population getting energy and protein below the minimum threshold has increased.

It is also true that the government should finally – after 60 years (or 6,000 years) – pay some serious attention to the vital health care role of women. First, nothing would reduce issues such as malnutrition, or child deficiencies more than the education of women, and their empowerment in the power structure. In addition, many small farms are now in fact run by women, because the men are in the cities trying to make money. Also, women have a very good record of work in the informal economy, and many of them are now running their own businesses. It still seems true that the official welfare programs, notably the Integrated Child Development Services and the Targeted Public Distribution System presently fail to reach large numbers of poor and nutritionally vulnerable people. If women who are the intended recipients of these programs were really listened to, the relevance of these programs would be strongly improved.

The health insurance market in India is very limited covering about 6-10% of the total population. The existing schemed can be categorized as:

1. Voluntary health insurance schemes or private-for-profit schemes;
2. Employer based schemes
3. Insurance offered by NGOs/community based health insurance; and
4. Mandatory health insurance schemes or government run schemes.

In the public sector, the General Insurance Corporation (GIC), a state owned enterprise, has five subsidiaries: the National Insurance Corporation, the New India Assurance Company, the Oriental Insurance Company, and the United Insurance Company, and the Life Insurance Corporation of India. All provide voluntary insurance. Mediclaim is the major program of the GIC and it was initiated in 1986 to cover both individuals including dependents and groups.

HEALTH CARE CHINESE STYLE

The Chinese Communist Party (CCP) has always refused to accept responsibility for social services programs. China trapped itself: it based the delivery of critical social services like elementary/secondary education, health care, unemployment and retirement insurance on the system of 400,000 State Owned Enterprises (SOE) but at best, they provided inadequate services to only about 20% of the workforce, and they never reached the 80% of the urban poor or the people who live in rural and village areas. Then to make matters much worse, it became apparent that the SOEs themselves were a failed experience. More than half were running at a deficit, and most had to be subsidized by the government or by the banks, thus diverting money from other urgent pubic purposes. The CCP had no choice but to work its way out of this SOE cull de sac in two ways. First, it initiated a program of divestiture of SOEs, keeping only those that were key elements for control of the economy, and either dumping others off on local governments, privatizing them, or killing them off. Second, the social services provided by SOEs were dumped on local governments who then had to struggle to provide staffs and funds to carry them out. As a consequence, local governments have been struggling for more than 20 years to recover from this blow and fill in the social services gaps. The reality seems to be that the SOEs transferred were mostly the losers; many are still operating at a deficit, and most were heavily in debt to State banks.

But the collapse of the SOE base has caused a mammoth timing gap. Provinces, cities and township/villages simply have not yet been able to develop social services delivery mechanisms fast enough or broadly enough. The result is that health care or retirement insurance are still not available for the great bulk of the population, and these services are worse now than they were under the old SOE system. This has greatly discredited governments and contributed to public outrage over the inherent unfairness of almost every form of government activity.

Health care, like education is one of the greatest failures of the Chinese Communist Party.

Even China's leadership is now admitting that the former socialist ideal of a "cradle to grave" social services system was an unworkable fiction and could never be achieved, and it was officially abandoned even for the SOEs in 1998. According to Becker, "As with education, state spending on health has shrunk steadily since 1979. Although the central government's health budget has gone up in absolute terms, as a proportion of total spending it had shrunk from 32% to 14% by 1993. By the late 1990s only 4% of the recurrent health care budget came under the direct control of the central government. While total health spending rose from 2.3% of GDP in 1980 to 3.2% in 1987, and is expected to reach 5% by the year 2010, 80% of health funding goes to big city hospitals." [30] The government seems to have given up on rural health care.

The general philosophy of reform now lies in three directions – first, it is now asserted that the people must "do more to take care of themselves and their own interests" (which they have always done, no thanks to the government); second, the whole health care system must be "rationalized" in operational terms; and third, the private sector must be brought into the health care system at least through the provision of health care for their employees, and also as manager and implementer in meeting more public needs. The most important tide running in health care in China seems to be a slow and inadequate movement from any form of government provided services to a system that relies far more heavily on private enterprise and individual cost burden. Hospitals are going private at the township and village levels, and they are anxiously searching for private funding, either from patients or from employers. Doctors and nurses are increasingly in business for themselves. Village level medical practitioners are abandoning the vestiges of the commune/cooperative structure and are privately employed. There are new experiments for the provision of health care through some form of cooperative, but these are just getting under way. All such efforts in rural and small town areas are still very oppressed by the lack of money among their clients.

There have been a series of schemes over many years to provide health care, all of which have failed. [10] In the 60s, there was a program through rural collectives based on communes, and while these collectives did manage to reach almost 90% of the population, the actual level of care was extremely low. In 1998, the government instituted a new health care scheme: employees now contribute 2% of their annual wages; employers contribute up to 6% of the total wage bill. The employee contribution and 30% of employer contributions are put into individual accounts, and the rest in a pooled account. Individual accounts are used mainly for smaller medical expenses, and the pooled accounts are supposed to pay for major expenses, but with a maximum of 400% of an individual's wage which is usually very low. The funds are put in the Social Security Fund which is supposedly managed by experts. Most of the money is invested in government bonds or bank deposits. Fund managers are free to invest funds elsewhere, but it must be remembered that these funds are politically controlled by a government that does not hesitate to dictate the course of action that props up state banks. It has been announced that ultimately the system will be compulsory, but as of 2001, the rate of return on invested funds was far too low to cover costs, and the system requires repeated transfusions of government subsidy.

Resistance to date has been stiff. Patients see the costs as excessive, and the payouts skimpy, and the treatments that are covered are often very limited. Government refusal to provide money is so foolish that it generates all kinds of destructive consequences Doctors see their payments as painfully low; they prefer to devote their time to generating private paying patients (through "donations") and kickback deals with pharmaceutical companies. Hospitals also feel under-compensated, and are doing better by retailing drugs, renting their facilities or charging illicit fees. Meanwhile, in rural areas, the service disparities have grown even worse. While access was available to only 22% in the richer urban areas, it was a pitiful 1-3% in rural areas, and most of the people in the unofficial urban economy have also been excluded. In 1998, the unit cost of an outpatient visit at a local hospital (county) was 400% higher than it had been just 5 years earlier. If workers use up all the funds in their accounts, they can be reimbursed from a social-pooling fund, but it will pay only about 40% of expenses. Even for those who use such a plan, the costs are rising, and more than 50% of people don't seek medical care when ill. Medical or social services for special problems such as those of the handicapped or drug or alcohol addicted are extremely rare, in large part because they cannot be made profitable.

Local governments have punted; much of simpler health care has been privatized, but these private providers lack the knowledge, the trained staff or the service delivery structures to be effective and health care remains of very low quality. At the village level, there are some 1.4 million health care workers trained in the basics of care, and they can prescribe certain basic medicines, and can charge a fee for their services. The 52,000 hospitals at the township level can do basic surgery and treat things like injuries and infections. At the county level are the first hospitals – about 4,000 of them – that are capable of major and more sophisticated medical care. In total, there seem to be about 175,000 more or less professionally trained medical personnel. But the physical plant ranges from moderate to primitive; most staffs are virtually untrained by Western standards, modern testing and analysis capabilities are poor, diagnostic capabilities are especially weak, and even these inferior services are increasingly too expensive for most people. There is a lot of corruption because "that's where the money is". Assessments made of this system in the late 90s and early 2000s suggest that the whole thing continues to be "high cost/low value" and that little progress has been made over almost 20 years.

The fault for this disaster clearly lies with the political leadership. The whole area has also suffered from serious price inflation. The rise in medical costs by some 25-30% per year took place throughout the 90s, and soon medical costs were so high that they could be afforded by only 15% of the population. More than 75% of women gave birth to their children in the home, with little or no pre-natal or post-natal care.

The only partially effective health insurance programs were those provided for the elites in government bureaus and in the SOEs, and even there, the services provided were weak. The failings of the SOEs and collectives were concealed, along with the absolute failure to provide health care at all in rural and village areas. Even the supervising Ministry of Labor and Social Security admits that only 6% of the people can actually afford health care even if it is available. China is still ranked 144th in overall performance in the world and 139th in terms of heath care finance per capita. The World Health Report 2000 ranked China at 188th out of 191 countries in terms of the fairness with which the health care system operates. **[31]**

In a typical Chinese political utterance, the Minister of Public Health has "mandated" that 8% of rural budgets be spent on health care, but this is obviously ludicrous. The national government itself is notorious because it allocates only about 2.4% of its budget to health care, plus some additional funding for construction. The wealthier provinces might reach 2%, but the poorer ones are capable only of less than ½ percent.

Meanwhile, the CCP's family planning program is heavily financed. Family planning involves the notorious "one child" policy which is aimed at reducing population, Administration of the family planning program requires a major bureaucracy at all levels of government, including 400,000 officials at the township level and more than 1 million at the village level. There is a National Family Planning Commission which sets birth rate targets, and doles out quotas to provinces. Zealous local officials have turned to seriously coercive means to meet quotas including administrative punishments such as job loss or termination of social services. In other cases, women have been forced to have abortions, husbands have been sent to jail, and there have even been executions for violators whose added child has been ruled a "threat to national stability" whatever that means. Officials have often diverted lush family planning funds to other purposes and then simply lied about statistical achievements.

Under the CCP, there has been a decline in public sanitation. In 1997, 400 million people still lacked access to safe water, and 76% lacked access to adequate sanitation. Infectious diseases have resurged, including tuberculosis, hookworm disease, and diarrhea. There are 16 million mentally ill patients, and only about 110,000 beds. Even so, half of these beds are unused, both because people cannot afford the treatment, and also because mental illness still is the victim of deep seated social stigma. Even official statistics report that China has the highest suicide rate in the world, and it is the only country in the world where the rate is higher for women than for men." [32]

The expenditure on health care is deliberately being concentrated on a few facilities in major cities for the elite. Most of the State's expenditure is going to provide for just three groups of people – 25 million government officials and party members, 75 million SOE workers, and 50 million workers in collectives. 80% of health spending goes to big city hospitals which over-spend on prestige modern equipment. Similarly, health insurance is usually only available to the same elite, including a program for collectives that covers 50 million people. The Chinese are notorious (as were the Russians) for neglecting, and never really understanding the whole concept of preventative medicine. For example, there are 320 million smokers, the great majority of whom are highly vulnerable to lung diseases and deaths from tobacco related causes, along with foul and dangerous air in most cities. And at the same time, all aspects of the tobacco trade are controlled as a State monopoly and it is the government itself that collects huge profits. AIDS threatens to become a major problem, compounded by a large traffic in illegal blood donations. There is a serious problem of fake or substandard drug manufacturing – the fastest growing problem of its type in the world. The sale of drugs is huge in hospitals (much of it illicit) because it has become their largest source of income beyond patient fees. Doctor/nurse salaries are often dependent on this trade, and there is therefore a strong pressure to over prescribe.

The Chinese people will never have adequate health care if they have to wait for the government to provide it. It may be acceptable to retain some elements of the old State system, especially as it relates to SOEs, but what is needed is a whole redesign of the health care system which combines government, private businesses, and individual responsibility. For the foreseeable future, it will be critical that governments at all levels come forward with large amounts of money for "system building"; the construction of hospitals, the education and training of many more health care professionals, the creation of new and more professional technical skills, and the purchase of modern hospital equipment. This surge is most needed in rural/small town areas, and there should be a concentration first on some of the simpler capabilities such as small local clinics, more and cheaper outpatient facilities, store front operations for things like pre-natal care, new clinics for dental care, and expansions of good quality technical support services. There is nothing wrong with the present system of concentrating the more complex kinds of medical treatment at the county and province level except there are far too few hospitals at these levels for the huge population. There needs to be 20-30 years of upgrading the performance of the heath care profession. The poorly trained amateurs must be phased out, and thousands of fully trained professionals developed so that all Chinese citizens can get health care which approaches world standards.

There does continue to be a vital role for the central government to play. There is a serious need for a national campaign to educate the people about preventative medicine, the importance of proper life styles like the avoidance of alcohol and smoking, proper diets, self care and self reliance. New or better packages of public regulation are needed. The government must broaden its ability to test and certify drugs, certify hospitals, examine professional qualifications, enforce occupational safety, regulate air and water purity, and all of the other protections that the people have a right to expect from their government, but which have been largely ignored for 60 years.

RETIREMENT INDIAN STYLE

India is a very young country: the average age is in the mid- twenties – but the government has routinely ignored both the young and the elderly. The general philosophy is that care of the elderly is the responsibility of the children. Having bought into this philosophy has allowed the government comfortably to ignore the obvious flaws in this public policy. Social welfare for the aged as a role of government has never evolved and has typically ranged between 0.1 and 0.6% of government budgets. In essence, the government has done next to nothing about people's needs in their old age. Despite several forms of retirement programs covering certain elites, the bitter fact is that these schemes cover only 11% of the national workforce in two elite groups: 25+ million employees of national and State governments; and another 15 million workers, primarily in state owned enterprises. [33] In 2001, 18% of all government's expenditures were on salaries, and another 6% on employee benefits. This wage bill grew rapidly in the late 90s because of the added costs for the implementation of the recommendations of a special wage commission which is vividly remembered because it produced "the single largest shock to India's strained public finances in the last decade".

While India does have pension funds, their assets amount to about 6% of GDP, compared to 22% in S. Korea, 61% in Singapore, and 64% in Malaysia. Even Thailand is at a level of 10%. The law requires investment of pension funds in instruments of the government and opposes investment in commercial stocks, and most funds are actuarially unsound, and will eventually become new problems. This policy deprives the fund of billions of dollars of potential revenue. To an astonishing degree, this is a function of the heavy residual Socialist aversion to private business; the arrogant feeling that government officials are all wise and noble, and all private sector people are scheming villains out to rob the public. The government seems able to ignore the fact that even the pension funds of other countries are investing in the Indian stock market. The government sees low risk-low return investments in government securities as politically preferable to higher risk-higher return investments in private equity.

In general, the total employment of civil servants is low in comparison with other countries, but there are strange stupidities that exist in the patterns of employee utilization. The teacher/pupil ratio is horrendous. Inspectors of foods, drugs, drinks, safety, health, and almost everything else are all deliberately in short supply–so bad that those who wish to violate the law seldom need hesitate. Food inspectors in Delhi itself number just 37 in a city of 12.5 million people, and their number has not increased since 1960. Irrigation systems, many of them run by or financed by the government are seldom inspected, and are polluting and highly inefficient.

There is a long and unsavory history of civil servants and employees of
SOEs that do little or no work, and many don't even show up a good deal
of the time. Thus, the whole arena of public employment is seen as one
huge populist political subsidy. There is also almost no unemployment
compensation provision for these favored groups, since there is almost never
any unemployment. Powerful unions are heavily resistant to workforce
trimming; once hired, jobs are forever. For the rest of the population, the
policy of the government has been either neglectful or punitive: there are
laws that punish children for failure to take care of their parents. As recently
as 2007, Parliament passed a law that allowed the state to put neglectful
sons and daughters in jail -- but not neglectful politicians.

But reality makes this approach a farce. Many grown children can
scarcely afford their own families. For the new middle class, they are
abandoning many of the old motivations, including a personal responsibility
for parental support. As a result, sociologists now speak of the "new despair
and sense of helplessness" felt by the elderly. More of them are descending
to depths of poverty, even as street people. Many simply die for lack of
ability to cope. Those old age homes that do exist are primarily provided
by charitable organizations, including foreign NGOs. As for the unions,
they all gang up to oppose change from the current defined benefit system.
The politicians are cynically neglectful. It does not help that the board of
directors that supervises the Employees Provident Fund Organization has
many union and civil service members. The elderly are not sources of either
votes or bribes. Then there is the reality that even eligible pensioners can't
get their payments approved until the appropriate minor official is paid off.

The current systems are really very bad, even for the 11% covered.
Benefits at retirement range from small to tiny. The management of the
funds themselves is increasingly suspect, with even audit reports required
by law seldom prepared. Poor accounting means that it is never publicly
clear what is happening to the funds paid into these plans, but managers,
as in the rest of government are suspected of wide ranging corruption.

Time and time again, there are reports of good programs and
innovative approaches, but almost always, they turn out to affect only

a few thousand people, and time and time again, it turns out that it is governments themselves that are the strongest resistors to reform ideas. It was not until 2003 that the government made any general commitment for development of a pension plan for all employers and self employed people. But at best, progress is "slow" – i. e. non-existent, and Indian politicians love to quote facts about the high costs of social services including pensions in developed countries.

Even if the government wanted to move toward a universal pension system, the country lacks even the rudiments of a "delivery system" to deploy such a program. A whole new process for pension deployment would have to be developed in millions of employers. India has a couple of hundred million people who are self employed, many of them in the informal economy. How would they be reached? The whole agriculture sector involves huge numbers of people and almost no public infrastructure.

The official Old Age Social and Income Security (OASIS) is a program administered by the Ministry of Social Justice which was intended to focus on the uncovered, informal sector which is estimated to employ about 300 million workers. It is a defined contribution social security scheme, and the financing arrangements would allow employees a choice of investments for their pension savings under an independent administrator/regulator, along with a high intensity IT system to drastically reduce transaction costs. The National Pension Scheme (NPS) applies to government employees and a shift to a defined contribution basis was made applicable in 2004, and it was also extended to most of the States for their employees. It is administered partly by distribution of funds at very low cost through existing organizations such as post offices and banks. It represents a rare thing in India: a successful change in a government program, based on rationality and not politics.

But according to Nilekani "overall, the pension system despite recent improvements, has stayed unsolved and remains largely a mess; and reform has repeatedly foundered. Every new government, coming into office, promises some bright new beginning; six months later, all has been forgotten. Sage advice is abundant; all is ignored. Brilliant innovations are well understood; but not initiated. Plans are announced; and then sink into oblivion. Increased budget amounts are proposed; and the money is not appropriated." [34]

PENSION REFORM CHINESE STYLE

China has one of the fastest aging populations in the world. In 2000 there were 87.9 million elderly over the age of 60, or 7% of the population. By 2005, this number was 105 million; by 2030 it will exceed 330 million or nearly 22% of the nation, and the largest percentage increases will be those 65 and above. The ratio of workers to retirees will shrink from the current 6:1 down to 2.3:1.

By 2050, the Chinese population of elderly will rise to over 400 million or 25% of the population, and will exceed that of all of N. America and all of Europe including Russia, plus Japan. It will be more than 50% of all of the elderly in the world. Increasing life expectancy is a big contributor. In 1949, male life expectancy was 42.3 and females could expect 44.8. By 1995 these numbers were 68.1 for males and 71.8 for females. [14] This is a remarkable achievement, but ominously, it means that the elderly population is increasing faster than the national capacity to deal with the problems that are emerging. At the same time, the old social services system, which provided services through the SOEs, is rapidly being divested because of the economic failures of the SOEs. Thus, China is entering an era of increasing demands for retirement pensions and health care without a functioning social services delivery system.

The new policy emphasis has shifted to provision of social services by local governments or private employers, but both are still financially too weak, and most of the population is still too poor to finance their own retirements. It is also very worrying that the one child policy has seriously undermined what was the real basis of care for the elderly, which was through their children.

China is faced with the enormous consequences of 60 years of neglect, leaving it with the problem of creating, administering and financing several of the largest and most complex social services programs in the world. The key question has become "how can China create a delivery system not for just the industrial elite, but for the bulk of its 1.3 billion people? Where is the delivery system for the administration of a billion pensions? There would need to be hundreds of thousands of trained people, and thousands of offices. And how will the government enforce fairness and honesty in any system that has been deliberately decentralized to thousands of local governments, which lack reasonably educated people to administer them? The Great Leap Forward and the Cultural Revolution seriously damaged local government, and the more recent regimes have just thrown new problems on local governments without much help in financing them. It appears that currently 55% of urban workers (252 million) and 11% of rural workers (86 million) have some form of (inadequate) retirement program. That means that about one billion people have no pension coverage.

The CCP has never ever faced up to this human necessity. It has known for almost 30 years that the previous system, based on state owned enterprises had largely failed, but after more than 30 years of fumbling around, the CCP has yet to come up with a viable replacement.

China does in fact have an official pension insurance system. In 1995, the State Council mandated a 3 tier system involving individual accounts with both employers and employees contributing. This was designed to replace the old SOE system which guaranteed 80% of wages, but which was finally admitted to be financially unsustainable, especially with the divestiture of SOEs. To pay for programs, both employers and employees are expected to make contributions, defined as percentages of total wages. For employers, there is a 20% contribution to the pension fund and a 6% contribution to the medical fund. For employees, the numbers are 4-6% for pensions and 2% for medical insurance. Including lesser contributions for other programs, it is estimated that the social services package amounts to about 38% of total wages.

In general, part one of the system is some form of public annuity, mainly for the poor, and vaguely resembling the U. S. social security system. Part two is the job based system, and part three is personal purchase of insurance or self savings. This system was made a national requirement in 1997, but it promised pensions of only 20% of average urban wages for the first tier payment. The second tier was based on employer/employee contributions of about 11% of wages, placed in individual accounts. All employees in official urban employment were required to participate, but they hate the system; it is too expensive (too much overhead), payments are way too small, and mandatory membership cuts them off from obtaining better plans through the private sector. In 2000, there were about 106 million workers covered, plus 34 million retirees in a separate system for Civil Service employees. In effect, the government set high costs because they wanted to get the "rich" to subsidize the poor, but the better off workers are too smart to sign up. It is only in very recent years that the new middle class has had the money to consider buying their own coverage, but they are a very small percentage of the workforce, and such costs are way beyond rural residents and the 180 million in the workforce "float". As used here, the "float" consists of migrant and seasonal workers, the underemployed, those in part time or temporary jobs, those in the unofficial urban workforce, those in the informal economy, and those who are simply unemployed.

The system was designed in the first place to avoid direct government commitment for pension program costs and it sought to confine those costs to employers and employees. In general, the immediate demands for assistance have outrun the increases in funding, and pension/retirement payouts have gotten relatively smaller. The World Bank has found that the urban pension system is heavily in debt. The deficit incurred in 2002 was 68 billion yuan; by 2010, it is estimated to rise to 115 billion. In the system of individual retirement accounts, local authorities have a bad record of using the funds to pay for immediate worker costs, leaving the "funds" empty and in deficit. Thus, most Chinese, even those in the official urban system must still save for their own retirement without benefit of tax deductions or tax free gains. Commercial insurance programs were not even allowed before 1978, and are not widespread even 30 years later. Over time, the contributions of individual workers are increasing and those of employers declining, but workers see the empty shells and the low pension payments and are too smart to participate.

Programs in rural areas are a governmental scam. Less than 3% of the population is covered; only ½ of those enrolled can contribute enough to earn a useful monthly payment on retirement–minimum of 50 yuan ($6.04). Thus, only about 1 million are collecting any pension. Nor is there any government sponsored health program for retirees.

At this time, in China the government sponsored plan is available only for urban workers, but efforts are being made to extend coverage to other workers, especially to farmers and those in the urban "float". The official government policy is that they will gradually extend social insurance coverage to uncovered workers. But at present, only 16% of the workforce has pension benefits; only 14% have unemployment insurance; just 11% have any form of medical coverage; 6% have job injury insurance, and only 5% of women have maternity insurance. Even those covered receive very small benefits in relation to real need. Even those who are covered have jobs at poverty wages with little job security. The pay for work in villages and townships is about one half of the average wage of urban official workers. Each year, about 10 million young workers enter the workforce, but at the same time, there is a constant level of about 15 million workers or 10% in the official workforce who are unemployed. If you add up all of the people in "high risk" categories it numbers perhaps 600 million or 80% of the total workforce. There are huge pools of marginal workers: a rural surplus of 120-140 million; a population of urban floaters numbering about 80 million; urban workers in the informal economy, and a redundancy factor of 20-30% even in the government's favored SOEs. In China, there is a confusing "blur" between employed, unemployed, underemployed, subsidized work, and work in enterprises that are marginal or downright obsolete.

The level of pension coverage has not increased significantly in the last 10 years. Many of the people laid off with the divestiture of SOEs were promised help, but didn't get it beyond certain "starvation" payments. Local governments are still so strapped for funds that there is little realistic belief that these insurance systems will increase much for many years. There is no real plan proposed for how these problems will be attacked, much less solved. The funding of most of these social insurance programs are theoretically the responsibility of local governments, but the national government has been forced to subsidize up to 90% of expenditures in a large number of jurisdictions. Worker's have virtually no bargaining position in the market economy, especially where unions are useless appendages of the State, and governments are reluctant to side with workers against the interests of employers, either public or private.

Employer contributions are made into both the general social fund and to the individual accounts. Individual worker accounts receive a uniform payment each year determined by the Peoples Bank of China, but it is far less than might be earned in true private sector investments. That is, the rate of payments is controlled by the profitability of the government's investments, which are now primarily in SOEs which are in bad shape, and are being divested. Thus, the government is now forced to expand to more investment opportunities in other ventures to try and enhance earnings. On a positive note, the Chinese government is working its way out of most of its SOEs as fast as possible, and there is a huge divestiture market that will attract both fund management companies, and world-wide interest in selling company stocks and bonds to the pension funds. In other words, there is a very high potential for a successful privatization.

Local governments not only must cover the costs of social programs, but they still must transfer part of their revenues from employers and employees to the national government. The legal base for pension programs is still being developed. Most of the overall umbrella laws were drafted in the late 90s, and many of the enabling regulations are only 5-6 years old. But the real concern remains financing. Greater urgency is now being felt by the CCP because they have come to realize the consequences of the rapidly aging population and the inability of local governments to find adequate revenues or even to collect contributions owed. There is a lot of "holding out" on the part of employers, especially the SOEs, and there is a lot of corruption and fund stripping to divert pension funds illegally to cover costs outside of the retirement fund. The trade unions in SOEs that had previously administered those pension funds have been largely allowed to sink, and this is not a bad thing. The SOEs themselves have had a bad record of non payment, and even some cities and towns have refused to contribute in one or more years. As a result, the so called pension reserves are so low that they could not cover retirement payments for even a year. Many of the individual accounts are also empty; there has been no "real money" contributed, which means that current pension obligations have to be funded out of current revenues, and little financing is being accumulated against future needs. At some point, these demands on current revenues will overwhelm local government budgets.

The admirers of the development of the Chinese economy should wonder where the Chinese government gets so much money. The answer in part is that, for 60 years, they have spent almost nothing on the social services that are so critical to the individual Chinese citizen: education, health, and protection for the elderly.

CHAPTER VI

Urbanization

URBANIZATION IN INDIA

At the time of Independence in 1947, the population of India was about 425 million people. By 1991, it was almost 850 million. In 2001, it exceeded one billion, and by 2010, the population is estimated to be about 1.2 billion. Everything in India is, in some way a reflection of the need to cope with this enormous demographic reality.

Population has increased both in cities and in rural/small town areas, but the fate of India is increasingly locked into the fate of its cities and towns. India has about 285 million urban dwellers (28% of the total population), and this is expected to expand to more than 575 million by 2020. In 2001, there were 35 urban areas with populations over one million and 393 cities with populations over 100,000, and these cities averaged about 26% of their populations below the official poverty line. Growth has been absorbed slowly from rural areas to cities of all sizes, which have grown at about equal speeds, and it is estimated that by the year 2021, there will be 75 cities with populations over one million. [1] Right now, of the 100 largest cities in the world, India has eight. (Mumbai, Kolkata, Delhi, Hyderabad, Chennei, Bangalore, Almadabad, Pune).

During the 70's, more than 1,000 new towns were created and most cities were expanding rapidly. The growth rate however, has been <u>declining</u> during the last 20 years. Why has urbanization slowed down? Industrial development has not been as intensive as in China and it has not provided enough jobs in urban areas -- or anywhere. Economic development in Indian cities has not been primarily in factory jobs, which require large numbers of workers. Instead, most jobs are in the services sectors of the economy and many of these have been captured by the large numbers of people already in the urban informal economies. Thus, the opportunities for new workers off the farms and out of the villages are relatively limited.

But even more importantly, most Indian cities are horrible places to live. There is an estimated 72 million who are classified as "urban poor", (World Bank, 1997) and millions of these people live in miserable shacks lacking water and sanitation, crowded, dirty, and dangerous. 90% of these people work – if at all – in the informal economy doing everything from respectable crafts and small businesses down to the most menial tasks. Municipal governments have generally failed to deal with issues of housing, transport, food supply, and consumer services. People don't volunteer to live in slums and work in the informal economy; these decisions are forced on them by the failures of the formal economy. And it is not just that municipal governments cannot afford to help them; it is that they deliberately choose not to do so. The real uses of land, for example, are dictated by commercial development. Much more money can be made by developing high rise buildings than by building cheap housing for the poor. Population migration has become increasingly complex, mixing rural to urban movements, with shifts from poorer to richer cities, from smaller to larger cities, from the illiterate to the more a new population of the educated or trained. Still, most of the increase in urban population is among the poorest of people living in the worst of slums.

"Union" budget items mean programs funded by the national government. "State" budget items are funded by and for the 28 States. "Concurrent" budget items are those shared by both the central government and the States, and they are largely financed by the national budget but with some funding split with the States. Amendment # 74 to the Indian

Constitution defined a fundamental approach to the decentralization of responsibilities from the national government to the States, including technical provisions dealing with a range of legal and financial accommodations, most of which meant shifting financial burdens to the States. The amendment granted authority to vary the services provided in cities according to how much residents are willing to pay. Thus, it favors those financially better off, and became the perfect justification for officially ignoring the poor who can't pay for anything. But the abdication of the national government is not as drastic as it might seem because it never supplied very much money at the best of times, and what local governments got instead was more likely to be criticism and interference. Thus, the central government has found a way to avoid responsibilities for cities and the urban poor by "decentralizing" responsibilities to municipalities and towns essentially as huge unfunded mandates.

On the surface, there appears to be a record of improvement in urban poverty, which stood at 42.5% of municipal population in 1974, but is now down to about 28%. But while this number is down in percentage terms, it is up in absolute terms. A large share of this improvement has been achieved not by the success of government programs, or even by the expansion of the private sector, but by the strengthening of the informal economy. This still means the survival of millions upon millions of people who are in high risk jobs, with no job security, earning a bare living, surviving largely without public facilities, and forced to live in horrendous debilitating slums, with an estimated 8 million or more who are absolutely homeless and live on the streets. As cities get bigger, so do their slums.

Housing provision has not nearly kept pace with demand and the shortage of adequate housing is outrageous and scandalous. Today, absent any really effective programs from governments, 90% of housing investment is from private sources. There are new housing financial institutions that allow people to get mortgages for home ownership, but the housing industry is reluctant to build low cost housing. Also, leftover socialist laws still make it difficult to own property in the first place, or to transfer ownership except through horrendous bureaucratic exercises.

But the truth remains that the real housing market is self- generated and 35% or more of the population is living in slum shacks put up illegally by individuals, mostly out of waste material. In urban areas, 67% of dwellings are permanent, 30% are semi- permanent, and 3% are very temporary. [2] 60% of units were owned by the occupants. In most cities, the percentage of temporary dwellings has been declining and the percentage of permanent dwellings has increasing. But these figures ignore the people who are living on the streets and sidewalks. Many of the dwellings, including temporary dwellings hold more than one family. "As for the facilities of drinking water, toilets and electricity for lighting, about 15% of the dwellings in urban slums and squatter settlements and 63% of other dwellings have all three, but 11% have none of them. About 18% of all urban dwellings lack proper sanitation facilities. [3]

It should be pointed out that a general look at national statistics, or the statistics for larger cities masks the huge discrepancies experienced by smaller cities and towns, much less villages. Being the owner of a dwelling in a slum area is not a sign of wealth, nor of access to public amenities. Most dwelling owners financed the construction of their homes themselves, or borrowed from usurious moneylenders.

Early Socialist rhetoric denied the reality of these slums and promised "slum free cities" within a decade. Official Slum Improvement Programs have been announced periodically and loudly since 1972. Then, in the 80's, policies seemed to change to approaches to achieve "slum upgrading". Again in 1996, a National Slum Development Program was announced. Ten years and hundreds of millions of rupees later, it had withered and died. 2005 saw the announcement, with trumpets from the rooftops, of the Nehru Urban Renewal Mission. In 2007, with more trumpets, the Total Sanitation Campaign for rural areas was announced, to provide universal rural sanitation by 2012. In almost all cases, the basic intent is the same: to provide necessary public facilities to support life in the slums -- water supply, sewerage, paving of pathways and roadways, electrical power, places for small businesses. After 40 years of bumbling and equivocation, slums are certainly no better, and some, like Mumbai, are worse. Officially, the government admits to 75 million slum dwellers nationwide, but this is thought to be a serious underestimation. More than 640 towns and cities in 26 of the 32 States or Union Territories report substantial slum areas.

Basic objectives for slum mitigation must also be accompanied by better security and law enforcement; set-asides of additional land that is free; subsidization of cheap construction materials; and some form of "ownership" or formalization of tenure as the basis for borrowing money. Many relatively decent homes can be created by a slow process of building up hovels as funds permit, but low cost financing must be provided to drive out greedy loan sharks and land owners, and other predators. Home ownership could be tied into another sound idea which is the sponsorship of small loans for women as self-employed entrepreneurs. Just above that level, there is a rental market for those who can't afford to own. But the rental market is bad for consumers -- too many people chasing too few places to live. There is a lot of crowding in urban areas. "India's cities need at least 25 million more homes. In Mumbai, more than 8 million people now live in shanty towns and have to pay substantial rents. It is estimated that about 180 million families have incomes between $2,000 and $4,300 per year. An additional 23 million have incomes between $1,400 and $3,000. Estimating the elimination of overlap, there are about 190 million families with incomes between $1,400 and $4,300. This is one measure of what might be called the "lower middle class". [4]

It is typical of Indian governance that dozens of laws have been passed, and hundreds of regulations promulgated, and thousands of plans and task forces and committees have been formed, but most generate pygmy solutions to gigantic problems. For example, in New Delhi, which has more than 100,000 homeless people, the government runs 14 night shelters with a maximum capacity of just under 3,000 people.

Nair [6] gives a compelling example of how the Slum Clearance Board of the State of Karnataka attempts to deal with burgeoning slums. There are two major angles of attack: clearances and "redevelopment". The governments of cities tried to use their role as planners to preclude slums from certain areas, but in their other role as developer, more and more central urban locations were sold out to commercial builders. The bulldozing of half a dozen slums and the relocation of their inhabitants into areas where they were deprived both of infrastructure and of opportunities to earn a livelihood demonstrated the futility of slum clearance as an objective in itself; slums exist because the inhabitants have nowhere else to live, and because residents conduct viable lives from them; improving slum conditions makes far more practical, economic, and indeed political sense than clearing them.

Unauthorized revenue sites proliferated with illegal building construction which the government periodically "regularized". Thus, slums were cleared only when they cluttered up properties being sold for commercial development. Nearby agricultural land was improperly seized and converted to city land and then illegally leased or sold. Thus, once again, economic development was deemed more important than the rights of the people. In effect, the government fell behind the power curve as it clung to outmoded Socialist thinking and at the same time chose instead to cave to high payoff private sector development. Each time some commercial interest overpowered limitations, the government simply revised its limitations. This weakness in turn allowed landowners and speculators to challenge the mechanisms of the government as flawed and possibly corrupt, and the government increasingly found itself unable legally to sustain its own regulations. The courts "showed a willingness to declare the acquisitions invalid when they were for low cost housing cooperatives, but when it came to large and prestigious projects which involved international capital flows, or more generally, the scope and direction of official economic development, the judiciary was unwilling to contradict the wisdom of government decisions. Inevitably, the builders succeeded in having government officials define even the most blatant of private ventures as "serving public purposes and public good" and thus to be entitled to exemptions.

Realistically, rapidly growing cities are becoming the new India and thus the wellbeing of municipalities is critical and cities are rapidly becoming more complex to manage. The socialist governments of the past 40 years have so deteriorated the capacities of local governments that the task of revitalizing them is almost mission impossible. And remarkably, none of these socialist governments appears to have made any attempt to build workable mechanisms for involvement between citizens and their governments. Every political party proclaims ideas for devolution of governance to local levels, and for greater citizen participation mechanisms, and yet there is little indication that any of this stuff is being seriously backed and implemented, because of the lack of political will. A heavy centrist socialist policy has acted to keep the financing of public services under central government control, with complicated formulas for categorical allocation of funds by program down to the State and municipal levels. This policy has also stoutly resisted any allocation of substantial taxing authority to local governments. In addition, States are required to ratify national laws, and there is a long history of interminable battles to get them to do so, with many laws floating in limbo for years.

Some large cities are still without any organized management worthy of note. Most cities are governed by municipal corporations or municipal boards; but many have been so bad that they have been suspended by the national government and their management taken over by a State government. Most cities suffer from a bewildering array of special bodies with narrow responsibilities and no real central direction. In addition to a municipal corporation, some cities will have a Council or Municipal Commission, and there may be a mayor or a city administrator who may be elected or appointed – and nobody seems to understand exactly who exercises what authorities. In addition, urban capital investment is usually controlled by an Urban Development Authority at the State level. Many of these cities have developed "master plans" which supposedly define and control the nature of physical development, but the fact appears to be that developers and builders simply ignore or buy their way past such Plans if they find them inhibiting. In addition, it is also true that cities are really collections of neighborhoods of religious, ethnic, caste, tribe and family groupings which control what happens in their neighborhoods, and resist the imposition of some government Plan. There is a long history of infrastructure projects, when completed, being turned over for management to local governments that totally lack the funds to maintain them. The main revenue sources for local governments are property taxes and a tax called "octroi" -- a tax on goods entering urban areas. The octroi is all but useless and is being abandoned. Property taxes have been growing, but there is heavy resistance, and it is obvious that this source alone -- even if well administered -- is far from adequate. An obvious alternative is the income tax, but strangely few people or institutions are asked to pay, and it is not clear why, beyond the usual political inertia and cowardice.

Intergovernmental relations – between the national, state, district and municipal government – are still dominated by the principles of State Socialism as interpreted by Prime Minister Nehru, and as in China, heavy centrist control resulted in weak and under funded local governments. This centrist philosophy runs counter to the approach in the United States and in many other countries which values local governance, believes that local governments should have a high degree of independence, and allows them independent sources of income. In India, the central (Union) government has always been reluctant to concede power by delegation even when the national Constitution requires it. The 28 States in turn seem to see themselves in conflict and competition with municipalities and resist power sharing, even where the central government requires them to do so.

Two forms of local government systems have been mandated by the Constitution and defined by law. Amendment 73 deals with rural governments, and Amendment 74 spells out the ground rules for urban governments. But note that 43 years passed between Independence and the passage of these Amendments, and it is difficult to see any rational reason for this delay except bad politics. There have never really been any compelling substantive reasons for not empowering cities, and the explosive growth and burgeoning problems of cities are compelling reasons to strengthen and support cities rather than inhibit them.

The growth of India's major cities is a sobering lesson in how growth has produced disaster. India now has more than 40 cities over one million in population, and six of these cities are over 5 million (Mumbai, 16.3 million; Kolkata, 13.2 million; Delhi, 12.8 million; Chennai, 6.4 million; Bangalore, 5.7 million), and all suffer from high levels of slum living, extreme poverty, filth, disease threats, and a scandalous shortage of even the most basic living facilities. Almost every Indian city suffers from the same problems, and the great fear is that the future will be worse because neither the government nor society in general is capable of solving these urban dilemmas.

The compelling quandary in India is the unwillingness and inability of the Union or State governments to finance public infrastructure development. There are a few big, and relatively successful government projects, but a recent new policy is to "expect private investors to contribute three quarters of the additional investment in infrastructure and 40% of the total." [6] But this is either naïve or hypocritical; much public infrastructure has absolutely no prospect of generating revenue that would justify private business investment, and in many cases, policy makers don't seem to realize this. There is a perfectly valid idea called "Public- Private Partnerships" which could, for example, take the form of build-lease-operate-sell contracts, but many governments still can't come up with the funds to lease or buy. So the government it turning more to hopes or expectations resting on the private sector. These expectations are of three types. At a minimum, the government may turn to the private sector to develop infrastructure under government contract, hoping that, where government bureaucracies have bumbled and fumbled, private companies will be more effective and successful. In a more sophisticated vein, the government is attempting the idea of "Public-Private Partnerships" where program management and costs can be shared, thus reducing demands on the public budget. Third, this may involve lease/purchase schemes where private companies invest in building facilities such as a port or power plant, operate it for some time under a lease with the government, and then sell it to the government after a fixed period. And finally, the government is conceding the idea that the private sector, entirely independent of government, may begin to provide some public goods for profit such as airports and shipping ports, power stations, electric transmission facilities and even universities.

In other words, the government is steadily withdrawing from the old Nehru agenda of a dominant and centrist socialist government. It no longer pretends that the public sector can create an adequate economy and it is enthusiastically looking for ways for the private sector to take up the burden. The private sector is not sure it wants the honor, and there seems to be a protracted and perplexing shifting of the respective roles of the public and private sectors, both in terms of who controls what elements of the economy, and who is responsible for the delivery of social services. India's economic financial stimulus package ended up having lots of public expenditures. An extra 200 billion Rupees will be spent on schools, roads, power plants and other development priorities set out in the last 5 year plan. In other words, the government is using the fiscal crisis to finance its regular plans but at an accelerated pace. But still: roads, ports, airports, and almost every other public facility are falling further behind demand.

In the last analysis, India and China are following very similar policies. Both have been forced to divest themselves of failed or ineffective SOEs. Both have sought to shift a larger share of economic development onto the private sector, where it is enthusiastically welcomed. Both governments have been forced to abandon major economic policies such as price controls, import restrictions, mandated resource allocation, and heavy burdens of economic regulation. Both governments now encourage foreign investment, and both would love to expand their economies and their government revenues with the wealth of foreigners.

Another idea is municipal bonds to finance capital projects, but local governments are so weak, and their sources of revenue so small that there is no credibility behind municipal bond offerings. One good idea would be to create a national government program of issuance of National Urban Development Bonds, backed by the national government, with the funds allocated to local communities. Repayment could be enhanced by allowing cities some additional income sources, either an income tax on corporations, or some forms of charges/user fees for public utilities. Another aspect of this tangle is that in recent years, much of the most crucial public infrastructure has in fact been financed by IMF loans and World Bank grants, but this is surely a limited option.

Another model might be public utilities where private companies build and operate and sell power to governments, but again, governments prefer to give power away, and private companies do not trust their government monitors. In addition, about 35% of power from government facilities is simply stolen, which destroys any possibility for profit. But any arrangement for the provision of urban services comes up against the cowardice of the politicians. Typically water and sewer service charges are kept so low that they do not even cover more than 20 – 60% of operating and maintenance costs. In a 1999 study, it was found that only 55% of users were even being metered, and many meters do not work or are sabotaged. A lot of water is simply given away as a political move. This failure means that the utility providers will not generate enough funds even for operations, much less for maintenance, repairs, upgrades or expansions of service.

There have been countless conferences, workshops, experimental projects, program reviews, technical assistance projects, regional tests, guidelines, standards, analyses, monitoring, urban demonstrations, etc. "Everybody thinks they know what to do; they just don't do it." [7] Even relatively prosperous cities like Bangalore have experienced big growths in their slum population (from 1.12 million in 1991 to 2.2 million in 2000). Many of these people make a living on the street: "push cart vendors, street cobblers, children selling toys at traffic lights, women who string flowers, or sell fruits out of baskets, refuse collectors, beggars, pickpockets and a host of other marginal occupations." Others are transient labor, working when and where they can, in jobs that are low paid, transient, irregular, dirty and often dangerous. The informal economy is flooded with a surplus of unskilled laborers, desperately looking for work.

Despite those 40 years of promises on pieces of paper, India is still rated the second worst place in the world for sanitation, second only to China. Urban sanitation is almost always horrible, slum neighborhoods are seldom connected to city sanitation systems, if indeed one exists, and large numbers of both residents and businesses must provide their own sanitation facilities and water supplies. Even where municipalities and towns provide sanitation facilities, they are allowed to deteriorate, and only about 27% of waste water is actually treated, and people defecate in the streets. In Delhi for example, the sewerage network has never been properly maintained or repaired, and it consistently allows raw sewerage to dump into open drains. Trash is seldom collected, and people simply throw trash out the window. Sewers are blocked, collapsed, and lacking in pumping capacity. Tragically, a staggering number of people – perhaps 700,000 - die each year because of unsafe water, inadequate sanitation, poor hygiene, lack of knowledge and lack of medical treatment. A World Bank study evaluated the impact of WB funding of urban water system projects and concluded "water supply and sewerage planning, construction and operations in Bombay posed daunting challenges to those who planned and implemented the investment program. At the outset, there was a huge backlog of unmet demand because of underinvestment. Population and economic growth accelerated in the following decades and the proportion of the poor increased as did the slums which they occupied. The intended impacts of the (WB) program have not been realized. Shortcomings include that "water is not safe to drink; water service, especially to the poor, is difficult to access and is provided at inconvenient hours of the day; industrial water needs are not fully met; sanitary facilities are too few in number and often unusable; and urban drains, creeks and coastal waters are polluted with sanitary and industrials wastes." [8]

Air quality in India's cities makes them among the world's worst. Mumbai is the 5th most polluted city in the world, with 97% of its people are regularly exposed to air that fails to meet World Health Organization standards. More and more, urban residents, even in better neighborhoods are forced to truck in water, even where they may be hooked up to the municipal water supply; there is simply not enough water in the pipelines.

Most cities have a relatively modern central core, and some protected communities for the well-to-do, while government policy for many years has been to try and limit the growth of cities and keep out the peasants. But the central core is surrounded by massive slums, plus an even more abjectly poor population that lives on the streets, in the alleys, on vacant lots and under highways, in fragile shacks made of tin and cardboard. Bombay has 18 million residents, and 60% of them live in these slums. In Mumbai 60% of the residents live in slums. Of 40 million urban slum dwellers nationwide, less than 60% have any sanitation facilities, and half don't even have tap water. Every city in India now fails the government's own emission standards. Slums are the home of huge populations of people living off of the informal economy. What do people do to live? Everything and anything: trades such as carpentry, electrical work, plumbers, construction, auto repair. Trash collection, trash "picking" and recycling. Manufacture of clothing, clay products, toys, leather tanning, small equipment repair and other services. Personal services such as maids, gardeners, cleaning people. All forms of transport. In addition, there are purveyors of liquor, prostitution, gambling and other vices. Finally, there are money lenders, landlords, sellers of water and electricity, "fixers" embezzlers and extorters. Governments, both national and local, see little advantage in enforcing even their lax laws and regulations for fear of slowing industrial development and cutting revenues. In other words, the urban environment is a great hazard physically, medically and environmentally, but it is most terrible in human terms.

A striking example of poor city management is Calcutta (Kolkata) in Communist ruled West Bengal. "The poverty and degradation in everyday life in Calcutta is legendary." The population density of its 4 million people is three times that of New York. In 40% of households, nobody has a regular job. There are some 200 "bustees" (urban slum neighborhoods) with an estimated 1.5 million dwellers, plus 5-600,000 who live on the streets. 60% of the population is Bengali; 15% are Muslim; the rest are a big mix. The Communist government supports the Party by channeling public contracts to Kolkata business men who then contribute bribes to officials and to the party. The city provides service primarily to the better-off people. [9]

The Communist "United Front Party" (UF) government made a huge political mistake in the late 60's when it ordered the police not to "interfere" in labor-management conflicts. As a result, within a few months, the industrial scene became totally out of control. Industrial production dropped drastically; factories began to close to shift elsewhere; invested capital dried up. It took Calcutta more than 20 years to recover from this disaster. This led to more general conflict between the unions and leftist allies (and often the Naxalites), and the Congress Party that hired its own "goondas" (goons) disguised as youth organizations.

Naxalites are Maoist terrorists now found throughout much of N. E. India. In Kolkata, its activities have declined because of police efforts; many of its leaders were jailed or killed, and their terrorist tactics alienated almost everybody. As a result of these pressures, the Naxalites also split up into many small, conflicting groups. But the movement seems to be expanding in poor rural areas.

The United Front Party in power has done little or nothing to deal with the horrible conditions in the city. It consistently uses the excuse that "Delhi does not supply enough funds". Local merchant interests avoid paying taxes or doing much to improve the city. While UF is bad, the opposing Congress Party is seen as worse because of its endless internal squabbling, poor leadership, and a nasty, arrogant attitude.

Investments in public infrastructure are seriously deficient. Despite obvious advances, it is felt that most Indian cities are still at risk in terms of both the safety of water supplies, and the availability of adequate sanitary facilities. According to the World Bank [10] water supply is available less than 2 hours a day in Chennai; 2-3 hours in Ahmadabad and Bangalore; 4 hours in Delhi, and between 5 & 6 in Mumbai. There is some data indicating that the hours per day are shrinking. This supply limitation is almost universal regardless of city size. Half of the supply in rural areas is hand pumped from wells. State agencies are supposed to maintain water supplies including these hand pumps, and often months will go by before a failed facility will be fixed, and as usual, the government's water facilities are seen as inadequate, incompetently managed and corrupt. Most urban dwellers have access to "safe" water, and 75% have access to piped water, but more than half of this piped water is through private connections. Public sanitation is better, but still only 36% of urban dwellers have access to sewers, 27% to septic tanks, and less than 20% to latrines. In rural/village areas, access to "improved" sanitation is only about 20%.

According to a report of the Paryvaran Mitra Foundation (2007), "India experiences more premature deaths due to air pollution than any other country, and New Delhi is one of the ten most polluted cities in the world. Over the last 20 years, car pollution has gone up 800% and industrial pollution by 400%. Government regulatory laws have been few, and implementation erratic and often non-existent. Even when the government does something, they often do it wrong. For example, a law was passed in 2001 that required all public transport vehicles to run on compressed natural gas. But this resulted in the removal of 10,000 buses and 15,000 taxis from service. Nobody seemed to have thought out the consequences to city commuters for whom this service was vital. Similarly, laws failed which banned all public vehicles over 15 years old. As is typical in India, the real failure was the absence of serious enforcement, even when laws were sensible which was not often. Government efforts to ban "plastic" disrupted a small but bustling plastics recovery industry of pickers, collectors, purchasers and recyclers, all functioning profitably in urban informal economies. But the banning of plastics was popular with New Delhi's elite, despite the fact that it damaged the lives of plastics workers, most of whom were Scheduled Castes living at the poverty line. Similar small enterprise sustains low caste workers who work in construction, auto and rickshaw cycle driving, food vending, domestic service, or as municipal sweepers and trash collectors." [11]

Lawmaking is an exercise in political populism, and seldom has much to do with reality. A good example is in the efforts to manage waste and water pollution. Everybody knows that the most serious pollution comes from industrial facilities, but there is not a city in India where waste water treatment is adequate. Presently, only about 10% of waste water is treated, and untreated water enters the underground water sources, much of which ends up as water for residential use. But finally the people and even the government are recognizing the threats to health from these environmental problems. Diseases such as nervous, circulatory, cancerous, respiratory, digestive and endocrine afflictions are traced to chemical pollution and have been directly related to specific patterns of industrial development.

India has in fact long had its three track economy: the public sector, the private sector, and the informal economy. Public enterprises remain very important, and recent liberalization, while now more extensive, has not really meant a fully free economy. Indian governments, especially at the State and municipal levels have long financed development through debt. But this in turn nearly bankrupted governments, especially at the local level. But public expenditure and debt patterns are slowly changing to shift to the private sector in any activity where the private sector can earn profits carrying out public operations. Upgrades of urban transport systems for example can be built and operated by private companies under contract with governments, usually containing purchase provisions. There is a growth of "parastatal" bodies which are semi-public and which include such entities as water or sewerage authorities, development authorities, housing boards, planning commissions, transit authorities, or private entities to furnish health care or primary education.

A recent UNESCO report [12] assessed the impact of the 74th amendment to the Indian Constitution which deals largely with the decentralization of responsibilities from the Union government to the states, including a lot of technical adjustments in legal and financial authority as a consequence. This Amendment also seems to abandon the theological concept of "all things equal" by permitting different levels of public facilities and amenities in large cities based on the willingness to pay. This is a way to cater to the well-to-do, but it is also a perfect excuse to further abandon the poor, who of course can pay for nothing. In fact, the whole new philosophy of decentralization and delegation seems to be in the face of the obvious lack of enabling finance at the local government level – which is perfectly well understood by the central government. Just like China!

The study comes to the general conclusion that this is a mixed blessing – but largely on the premise that it is not necessarily desirable (in the short run) for local governments to be more independent, since they are deprived of former central government support and assistance. But in fact, such assistance has been minimal and is a small loss in many arenas.

The study also concludes that generally, larger cities benefit more from new authorities, especially in the financing of public infrastructure, than do small or medium sized cities. The report seems confused as to whether growth is good or "healthy". It also generally concludes that the development of small cities is seriously inhibited by the inability to attract industry, or to afford supporting public infrastructure. The same kind of argument is made with respect to richer or poorer States.

During the 70s, more than 1,000 new towns were created, and cities in general expanded rapidly. But in more recent years, this growth has slowed, and it is argued that the decline is mostly because of slow downs in rural to urban migration. It further concludes that permanent migration is actually declining, and most people migrate for short term advantage, or are daily commuters. Further, it is concluded that employment in the informal economy is reaching saturation. This whole line of reasoning is very confused; things are better in villages, but they are worse in villages. Small cities lack funds to develop, but are developing. The percentage of workers in non-agriculture is growing but has slowed down. Urban population growth is slowing, but will increase from 28.6% in 2000 to 42% in 2020. A lot of this is seems mostly games being played with statistics.

There is a similar murkiness with respect to urban planning. Master Plans are cited as a means to reduce the expansion of uncontrolled slums, but realistically, Plans control nothing and slums and urban ghettos have grown very greatly. In larger cities, the center core is being upgraded and gentrified, (in large part by the eviction and banning of slum dwellings, hawkers and street merchants, pavement dwellers, and cheap businesses) and new commercial and industrial development is emerging in suburban areas around the central core. Then, low income housing and slums sort of grow up in the spaces between the two. A large number of the industrial units in the post liberalization phase have grown up in the villages and small towns around the big cities. The reasons for moving out of the large cities are easy availability of land, access to unorganized labor markets, or less stringent implementation of environmental regulations. Yet the report also says "The percentage of people below the poverty line increases systematically as one goes down the scale of urban population size. If nothing else, this is a reflection of the nature of political clout, which is closely tied to "who's got the money".

There is a strange anomaly in the debates over public finance. The 74th Amendment emphasizes the need for states and municipalities to "build cost recovery into municipal finance systems." Thus, municipalities are presumed to be able to find the money for capital investments on their own, and to give priority for those public facilities that make money, and/ or can cover their operating costs. And it is assumed that the tax base will be inadequate and thus development will be financed by borrowing from banks. Thus, if a government can't at least break even on an infrastructure project, it does not get done. It further assumes that bank financing gives new and ominous power for banks over the actions of governments. As usual, the Indian government has fancy schemes to "aid" beleaguered municipalities, but as usual, they are scarce and puny. One such scheme is called the "Structured Debt Obligation" (SDO) in which cities issue bonds backed by the income from some municipal property or revenue source. This is probably a good idea technically, but it is a safe bet that local governments will screw it up somehow.

A study conducted by the National Institute of Urban Affairs (1998) showed that the new authorities for local planning and taxation, which require explicit authorization by State parliaments, have seldom been used. The reality still is that local governments lack the income or the skills to use such authority, and the 74th Amendment has been dysfunctional. **[13]** The intellectually satisfying concept of Master Plans is treated much the same; developers and contractors simply pay to have it ignored, or they work around the controls imposed by the Plan. It also appears that, in a world typical of India, cities are not just economic areas, but they are "villages" of religious, ethnic, caste, tribe and even family enclaves which control their own part of the urban terrain, and resist some elitist form of Master Plan.

After the formal launching of the program of economic structural adjustment in 1991, and the consequent decline in public sector investment, privatization, partnership arrangements and community-based projects have emerged as the major options for undertaking investments in infrastructure and amenities. While decentralization has been sold as "liberation", it can also be interpreted as both "abandonment" and "abdication". The main problem remains the lack of profitable economic institutions, which in turn translates into inadequate public revenue. Part of this problem is that the tax base is so weak and stupid, that even when businesses are there to be taxed, they escape. This pushes cities into borrowing, which is obviously far more expensive.

The capacity of any government to generate employment through weak and temporary mechanisms such as anti-poverty programs is very limited, but it has taken Indian governments a long time to abandon this particular facet of Socialist theology -- as it did in the U. S. There is a new realization that loans to the poor are perfectly sound and very valuable. The idea of equal levels of public amenity has been abandoned. The Constitutional Amendment # 74 for decentralization of authority and financial powers does little to generate actual revenue. And many States still cling to their old powers and refuse the formal action of delegation to municipalities.

URBANIZATION IN CHINA

As in countries all over the world, there is an almost inevitable tide of people movement from rural and small town areas to cities. In 2009, for the first time in world history more people in China are living in cities then elsewhere. The Chinese urban population is now about 480 million or 38% of the total population. The rural population is about 800 million. The urban workforce is about 248 million, only about 114 million of whom are in the "official" economy as authorized by the government, and are thus covered by the social security system. 72 million are in SOEs, 11 million are in collectives, 8 million are in foreign funded facilities and 23 million are in governments, the professions or self employed. At the same time, there are an estimated sixty to eighty million workers in cities who are "unofficial" residents. In fact, there is a workforce "float" of around 180 million workers which includes those in the informal economy, those who are in casual or part time work, those who are transients, and those who are simply unemployed.

There are now 661 cities in China, of which 89 are over 1 million in population. Of 177 world cities over 2 million in population, 21 are in China and 8 of those are over 5 million. Thus, the urbanization wave has now become the most extensive in world history, and it is expanding beyond the largest cities to many others, and creating new massive suburbs – and shanty towns.

Article 90 of the Constitution guaranteed citizens freedom of residence, but typically, the government ignored its own Constitution and a directive in the '50s from the Ministry of the Interior and the Ministry of Labor set out rules to "control the blind influx of peasants into cities." This in turn led to a huge and elaborate control system aimed at limiting the flow of migrants. The Household Registration System was first initiated in 1955, decayed, and was then reinstituted in 1978. Under this policy, every individual is tied to his/her place of official residence, and social services are available only at that place of official residence. First and foremost, this was a policy to monitor and control people. And most importantly, it was the principal means for controls against free movement, especially from farms to cities but also between work places. Under the Socialist regime, all workers were assigned to specific jobs by the State. Huge numbers were allocated to work brigades, state collectives, and special work cadres in which direction and control was exercised by government officials. Linked to this work allocation was the allocation of other resources. Almost everything was rationed – food, shelter, health care, housing, education beyond primary, child care, fuel, and almost everything else. There were three main classifications: rural, "non-agricultural", and collectives. In many cases, workers and their families had no individual property but were only listed as a member of a collective or commune. Ration coupons were issued and often valid only at the official place of residence. Thus, migrant workers who could not yet get "formal" jobs in cities were considered illegal and could not receive any social services, and were usually harassed and often ejected by the police.

But this whole elaborate system proved to be totally unworkable, and like so many communist/socialist blunders, has had to be abandoned. Many of the special rationing and food controls are no longer justified, and have been phased out, but could be reinstated in selected situations if the government chose to do so. But strangely, this elaborate array of Maoist era controls has not so much been repealed, as it has simply been quietly allowed to dissipate. The far looser rules for migration to township and village enterprises (TVEs) and to smaller cities permit more and more rural workers to obtain official urban residence permits. As a result of this loosening up, millions of poor rural workers have been able to rise up out of poverty into life-sustaining jobs, often despite the government.

Many environmental problems are ancient: floods, droughts, overgrazing, desertification, soil erosion, mining wastes. But there are also new problems that are a direct consequence of the economic development programs and most of them are urban such as hundreds of thousands of new industrial sites dumping pollutants into the air or water; millions of new automobiles; accelerating exhaustion of water resources; and wastage of energy and raw materials and rapidly expanding urban slums. Over expansion of cities has created rapidly growing urban problems. Lack of raw materials and energy tends to drive up prices. While China's government benefits greatly from foreign sales, it has not yet made satisfactory progress in meeting the consumer needs of its own people.

The success of economic development is vital to the survival of the CCP itself, and this cannot and will not be changed any time soon. Economic development has been the compelling and overpowering driver in China for almost 35 years. Because of this, China will not stop burning coal and creating acid rain. It will not willingly close industrial plants that pollute the air unless there is the risk of fatal political disaster. The CCP will not reverse its policy of dumping environmental problems on local governments, nor will it fund these governments. Neither the CCP nor anybody else has any idea of what to do about desertification, soil erosion and river silting, and even if they did, these problems are so enormous and complex that they are simply "mission impossible". Urban air pollution is not being dealt with, and in fact, is getting worse every day, and in more cities and lung diseases now kill more people than any other cause. The depletion of urban underground water aquifers is permanent and irreversible, and the exhaustion of these resources is speeding up. Urban expansion requires more water resources, urban sanitation, waste water treatment and other public services which are not being developed. It also means the rise in the number of households, millions of urban transportation trips, huge truck traffic to bring in supplies, vastly increased oil and gas consumption, and heavy and unremitting construction activity.

Most of the older industrial base and energy production facilities, and even the newer manufacturing plants were designed and built with absolutely no thought to their environmental impact. Many are highly inefficient, environmental issues aside. Most are energy guzzlers, using 8 to 10 times the energy per unit of output compared to that of modern plants elsewhere. In other words, "fixing" the environmental problems of SOEs is a monumental problem embedded in an even more monumental problem of upgrading the SOEs themselves. SOEs, which provided the great bulk of industrial production through the early 90s, were never even permitted to deal with environmental concerns because of the potential costs; the government recognized that up to 50% of SOEs were operating at a deficit, and many others were economically marginal. Few could bear the additional costs of environmental protection. In fact, the government often subsidized these SOEs not only with money, but with free water, free land and highly subsidized energy. As a result, the industrial and energy sectors of the economy were highly wasteful and polluting, and environmentally threatening.

Much of what is now being developed such as farming, pulp and paper mills, coal mining, chemical factories, tanning and dyeing plants, small scale manufacturing are high polluting enterprises, and their runoffs are going untreated into rivers and streams, and their solid waste is forming new mountains. There are hundreds of thousands of these little operations in the huge industrial areas in and around cities, or as township/village enterprises (TVEs) running on the thinnest of profit margins. What is the prospect of fighting through local political resistance and getting all of these little marginal enterprises to clean up their act?

Two thirds of the water in underground aquifers in 118 major cities is severely polluted, and these aquifers are also being exhausted. Almost every city in China faces an increasingly ominous future about the adequacy of its water supply. In some coastal cities, when underground aquifers are drawn down, they may be penetrated by seawater pollution which is permanent and irreversible.

The Chinese government is developing what is called the "South to North Transfer Project" which proposes to set up three transfer routes from the Yangtze River in the south to the Yellow River in the north. One transfer route is near the end of both rivers, where an existing reservoir will be enlarged and a 200 foot wide channel will be dug. The second route will be from Shandong to Tianjin. The third will be near the headwaters of both rivers where a 65 mile tunnel will be dug. But this whole scheme has a certain fantasy quality about it. It would take almost unthinkable amounts of money (about $16 billion has already been committed) and long periods of time for activation, and it is not yet been made clear how more water would solve the pollution problems that are the major dilemma. The main objective of the project seems to be to solve the water shortages in Beijing and other northern cities, all of which are in trouble, but it is difficult not to conclude that the grand scheme is not likely to be a serious solution to anything.

The most "modern" of China's environmental disasters is in the air. The amounts of dangerous chemicals pumped into the air are now staggering and the air in China's major cities is almost toxic. China is now the world's largest producer of carbon dioxide. Air pollution also includes excessive and illegal levels of sulphur dioxide, chlorofleurocarbons, smoke, dust and soil. Even the government's own State Environmental Protection Administration (SEPA) admits that this is true, and that air pollution is getting worse, not better. It is typical that the Chinese government now has a full array of nicely drafted laws and regulations "controlling" air pollution, and there are standards setting limits for every form of emission. But two thirds of China's cities that have been tested cannot meet these standards, or similar standards set by the World Health Organization. Nor does anybody seem to have a clue how this pollution can be brought under control. On the contrary, the whole vast tide of industrialization and urbanization is guaranteed to make matters very much worse very fast. One needs only to think about the millions of new automobiles and trucks and airplanes, and the development of an additional 562 new coal fired power plants, and the addition of many thousands of new or expanded industrial facilities to realize what is making air pollution worse.

Finally, and most typically, these environmental disasters pose ever increasing threats to the health of China's citizens. An estimated 190 million Chinese have had illnesses connected with drinking contaminated water. Cities and villages alike have suffered from repeated epidemics of diarrhea, and heightened rates of cancer, tumors, poisoning from lead, mercury and other heavy metals. Air pollution alone is said to have been the cause of up to 300,000 deaths. Once again, China's record is worse than any other country on earth. Beijing has six times higher air pollution rates than New York. Past dust storms are so persistent and severe that many people in cities wear face masks against dust and chemicals. There are huge worker time losses from lung diseases, blood infections, heart diseases, strokes and diabetes. There are about 24 million cars today, but in 20 years there may be upwards of 100 million, most of them in already choked cities. 60-90% of rain in Guandong province is acid rain, and farmland losses would equal the farm land in Britain, Germany and France combined.

But the disasters are building. Shanghai is in many respects modern China in miniature. Consider this example: in the late 90s, the river basin northwest of Shanghai, which contains 110 million people, suffered from a further massive pollution of an already polluted river. "Hundreds of thousands of people were left without drinking water, several thousand were treated for dysentery, diarrhea, and vomiting, and 26 million pounds of fish were killed." [14] Pollution came from several thousand factories: paper factories, leather, cloth dyeing, many more. Most factories were Township and Village Enterprises (TVEs); most workers were migrants and moonlighters at slave wages. While the government forces the closure of these small business plants (60,000 in 1999), the larger SOEs are left alone. And still Shanghai continues to grow.

Now, reluctantly, the official policy has flipped. Officials now concede the fact that an additional 300 million farmers are expected to move to cities in the next 20 years, and they cannot be prevented, and thus efforts had better be made to prepare for them. In recent years, urban housing has been largely privatized meaning that the government continues to own the land but the housing itself can be acquired either by purchase or long term lease. This creates two improvements: the government has shed itself of much of the huge costly obligation to maintain the housing stock, and cities have gained a whole variety of new forms of income – rental income and property taxes, various land use taxes, leasing fees, construction fees and other levies.

On the negative side, much of this housing was neglected and now needs costly repairs and upgrading. Mortgages are not easy to obtain, and are still available only through state owned banks. Nevertheless, governments at all levels and both public and private developers have been pushing forward with very large programs to construct housing, all the way from basic apartment blocks to opulent gated communities in the American style.

Chinese cities have never been officially established entities with their own legislative bodies, and they are governed under heavy and detailed instructions from the top conveyed through both government and CCP chains of command. The municipal offices in Canton were not established until 1921, and those in Beijing itself in 1928. [16] Until very recently, it was the police who kept order, and largely supervised city operations. During the 20s and 30s, the first real efforts were made to overcome centuries of stagnation. With the ascent to power of the communists in 1949, efforts to professionalize local governments were stopped in favor of combinations of Communist-style rural collectives, work brigades, communes, and government supervised cooperatives. While these were politically "correct" they were mostly economic and administrative disasters. Urban expenditures were held to a minimum for many years, largely because Mao did not trust cities or urban dwellers or bureaucrats. Thus, Mao precipitated the CCP's own period of stagnation for cities that lasted about 30 years. The only real urban activity lay in the construction, at enormous cost, of new industrial cities in the interior mostly based on the perceived need to protect military industry from unspecified foreign attack. When the collectives system was discontinued after Mao's death in 1976, the CCP finally had the courage to start rebuilding urban governments. The Household Responsibility System was reinstituted in 1978 under which the government set quotas for every kind of enterprise from farming to medical practice. Products/services up to the limit of the quota had to be furnished to the government at government dictated prices, but still, the change stimulated productivity to a remarkable degree because any such surplus above the government quotas could be privately sold at a better profit.

The official urban workforce were "entitled" populations who are given access to subsidized housing, food, state-sector jobs, and many fringe benefits including health care, disability benefits, schools, pensions, and unemployment compensation. Throughout the 50s the newly formed state enterprises actively recruited rural labor in large numbers into these official jobs. This was a means of promoting the shift of populations from agricultural to manufacturing. At the same time, the government foolishly refused to allow workers to bring their families to the cities, because that would drive up costs to the State in the form of housing, health care, education, food subsidies and urban infrastructure. Only about 20% of the population ever achieved this full official urban status. Beginning in the mid 80s however the dam broke and an estimated 60 to 80 million workers came flooding into the cities despite official disapproval and active measures to prevent it. Thus, half of the urban population was illegal and technically guilty of breaking the law.

The old nature of core cities, or even core suburbs, has been dramatically expanded to become endless huge sprawling complexes of industrial and commercial enterprises, public facilities like ports and power plants interwoven with residential enclaves ranging from glittering towers to intolerable cardboard hovels. Chongquing has a central city of about 3.3 million but a huge regional area population of almost 31 million. The Shanghai river basin region contains 17 to 20 million people. Beijing has about almost 15 million and Tianjin about 11 million.

It proved difficult enough to implement new economic freedoms because some of the old guard in Beijing and elsewhere continued to raise political objections, most of them doctrinal, and the local governments and SOEs tended to hang on to native vices. Also, quality has often been poor, labor productivity low, transport difficult and expensive, and it was not always clear how well the legal system would protect commercial rights. In addition, cash poor local government officials invented many additional fees and charges just to raise money. The bureaucratic burdens were great, and the likelihood of bribery was always high. What probably saved these early experiments was the willingness of expatriate Chinese in Hong Kong and Taiwan to take these risks and invest. By 1987, it was estimated that from 1 to 2 million Chinese were working in Guandong Province in businesses financed by Hong Kong companies. Most of these business opportunities were in manufacturing, with a big emphasis on consumer goods, and by the mid 90s, manufacturing exports had risen from about 50% of total exports to more than 80%. The sophistication of exports tended to move up the "value added" scale to include electronics and home appliances. These coastal cities continue to have economic advantages, including an inside track on much foreign direct investment, and they have become rich at the expense of other areas of the country

The Yangtze Delta around Shanghai is the epitome of Chinese style development. The whole vast region has simply exploded. There are hundreds of new factories that cover an area slightly bigger than Portugal, and it produces 20% of the value of the Chinese economy. Land grabbing by the government continues in almost every city in China. The bigger problem however is taxes because most cities are desperate for money so there are road taxes, a population tax, a grain tax, and every other kind of tax, applied rigidly and enforced ruthlessly. There are few central government subsidies for public programs and local officials are always desperate for funds to try and keep up with this enormous expansion, so they impose every tax they can think of and supplement their income through land grabs and the time honored manner of gouging the peasants for more taxes.

The initiation of the national reform program in the mid 80s, and the divestiture of SOEs led to the resurrection of something like full time professional city management. In many cases, cities were allowed to annex neighboring rural areas despite the Constitutional provision against such actions. In the process, they acquired access to land, which remains owned by the government but was generally controlled by collectives. Part of this resurrection was the institution of local People's Congresses that had authority to pass laws, make regulations, and approve certain administrative actions. Cities have been quietly jettisoning their communes and collectives, restructuring themselves, adding more professionalism to the staffs, and in general acting like real governments. The City Planning Act of 1989 required the preparation of comprehensive urban plans, which was a good idea, but it also provided a new means of upward political control. Cities used subsidiary offices called Street Offices and Resident Committees.

Street Offices were really administrative sub offices, mainly concerned with streets, sanitation, and sewers, but were also involved in enforcement of the family planning law, fire protection, law enforcement, and other community services. Resident Committees were mostly voluntary, but often headed by one or more paid staff. They too dealt with community matters, including turning out people for political rallies but they are now mostly moribund. Both of these mechanisms are classic "CCP" think. They allowed the Party to meddle deeply in the lives of people without appearing to do so. The Chinese government has not granted new rights to individuals; it has merely eased off in some areas from it's tendency to interfere in people's lives. And whenever it may wish to do so, it can re-impose controls. The real life performance of local authorities continues to be highly suspect and often vicious. As reported by Pei **[15]** "Of 632 petitioners filing complaints interviewed by a research team, 55% reported that local authorities had retaliated by ransacking their houses and seizing valuables; 50% said they had been beaten by local officials; 50% said that they had been illegally incarcerated; 72% said that they had been falsely charged with crimes; and 54% said that local officials used the mafia to retaliate against them."

Authority written into the Constitution of 1982 declared that all urban land was the property of the State, while all rural land was ostensibly the collective property of local governments. Thus, land has remained under the control of governments, and again in typical Chinese fashion there are both formal and "informal" means of control in which money changes hands. Cities are required to maintain a system of land use approvals, building permits and control over development – all good management tools, but also political control tools. In general, the policy of the government was almost wholly concentrated on development of large scale manufacturing, most of it in SOEs. It was anti-urban, in the sense that it tried to limit the growth of cities to the pace of industrial development. There has been little or no policy of rural development, but there is little or no policy for urban development either except to push responsibility for most SOEs, social services and environmental problems down to towns and city governments.

In typical CCP style, most of these SOEs assigned to local governments were the "loser" enterprises that had been operating at a deficit. There was also an effort to divert militarily important facilities away from coastal areas into the interior.

As the Chinese economy develops, barriers against urban migration are deteriorating. SOEs themselves are mutating and being liberated. The all-absorbing concentration on the growth of the manufacturing economy proved not to be enough to absorb even the entitled workers. The government officially discourages the workforce "float", but on the other hand, these workers contribute to the urban economy without the added costs of the service entitlements, so they are largely tolerated. There is no question that in whatever job they do, migrant workers can expect to be exploited. Working exceptionally long hours, they are usually paid below the mandated minimum wage. If they are young women, they can expect to be sexually harassed. Beyond that, health conditions at work are often in violation, with workers having virtually no protection against potential hazards such a chemical fumes. If overcome by tiredness or sickness, they can be dismissed at a moment's notice. In other cases, their identity documents can be withheld to insure that they work out the length of their work contract, which may be anywhere from one to three years. Many workers are housed in cramped dormitories, managed by the factory, where their grievances may be without recourse either to the government or to the unions, both of which will nearly always back the employer. So long as there is an unlimited supply of unskilled labor, these conditions of work are likely to continue.

The government is now actually promoting a second great wave of urbanization, and that is the movement of rural workers to townships, villages (really small towns) and second level cities. Often misnamed "rural industrialization" it is the Chinese equivalent of the development of small and middle sized business development that would be left to the private sector in developed countries. Employment in rural industry has grown from perhaps 50-60 million to 90 million in 1990, and perhaps 110 million now – some 25% of the entire national workforce. The political and management leadership of these township and village enterprises (TVEs) was handed the job of economic development with little or no funding from the central government, and as a result, they have been forced to become entrepreneurs, usually with tax money. Major investments in light industry have been undertaken, often with pubic tax money used to upgrade the SOEs foisted off on local governments. This policy is working, but Chinese cities are about 50 years behind their Western contemporaries. Many of these new enterprises at the TVE level are created and managed by a strange amalgamation of public officials, regional and local Party leaders, and new private sector entrepreneurs. National economic development is in fact largely the result of this TVE level of enterprise development. In most cases, the number of small enterprises exploded in the 1980-1990 period. These enterprises then went through a period of rationalization where many of the weaker ones went under, and there was a wave of consolidations. But it appears that the process left a substantial number of more economically viable survivors.

There has been a remarkable boom in urban construction. According to Campanella, "In 2003 alone, China put up 28 billion square feet of new housing –equal to one eighth of the housing stock of the United States. In the year 2004, $400 billion was spent on construction projects. There were virtually no modern high-rise towers in Shanghai in 1980; today it has more than twice as many as New York City."[16] In the late 1970s, Shanghai followed national trends in that most of its 6 million residents lived in crowded apartments with few amenities. A majority shared bathrooms and kitchens with neighbors, and many had to use public latrines. Three generation households were typical. Even married couples that lived independently of their parents or in-laws rarely had the luxury of a bedroom separate from their children. In the entire metropolis, only five buildings exceeded twenty floors. The explosion of building in so many cities is addressing these housing needs as well as breakneck speed in industrial and commercial construction as well. But consider the formula for disaster that may be building: first, the government continues to own and control almost all of the land. Then, public officials at local government level have world class reputations for corruption and pathological practices. Next, both public sector and private sector commercial developers have an even worse reputation for greed based corruption. There is heavy competition for land lease deals with public officials, in which developers will "do anything" to win a lease. Next, there is little or no oversight over construction work, and even where there may be inspectors, it is likely that they can be bought off. Thus, a number of results are likely. There will be extensive bribery of public officials (in fact, due to recent reform activities, hundreds have already been caught, tried and convicted). There is the high likelihood that large numbers of buildings will be shoddy construction, and indeed examples of deterioration are already appearing. In addition, there is massive overbuilding, and as in Japan in the 90s, property values are being artificially inflated, and at some point, one can foresee heavy value losses as the market recedes to more realistic levels. If these problems are as serious as they appear to be, at some point they will start to scare off development money. And shoddy construction portends heavy unanticipated expenses for the unlucky owners in the form of either renovation or abandonment. Any slacking off of the miracle construction boom will mean serious unemployment among the part time and seasonal workers who need employment the most. As this was written, the world-wide financial and economic crisis had begun to sweep over China, and 3-4 hundred thousand marginal businesses have closed. The next few months may well be difficult for the Chinese economy. But the government can probably weather the storm largely because it extracts a huge percentage of the country's wealth, which can now be used for financial crisis management.

But nevertheless, the changes made in this construction environment after 1978 are mind boggling. Between 1979 and 1989, 830,000 households occupied new or renovated apartments; and between 1992 and 1996, another 800,000 moved. More than 4.5 million people changed address, and the average space per capita doubled. Housing has improved vastly over the last 25-30 years. Average space is increasing: from 3.6 square meters (6' X 6') to almost double that now. Older housing remains a big problem. Much of it was shoddy construction, and the State as landlord sadly neglected maintenance and repair, and many units provided by the State are being fixed up by their occupants or by managing cooperatives, at their own expense. But over half of all housing continues to be under the SOEs or government bodies. Rents are heavily subsidized, but the pattern is bad housing at low cost. Proposals to "marketize" rents are under way, but are stiffly resisted.

The number one complaint of urban dwellers is lack of commercial services. But more latitude for private and "informal" enterprise is reducing the past failures of the tight restrictions imposed by the government over the marketplace, and the older Communist communes, labor brigades and union cadres, while never officially repudiated have been allowed to wither away. Most cities still suffer from lack of transport, and lack of child care. Also, millions of readers eagerly snap up the skyrocketing numbers of newspapers, journals and books. And wave after wave of new enthusiasms swept across China such as hobbies, tourism, fitness, computer games, or the Falong Gong. And gratefully, the older communist organizations such as communes or labor brigades or union cadres simply faded into the sunset.

The urban destitute are denied a political voice because the leadership doesn't want to hear the complaints, and certainly does not want to do anything expensive to deal with them. The "cradle to grave" commitment never meant much except to those in the favored sectors of the economy; and as State resources have withered, things have only gotten worse. China's analog to the informal sector -- new neighborhood-run collective enterprises, urban private enterprises, and rural subcontracting -- are the most dynamic part of the economy. In truth, these sectors are faster on their feet than the SOE's as well.

CHAPTER VII

Rural Life and the Environment

RURAL LIFE IN INDIA

India has been forever an enormous and infinitely complex kaleidoscope of life in villages and farms. Only China of all the major countries of the contemporary world comes close to the degree to which it is dominated by the rural world. Chapter VI discussed the extraordinary evolution of cities in both countries, but neither country can be understood without understanding the rural/village world. In India, each of its more than half a million villages is a world of its own, a blend of class, caste (jati), clan, family, religion, language and local customs and social rules. There are thousands of castes into which people are supposedly born for life, and they can dictate who can be married, who can deal with whom and how, who does what work, and who is subservient to whom. There are additional overlays of religion, race, wealth and prejudice. Thus, village life is far broader and more complex than the issues of agriculture as a sector of the economy, but yet, two thirds of India's population, or about 750 million people, including

240 million who are classified as "rural poor", depend on this rural/village/small town sector for their living, and villages are the strong bastions for the preservation of all of the old traditions and prejudices. Many rural workers have moved to cities, but still return to their home villages during periods of unemployment or to celebrate major holidays. As for farms,

they average only 2½ acres, yet they support a very large population including huge numbers of unemployed or underemployed workers, and workers who earn only about $1 to $3 a day. About 60% of current food production is consumed by farm families and village residents. But farms are getting smaller, the costs of farming are rising, and the gap is filled by expensive government subsidies which are politically popular, but which seriously overloaded the government's budget

An Intensive Agricultural District Programme was launched in the closing years of the government's Second Plan (1960). It aimed to concentrate resources and efforts in specially designated areas with adequate production potential. In other words, narrow the focus of government aid, lavish high subsidies on a limited number of favored areas, and ignore the rest of the country. Subsidies included at least fertilizers, seeds, insecticides, large expansions of irrigation systems, water subsidies, and power subsidies. Larger scale farmers could take advantage of this policy, and the poorer, smaller farmers were largely frozen out. This policy, almost predictably seemed to produce inefficient use of scarce resources, and poor usage practices which also ended up endangering environmental conditions.

This failure to help the small farmer was recognized again in a National Commission on Agriculture in 1974, but in typical Indian fashion, most of the commission's report was ignored and nothing substantial was done for small farmers. Once again, the latest Five Year Plan (2007-2012) seems to be making the right noises. It says that agriculture and allied activities are the main stay of state's economies, not only because they contribute about 26% of state domestic product but more so because they employ about 71% of the total workforce. Irrigation remains the key to increased production, but the government persists in declining to irrigate in what it calls "rain fed" areas where irrigation is seen as unnecessary – and where most of the poor farmers live and work.

Historically, rural/village life was seldom considered in the aggregate because it was, in fact, a world of more than 550,000 separate villages each with its own separate cultures and characteristics. Thus, the "agricultural sector" of the economy is a modern concept that may or may not reflect the real world. But it is probably true that slowly and often reluctantly the farmers and villagers are entering a new and broader economic world, because they are coming to realize that it may offer them some vital advantages. Also, they have long been tired of the hypocritical attitudes of politicians of all parties that regard villagers not as citizens or clients, but merely as reservoirs of votes that can be lured or bought. The richer states have no interest in dealing with their agriculture. There is no connectivity between increasing wealth in the industrial sector, and the lagging agricultural sector. Strangely for a country that remains predominantly rural, there has never been a conscious, consistent, substantial strategy to increase agricultural productivity, build up non-agricultural employment, or find ways to enhance life quality.

India remains a totally fascinating but befuddling and inexplicable overlay of many elements of society: cultural, religious, caste, tribal, geographical, repressive, divisive and increasingly political in very partisan ways. This diffusion complicates both self help and government outreach efforts. Typically, there are still large land owners, plus millions of land holdings that are already too small to be effective economic units. About 5% of the population belongs to one of hundreds of elite Brahmin castes. Another 20% are in the Dalit lower castes, and according to Wolpert, "The vast majority of India's Hindu population were born somewhere between exalted Brahmanic sacrosanctity and traditionally shunned Untouchability. Most of these middle castes are twice-born merchants and landowner farmers, many of whom have in recent generations moved into urban professions attained by modern and higher education. The remaining quarter or more of India's Hindu majority are landless laborers and urban menials, whose lowly birth, darker skin or lack of resources have long relegated them to the bottom rungs of hierarchical social ladders, once more rigid that they have recently become but still very much in evidence across the landscape of village life and urban poverty that fill India's complex continent with long-suffering struggling humanity." [1] The Indian Constitution (Article 15) explicitly states "The State shall not discriminate against any citizen on grounds only of religion, race, caste, sex, place of birth or any of them. No citizen shall, on grounds only of religion, race, caste, sex, place of birth or any of them, be subject to any disability, liability, restriction or condition with regard to access to shops, public restaurants, hotels and places of public entertainment; or the use of wells, tanks, bathing ghats, roads and places of public resort –". The Constitution further states (Article 17) that "Untouchability" is abolished and its practice in any form is forbidden. The enforcement of any disability arising out of "Untouchability" shall be an offence punishable in accordance with law."

There is a historical legacy of a large powerful class of land holders that has long dominated local affairs, and who continue to benefit disproportionately from government programs intended to help the real poor. But typically, most land holdings are already too small, but the enlargement of small farms requires government permission to combine or consolidate, and these permits somehow end up in the hands of large land holders. It is often through this layer of landed rich that politicians find their greatest leverage. At the same time, popular resentment of this oppression has created an outraged backlash among the disadvantaged and neglected, and which, increasingly, is leading to highly emotional political activism and armed resistance. Also, the new economy of India includes highly successful surge of rural/village industrialization, but it has also retained the same plague of brokers, middle men, "fixers", lobbyists, influence peddlers and rapacious loan sharks that swarm in the larger cities.

Farming in India is critically linked to irrigation. Land that is irrigated can be profitable and productive. Land that relies solely on rainfall is marginal at best and is highly vulnerable to disastrous water shortages. Therefore, the expansion of irrigation is both an economic necessity and the source of endless gaming. Political allies get government irrigation help. Others are largely ignored. Yet the thousands of miles of irrigation systems are expensive to construct and maintain, waste staggering amounts of water, drain the public budget, and are poorly managed and corrupt.

India has also historically been the victim of periodic famine, starvation and malnutrition. A remarkable miracle was brought about in the 1960s which became known as the Green Revolution. This revolution started with the introduction of certain forms of low water and rust resistant wheat that uses little water. The American Norman Borlaug first used these seeds under a grant from the Rockefeller Foundation, working through the International Center for Wheat and Maize Research in Mexico. The results of these experiments were so outstanding that Borlaug was able to convince the Indian Minister of Agriculture C. Subramaniam in 1966 to initiate experiments in India involving high-yielding rice and wheat seeds, along with fertilizers and pesticides. According to Anderson [2] "Benefits were widely shared, with farm incomes substantially enriched. Between 1970 and 1995, while population increased by 67%, cereal production grew by 88%. By 1995, there was enough food for every Indian to meet her or his minimum calorie needs – if food was distributed according to need. The proportion of Indians who are chronically undernourished has declined from 38% in 1980 to less than 23% today. Rural poverty declined from over 50% in the mid 60s to 27% today. And it was largely the small farmers that benefited because of increased yields and lower unit costs."

This whole major agricultural technology reform program not only ended India's history of famines, but for the first time, it became clear that India could feed itself, if its leaders were wise enough. But there is a growing concern that they may have flunked that test. The Green Revolution had its limits and needed to be followed up with a continuing program of agricultural development, but there has not really been any second wave of reforms and productivity enhancements in the last 20 years, and as the national population has surged beyond one billion people, and as a result, food production has once again lagged behind demand. But the most knowledgeable of observers continue to insist that India, which has the second largest area of land suitable for cultivation among the world's nations (after the U. S.) could, with proper stimulation and leadership, not only meet its own food demands but could become a net exporter of food to countries that badly need it, at great profit for the Indian economy. The problem is that the government has never ever seemed interested in, or capable of, providing such leadership. As for the private sector, it thinks in terms of large "agribusiness" operations that may actually be a threat to the small farmer rather than a salvation. [3]

Unfortunately the great blessing of the Green Revolution, when pushed to the limit, has generated growing environmental repercussions.

For example, pesticide use in India is among the heaviest in the world. Pesticides were a key ingredient in the Green Revolution, their use plus new hybrid seeds, synthetic fertilizers, irrigation raised crop yields dramatically during the 60s and 70s. DDT, now banned, nevertheless reduced the annual incidence of malaria from 75 million cases in 1952 to less than 3 million now. But new testing is revealing high levels of dangerous chemicals in Indian food and water, and it has become another serious problem to face. Politicians lack the guts to ban some chemicals that favor agricultural production. Pollutants were found in foods and bottled drinks such as Coca Cola, and the government took and increasingly negative regulatory attitude, which apparently inhibited some economic development. [4]

Fruits, vegetables, oilseeds, milk and milk products, or cut flowers all offer new and higher value added farm opportunities in meeting the demands of both foreign and domestic markets. And the benefits could accrue to small farmers and not to large corporations. Despite government concentration on irrigation, which benefits larger landholders, more than 80% of India's rural poor live in what are called natural "rainfed" areas.

There many opportunities for the involvement of the private sector in agricultural production, processing, marketing, transportation, storage, input supplies, infrastructure, housing, and consumer goods provision and retailing. The role of the government is crucial, but it should be remodeled to concentrate on promotion, safety nets, standards, legal bases for contracts, investments in public goods, and R & D. One of the first and best things that the government could do would be to form an alliance with private interests to design and implement an optimum agricultural distribution system. Alternatives are needed from the Indian government for the current obsolete and dysfunctional system of input cost subsidies, and the whole obssolete philosophy of import substitution. Too many of the government's enterprises are State monopolies that are notoriously inert and inefficient. The Food Corporation of India should either be abolished or confined to a limited role for emergency protection. An ideal alternative is available: there are thousands of examples around the world for the use of agricultural cooperatives for everything from input purchases to product marketing.

It seems blazingly obvious that the high costs of politically popular subsidies drives out money from far more valuable activities such as rural community development, rural health and education, rural roads, and more efficient power, soil and water management. Studies show that roads and agricultural technology are all win and no lose. Studies also show that, while irrigation does raise production output, it benefits mostly the large landholders and not the rural poor. Small farmers should look for niche markets (e. g. cut flowers), or for new markets created by the new urban middle class.

India, like many other countries is facing a crisis over water. Water management is a government responsibility as defined in the Constitution, but this responsibility has been delegated to the 28 States, and water usage is highly inefficient. The central government concentrates on such national issues as the management of river basins, the resolution of disputes, and some environmental problems. The government seems not to have any really coherent national strategy. It has several options: water can be treated as a public utility, run a set of regulated private sector monopolies; or it can be provided by various forms of public- private partnerships. Already, private entities (both organizations and individuals) who find that they can't rely on the government are running their own private water supply.

So now, India must undertake major very sophisticated programs to strike a new balance. It cannot afford to reduce agricultural production, so the government will try to keep the fertilizers and pesticides that work and are not environmentally threatening, and it is moving to ban worst offenders. In a similar vein, increased irrigation has also been vital, but it consumes so much water that the availability for other uses is threatened. Even as canal irrigation projects have been largely unsuccessful, government budgets have allocated massive amounts to them – along with the mentality of heavy subsidy for fertilizer, pesticides, power and fuel, and attempts to cut subsidies usually results in cowardly politicians who react by raising them instead. The policy of "free water" is a disaster, and soon India will have to figure out how to manage increasingly inadequate water supplies. Electric power is often free, especially to encourage the pumping of irrigation water. In addition, many in both rural and urban areas are skilled at tapping illegally into water and power sources, and there does not seem to be any will or ability to stop it or punish the culprits. But strangely, all of these public subsidies have not led to financial stability for farmers: over half of them are into serious debt to the point that many are driven to suicide. Land degradation, water wastage, obsolete practices and corruption seem to cost India 20% of its agricultural output each year. **[5]**

And dramatically increasing the food supply did not really eliminate hunger, and more people still go hungry or malnourished than in any other country. There are said still to be 200 million malnourished children, both urban and rural. The solution to this problem is more economic than agricultural – how to make the economy provide food to these people and get it distributed.

Nor is it likely that a significant next wave of agricultural expansion can happen with the present transportation/distribution system. Few adequate roads exist away from the urban areas. Warehousing, wholesale distribution facilities, food processing centers and refrigerated trucks and rail cars are simply not available. The government's long standing monopoly on the purchase of many farm products inhibited the evolution of the whole dynamics of marketing and sales promotion. In fact, the government's tendency to pursue dysfunctional policies of import substitution has seriously inhibited agricultural modernization and competitiveness.

In addition, the government got committed, especially during the Indira Gandhi regime, to heavy subsidies for populist political reasons – irrigation systems, fertilizers, pesticides, water, power, and seeds. These subsidies were often pernicious. Irrigation systems were very costly, and were not maintained; fertilizers and pesticides were used in excess and created environmental risks; water and power were so cheap that they were heavily wasted. These subsidies acquired a life of their own, and no politician now has the guts to advocate cuts. They have become a heavy fiscal burden, and have strained the tax system. The direct tax base is too small (80% + of taxes are indirect). Rural/small town people are seldom taxed at all, and millions in the informal economy escape taxes too. There is very little latitude to expand the tax base, because even where people have risen out of "abject" poverty, they are still very poor. And the new middle class is constantly fearful that political ambitions will result in higher taxes for them.

Promises of rural development turned out to be that the government simply offered higher subsidies, along with a few respected programs like the Food for Work Program. But the real problem was and is that, with 680,000 villages and more than 750 million rural/village residents, every effort was puny in comparison to the enormity of the problems.

Even the very expensive subsidy programs of the government have not had the galvanizing effect for which the government had hoped. That is, these subsidies have helped greatly to improve the circumstances of farmers in the short run, but they have had little developmental consequence for the longer term. The next "Green Revolution" will have to come from sources other than the government. The government seems surprisingly slow to recognize the fact that, in addition to technology, part of agricultural development must stem from better management – crop diversification, better crop management, better water management, precision farming, integrated pest management, pest resistant crop varieties, improved soil management, use of cooperatives, serious productivity management, more agricultural machinery, and perhaps even genetic crop modification. The point is that all of these management improvements are well known and relatively inexpensive, and a lot of progress could be achieved in a relatively short period of time. These are programs that can be easily taught, and can involve a lot of private sector help. Why is the Indian government so stubbornly opaque to these opportunities?

The politicians seem also not to realize that the economic conditions for export encouragement are surprisingly strong. According to Anderson, "Most domestically produced commodities enjoy a comparative advantage in the home market. Many are, or could become, competitive in the world market, since the productivity gains of the Green Revolution resulted in real cost reductions. Both Indian wheat and rice are competitive, despite government interventions which have hurt exports because they keep domestic prices higher than world prices. Much of the import substitution policy preference continues, and grain, oil seeds, and edible oils remain protected. If India could mount a serious and sustained program to help and encourage agriculture exports, it could probably enjoy considerable success. **[6]**

It seems richly symbolic that the first ever national agricultural policy for India was not even formally announced until July of 2000 – 50 years after Indian independence. All of the stated objectives in that policy seem reasonable if somewhat pompous, but one cannot help but feel that they represent a piece of paper rather than a committed government intent. These objectives were stated as follows:

- Actualization of the untapped growth potential of Indian agriculture.
- Strengthening of rural infrastructure to support faster agricultural development.
- Promotion of "value added" agriculture.
- Accelerating the growth of agribusiness.
- Creation of more employment in rural areas.
- Securing a fair standard of living for farmers and agricultural workers.
- Discouraging migration to urban areas.
- Facing up to the challenges of globalization and economic liberalization.

The political mix master also approved a few more specific objectives for the next 20 years, including producing a growth rate of 4% per year. Also, and for almost the first time, a policy was adopted to "maximize benefit exports of agricultural products in the face of challenges arising from economic liberalization and globalization." Pleasant thoughts are uttered about the virtues of equity, efficiency, and agriculture that is "sustainable technologically, environmentally and economically."

Notwithstanding the blandness and vagueness of these objectives, they represent a very valuable retreat from past government failings and a willingness to move toward more realistic policies. A standing policy which is now largely unspoken is to continue the record of avoiding famines and feeding all Indian citizens. But the government never wants to discuss its shameful record of tolerating the malnutrition of millions of people, including children and pregnant mothers.

The government's policy objectives need to be far more specific about the critical neglect of much of its irrigation systems which includes widespread maintenance and repair failures, and the disturbing waste of valuable water resources. It should also produce a realistic and specific plan, including funding, for the repair, upgrading and expansion of the food distribution and marketing system. This is one area where there is the opportunity for some very productive partnerships with the private sector.

Perhaps the greatest challenge for the government lies in the need for complete restructuring of the whole gigantic structure of rural subsidies. "Explicit subsidies include petrol, food, fertilizers and water, and these constitute 38% of all government subsidies, and food subsidies are 60% of rural subsidies. India has a "national distribution system (for food) that guarantees that a third of its goods will never make it to market. Until recently, farmers were required by law to sell their produce to mandis – a network of local markets originally introduced to protect poor farmers from exploitation, but now controlled by cartels of traders, petty bureaucrats and moneylenders. They are supposed to be paid the officially set market price, but many mandis cheat. While the produce is slowly shipped to retailers, 30-40% rots during transport." [7]

Part of this huge cost is created by the minimum support prices paid by the national Food Corporation of India (FCI), along with state agencies, based on the recommendations of a Commission on Agricultural Costs and Prices (CACP) [8] In addition to wheat and rice, the CACP recommends prices for corn, pulses, sorghum, millet, sugar cane, cotton, oilseeds and jute. But political pressure is brought to bear on the FCI to pay ever higher prices. The dismal fact is that produce prices set by the government are now above the true market, and the beneficiaries are not the poor farmers but rich farmers and agribusiness processors and various political "fixers". At the same time, Indian consumers are buying food at prices inflated by their own government, or they are obtusely benefiting from food at subsidized prices through a distribution network of 350,000 outlets operated by state governments. Along the way, the FCI has built up mountains of stored wheat and rice in government warehouses. This is exceedingly expensive, but the real puzzle is why nobody seems able to figure out how to use these mountains to help the truly poor in both the countryside and the cities

Especially under Indira Gandhi, these subsidies expanded, and were used as blatant political favoritism. As a consequence, they are one of the major contributors to the high cost of government, and the intractable deficits of local governments. Local taxes are equally rigid; the poor have no money to pay taxes, and the new middle class has begun to have the political clout to oppose tax increases. Even today, politics in rural India is all about buying votes for political parties, and not about improving rural life or culture.

The reform of this whole huge malfunctioning and incoherent system looks like a daunting "mission impossible" in political terms, but it is absolutely vital for any real hope of longer term development. But the politics of agriculture seem only to get worse. On the one hand, government policy urges farmers to grow more wheat and rice, ostensibly to maintain national "self sufficiency'. On the other hand, the government has actually created a situation of surplus, and it must buy all grain at a high "minimum support price" and store it. At the same time, over a quarter of India's electricity is given free or cut-price to farmers, and as a consequence, state power utilities are technically bankrupt, and lack funds for expansion or modernization. And still, an estimated 400 million Indians have no electricity.

Subsidy giveaways may help as short term welfare, but they are a budgetary bottomless pit. Irrigation systems cannot continue to be expanded if the current systems are breaking down and failing. Rural electrification cannot be expanded if the government continues to force power companies to sell power at below cost. Free fertilizers are cornered by the big landholders and profits accrue to big manufacturers. Meanwhile, agricultural chemical runoff is an ominous and growing problem. Government price controls and monopoly crop purchasing inhibit producers who can't earn a reasonable profit. The government at least appears to have stopped forcing farmers to grow low value wheat and rice and now allow, and indeed encourage, them to shift to higher value added products such as fruits and vegetables. Government storage facilities are still full of wheat and rice which has been purchased and stored at great cost, so new subsidies are simply pointless. Even the water itself is subsidized to the point that it is often almost free, and this has had the unfortunate effect of promoting water wastage.

Agricultural policy should have been very high on the government's policy agenda. Nehru's socialist theory led him to efforts to increase employment in agriculture and to manipulate prices to subsidize farm incomes. But both approaches proved to be failures, and his government never really understood the options of rural development, higher farm productivity, shifting of crops from low to higher income plantings, or any of the rest of modern agricultural development. Instead of prohibiting food exports, the government should have been trying export stimulation. The farm/village labor surplus was so enormous that no government program stood a chance of making serious inroads. In fact, it is hard not to conclude that keeping the prices of agricultural products deliberately high had a far more negative impact through higher prices for urban consumers than any populist vote getting among the rural population.

Amarta Sen, the Nobel Prize winning economists asks: "Why is it that large expenditures on food subsidy do not achieve more in reducing undernourishment? The answer centers around the fact that the food subsidy program is really aimed at keeping food prices paid to producers high, but the producers that benefit are large farmers and agribusiness enterprises. Thus, small farmers benefit little, and consumers of food actually pay more. It also seems that a lot of the subsidy money must go to other than producers – storage facilities middle men, transporters and processors. Also, huge sums are spent on the storage of food grains – now more than 50 million tons of grain for example - as well as to pay for a big staff of government employees to manage the system. [9]

Largely as a consequence of political intervention, there is a growing gap between the cost of power and charges to users. This gap has been covered by subsidy, but losses are now less covered by budget subsidy and more by borrowing, with ominous long term implications. The power sector is seen as plagued by inefficient operations, underinvestment, technical inadequacies, and the theft of power. Among customers, farmers and many urban households enjoy the biggest subsidies. Households pay about 60% of actual costs, and farmers only about 10%. Furthermore, lacking reliable population estimates or metering in many places, the power companies have been accused of "inventing" rural customers.

Not only are irrigation systems very wasteful of water but they rely far too heavily on groundwater extraction, and on electric, rather than diesel pumps. More than 26% of all water usage is for agriculture, and there is the special problem of the wide spread theft of water. Subsidies for water costs are all too often captured by the richer farmers who bribe water control officials. Many farmers or villagers figure they can simply avoid paying their bills, since they will probably get political backing against the suppliers. Both the allocation of water and the allocation of electric power are involved. The government is a lot better at water rationing than it is in development of greater water supplies. Indian agriculture is said to be very capable of water management technology. The subsidy cost of water and power is a potential target for big budget savings.

But around 450 million farmers must make do with normal rainfall rather than irrigation. The monsoon season is vital; it extends from June to September, and when the monsoon rains are inadequate, crop failure is highly likely. But monsoon rains supply 50% of the rainfall for the year in just a few days. Farmers need better ways to capture and store this water, but India suffers from a serious failure of overall water management. But beyond the main concern about the monsoon, India suffers from serious failures of overall water management. The monsoon rains supply 50% of rainfall in just about 15 days. The trick is to capture and store the water against the drier months. It is felt that there is enough rain water in general if it is intelligently captured, stored and transported, but on all three counts, India fares badly. In addition, there is increasing concern that global warming is melting the Himalayan glaciers which will reduce the summertime flows into India's three great river systems – the Indus, the Ganges and the Brahmaputra. There is a further growing concern that larger cities and more industrial users inevitably means ominous new competition for water.

India does have a water management organization starting with the national government Central Water Commission, but actual water management is carried out be state governments, usually at the district level. One big answer is seen as the construction of dams, and 390 new dams are already under construction. These dams are then linked to a network of irrigation canals and reservoirs. There are two major subsidiary problems. One is silting: each year, India is estimated to lose the equivalent of two thirds of the new storage it builds to silting behind dams and further upstream. The second problem is "India's corrupt, under funded and overmanned state irrigation departments. Uttar Pradesh's for example employs over 100,000 people, but still often provides no maintenance at all." "Between 1992 and 2004, despite the fact that India built 200 large and medium-sized irrigation projects, the irrigated area shrank by 3.2 million hectares." **[10]**

India is the world's biggest user of groundwater, with some 20 million bore-holes providing water for over 60% of its irrigation system. But nearly a third of groundwater areas are defined as in critical, semi-critical, or overused condition. In many boreholes, nonrenewable water is being extracted. And still, 220 million Indians lack safe drinking water. Many municipal governments also sell water at below cost, and must fund the deficit by diverting funds needed for other public programs, and still they fail to maintain their water distribution systems properly. It is estimated that in Delhi for example half of the distributed water is lost through leaky pipes. Boreholes supply at least 40% of the city's needs, but many are draining irreplaceable water. The poor end up with 1 ½ hours of muddy water a week, for which they must pay a high price to the "water mafia", often in league with corrupt water board officials.

These are not insurmountable problems. There are well proven techniques for far better water management including small dams, local catchments basins or small reservoirs, inexpensive water storage techniques, drip irrigation techniques and so on. A little more political guts and honesty could drastically cut back water corruption.

India sought weakly to move away from this regime of subsidized agricultural resources after Indira Gandhi. Such a retrenchment plan was approved in 1992, but 17 years later, little has been accomplished. Most jurisdictions still cannot meter either water or energy. Rich farmers are locally powerful; besides, few states have the money to invest heavily in expansions of service or costly retrofitting of irrigation systems, installation of meters or of drip water technology. Fees are still almost always subsidized to some degree. In what seems like a clever move, the Minister of Finance announced in July, 2009, a scheme to pay subsidies directly to the farmers, rather than to the big fertilizer companies. Fertilizer company stock immediately crashed. And the new rhetoric of "sustainable agriculture" is simply a cover for more development and "business as usual".

The most recent response of the Indian government has not been to reform existing agricultural subsidies but to add new ones. In 2008, the government instituted a program of debt forgiveness under which small farmers (less than 5 acres) would have their bank debts totally forgiven, and larger farmers would have their debts reduced by 25%. More than 43 million farmers have benefited; the losses suffered by local banks will be repaid by the central State Bank of India over a four year period. This program is counted as a political success, but nobody seems to have given much thought to the longer term implications of such a program. Farmers, who are not dumb, have figured out the difference between private bank "hard" loans and government bank "soft" loans. Even in the buildup before the loan forgiveness program of 2008, repayments of bank loans declined markedly. Now, farmers will expect government bank loans to be subsidized, uncollected, and ultimately forgiven. [11] But few Indian farmers have a clear title to their land and thus have trouble using it as collateral for bank loans, and they often have to pay big bribes to greedy bankers or money lenders.

According to a CARE report [12] "The government is (supposedly) implementing a special program to provide financial assistance for construction of dwelling units for the poor. When initiated in 1985, it was confined to families below the poverty line (BPL), and members of Scheduled Castes and Tribes. In 1993, the scope was expanded to cover non-scheduled castes, rural poor below the poverty line, some military families, and families with disability persons. Costs of the program are shared between the central and State governments on a 75/25% basis, but the program is administered by the States. This is in the form of a categorical grant program administered through district level Rural Development Agencies." There are estimates that put the rural housing shortage at about 14.8 million units. The government has put out statements about how they want to reduce this number by about 40% in the next 4 years, which is pure political nonsense.

Also, The National Rural Employment Guarantees Act (NREGA), initiated in 2009, guarantees 100 days of labor on public works at minimum wages to every rural household that asks for it. "This is not "workfare" since it guarantees work, and does not impose penalties for refusals. People in the program feel that they are earning their money and it is not charity. Often, at minimum wages, payments still exceed the market rate. The main problem with the program – in typical Indian fashion – is the "indolence and inertia" of the bureaucracy. [13] There are two official designations of consumers: those Below the Poverty Line (BPS)" and those Above the Poverty Line (APL). Studies show that too much of the subsidy purchase of food is by APL people.

AGRICULTURAL REFORM CHINESE STYLE

China's rural population is in excess of 900 million, and despite recent migrations to cities, China remains along with India as one of the most seriously rural/village societies in the world. Even many of those who are part of the "float" of urban transients remain legal residents of their original villages, and many return there when there is no work for them in the cities.

Throughout history, the peasants have been victimized by their leadership, and Mao Zedong was no exception. But the Communist revolution was supposed to change all of that. It was to be the triumph of the peasants and workers, but farmers have been more victims than beneficiaries even to the present day. Mao and local political leaders taxed the peasants unmercifully, forced them to grow low value crops and then paid them almost nothing for them. Farmers were forced into collective farms despite the fact that they had already been shown to be failures in the Soviet Union. Little effort was made to teach them modern agricultural techniques. Terraced farms and irrigation systems were used excessively, and many have deteriorated and failed. Farming in China has been such a marginal occupation that hundreds of millions of people lived in grinding hopeless poverty, and 90% of them were illiterate. Huge floods occurred every few years, along with droughts, dust storms and locust swarms.

The plight of China's rural and village people has been the same for thousands of years – too many people, too little land, too little value, too many overlords – ignorance, abject poverty, no hope, no future. Money gouged out of peasants was used as capital for industrializing China's cities, where city dwellers got subsidies for housing, education and health care not available to the rural majority. It was not until after Mao's death in 1976 that the CCP even began to think about how to help peasants instead of taxing and exploiting them. Several changes began to emerge which, over the last 40 years, have finally begun to energize the rural world. First, the failures of collective farming were finally admitted and a Household Responsibility System was initiated in 1978. If a farmer or farm collective produced more than a fixed quota for crops set by the government, they could keep the overage and use it as they chose. Village authorities negotiated contracts with individuals or with cooperatives of farmers that specified three critical things: the price of farming inputs like seeds or fertilizer; the expected crop quotas and targets; and the price that the government would pay for mandatory sales of these crops to government agencies. Because these contracts allowed some latitude about what was grown, farmers shifted from grain (at foolishly low government prices) to fruits and vegetables which are more profitable. Gradually during the 1980's, the government removed most of their artificially low price controls, and farmers were able to sell at greater profit to buyers other than the government itself.

One of the first and most momentous changes brought about by the Communist Party when it came to power in 1949, was a huge program of land reform, which involved the assumption of ownership of all land, the seizure of private land holdings from then existing land holders and the execution of literally hundreds of thousands of these people as enemies of the State and counterrevolutionaries. In total, almost 50% of all land had been "redistributed" by 1952.

By 1956, rural land had passed largely into the hands of farm collectives similar to those in the USSR. These collectives were an important element of control over the rural population but it was also expected that they would produce far more efficient farming results. This proved not to be true, any more than it had in the USSR, and 15 years of effort had produced little increase in either production or productivity.

Until the 1980s the Chinese rural areas were organized into communes which were large collective groups of around 2,000 families. Communes in turn were organized into work brigades of maybe 2-300 families. These in turn were subdivided into production teams of 40-50 families. Plans were formulated at the commune level by the Communist Party office. Work assignments were usually established by the heads of the production teams. The work brigades usually owned the equipment and controlled the allocation of land. Individual families could own their home, but the land remained owned by the government. Families could have a "private plot" and could grow for home consumption or for sale at market prices. The communes were charged with providing basic medical care and primary education. Production was very low, there was little incentive for "struggle", and social services were usually pitifully lacking and amateur. But the critical point is that total production increase was very slow and could not keep up with population increase. Prices were set by the government, which for 40 years was infamous for gouging the peasants. All of this changed when the household responsibility system was reintroduced in 1978. But even this system left the CCP offices with too much power. The government set deliberately low quota prices for purchases, and was endlessly manipulative. The CCP backed off of this archaic style only slowly and very reluctantly, despite the fact that the loosening of controls was clearly seen as achieving production increases. Beginning in the 1980s, reforms encouraged real rural development in the form of new industrial enterprises at the township and village level, including upgrading of many of the recently transferred

SOEs. Because of these policies, rural industrial production has vastly increased, perhaps by as much as 300% in some areas. A problem has been created by initiation of too many small and underpowered units, but these will gradually be worked out by rationalization.

Farming in China seems to fit the worldwide pattern: it is only marginally profitable when practiced at levels less than agribusiness. China may have to abandon its policy of food self sufficiency – just as the Japanese had to – and decide that moving resources into industry produces enough money to import needed food. Urban workers, at least in the formal economy, earn the equivalent of $3,000 per year, while rural incomes are about $950. There has been a cap of 5% taxation on rural household income, but this tax was eliminated in 2005. But in the usual Chinese fashion, local officials impose fees, tolls, fines, special levies, user fees, and service charges that add from 15 to 50% over the official taxes. This money is seldom visibly invested in local services or infrastructure. There is a huge discontent because it is perceived that much of this revenue is stolen, wasted in high living, or diverted to other purposes.

During the 80s, the township began to take the place of the communes/brigades/production units, and management of rural activities became better and more professional. Township/Village Enterprises (TVEs) were used to replace the commune managed structure. Some TVEs were government run collectives; some were converted SOEs that had been dumped on local governments. And out of a total rural labor force of 350 million, only 140 million were needed for agriculture, while another 90 million are working in rural industry and other non- agricultural activities. The 140 million who remain in agriculture are underemployed and tend to live in abject poverty. In addition, there remains another huge pool – perhaps as many as 135 million – who may have risen out of "abject" poverty, but who remain poor or near poor.

It now seems clear that the best way – perhaps the only way – to solve the problem of rural employment is to accept the fact that rural workers have to be allowed to migrate to the cities and towns. The rural workforce still contains an estimated 150-200 million surplus workers, and no amount of rural assistance is going to dent this enormous fact. Migration to cities is still crucial. It can be either permanent or temporary, but the government's attitudes must be changed to assist migrants to find jobs rather than punishing them as illegal, and they must be allowed to have at least limited access to social services, especially health care. In addition, some of the new construction in major cities must be shifted from opulent new apartments and office buildings to better housing for the general population. Eventually, the government must deal with urban/rural wage inequities as well. The government has begun to accept this line of thinking. In 2002 and 2003, new policy documents have been issued to redress some of this unfairness and accord equal treatment to migrant workers in most urban settings, but as usual in China, these policy documents may not be worth the paper they are written on, and it all depends on getting the leadership in cities to face up to the demands of their "floating population".

If the Chinese government wants to subsidize their agricultural sector, there are many ways by which this could be done:

1. Crop price supports and subsidy payments
2. Government development of the distribution system
3. Land reforms
4. Targeted import quotas
5. Low taxes for farmers
6. Subsidized crop insurance
7. Subsidized farm home loans and loan guarantees
8. Irrigation, soil conservation and land reclamation
9. Subsidies to shift crops
10. Education and training programs
11. Purchases for food subsidies for the poor
12. Promotion of agricultural cooperatives and even private sector "agribusiness"
13. Development of rural villages and towns.

But the government, driven by traditional centrist socialist doctrine, is not interested in rural development. Other poor countries such as India and Bangladesh have developed innovative techniques such as micro-credit programs, Food for Work schemes, broader use of agricultural cooperatives, encouragement of more profitable crops, and subsidized fertilizers and insecticides. Even though such programs are not particularly expensive, the CCP continues to show little interest.

An important alternative strategy would be to open up the market and see if Chinese farmers could produce enough grain to satisfy domestic needs and produce a surplus for export. The same dilemma is reflected in government involvement with sugar beets, sugar cane, fruits, and other commodities. Commodities sold in the informal economy would usually earn 3-4 times the price for the seller. Finally, when urban dwellers became more well-to-do, the government had the courage to let more grain and other prices be set by the market.

THE ENVIRONMENT

INDIA'S INSURMOUNTABLE ENVIRONMENTAL PROBLEMS

India is home to many of the world's most polluted cities. The air in Calcutta or Delhi is all but unbreathable in winter when exhaust fumes, unchecked industrial emissions, and smoke from countless charcoal braziers in the street rise and are trapped by descending mist and fog. Thus, respiratory diseases are rife in India. Factories belch noxious black clouds; effluents pour untreated into rivers; sewage systems reek and overflow. Deforestation and over cultivation take their own environmental toll in rural India. Environmental consciousness in both countries remains very low, and even when their governments get around to passing regulations, they are largely ignored. Billions of dollars each year are incurred in health costs because of air and water pollution, amounting to more than 4.5% of GDP. Yet green politicians still try to use environmental threats for political leverage.[14] Welcome to environmentalism Indian style.

India, with about 1.1 billion people continues to justify much of its official policy on food self sufficiency. But tragically – and typically – this obsolete fear has driven the government into a whole series of wrong and dysfunctional policies affecting its agricultural and village world, and leading to the worst ecological consequences: degradation of agricultural land, over usage of fertilizers, pesticides, and insecticides, overgrazing, deforestation, squandering of precious water, give away electric power leading to more coal driven power plants – all at huge public cost while actually reducing rather than increasing the ability of the country to feed itself.

In fact, it is perhaps the most compelling irony that, in both China and India, economic expansion is absolutely vital, and India has finally joined China in recognizing that fact and abandoning the old socialist past as rapidly as possible. But the financial demands of economic development leave little money for curing the problems of the environment and natural resources, all of which are being made worse by the burgeoning economies. In both countries, this inherent conflict will play out for several more decades. [15]

But for a long time, the response of the Indian government to environmental concerns was hypocritical and rather foolish. The government found it convenient to assert that environmental issues were a "Western problem", especially relating to global warming, and that India was a victim rather than a perpetrator. Some extreme opinions were that the whole thing was somehow a Western, mostly European, plot against India. The Kyoto treaty was rejected, and it was thought that the 2% reduction target by the end of the century was pointless. Official Indian thought has been slowly changing, but as usual, change in official utterances is not the same as action. India's leaders see the current world pressures as coming at a very bad time for India, just when their new economic policies are paying off. But they concede that economic development is in fact making many environmental problems even worse. In reality, the effects of environmental neglect are so serious and obvious that even the government can now see them, usually through heavy banks of polluted air. What has been hypocritical has been the cheap skate policies of financial neglect, and the assignment of responsibility for environmental concerns to local governments ill prepared to deal with them. There is a growing recognition that past neglect now means that India lacks the political will, the money, and the managerial competence to deal with any of its environmental problems. Nor can it stop or mitigate industrial growth and heavy urbanization.

In 1944, a project sponsored by the Rockefeller Foundation and led by Dr. Norman Borlaug, a plant geneticist led, to the development of extraordinary new plant hybrids in basic food grains in Mexico. Within two decades, Mexico was able to shift from an importer of wheat to an exporter. The Green Revolution was then brought to India also by a Rockefeller Foundation grant starting in 1960. At that time, India was in such a desperate situation that severe food shortages made the prospect of wide- spread starvation a real possibility, avoided only by international help, primarily out of the U. S. Borlaug's seeds were planted in the Punjab, and the yield increases were so dramatic that it triggered a national expansion of the plantings, sponsored and led by an extraordinary Indian Minister of Agriculture Mr. C. Subramaniam. India went from a net grain importer to producing a bumper crop of 131 million tons of grain in 1978, and making it one of the world's largest grain producers.

India, like many other countries is facing a crisis over water. Water management is a government responsibility as defined in the Constitution, but this responsibility has been delegated to the 28 States. The central government concentrates on such national issues as the management of river basins, the resolution of disputes, and some environmental problems. The government seems not to have any really coherent national strategy. It has several options: water can be treated as a public utility, run a set of regulated private sector monopolies; or it can be provided by various forms of public-private partnerships. Already, private entities (both organizations and individuals) who find that they can't rely on the government are running their own private water supply. Governments themselves can develop water supplies and sell water for a profit. [15]

So now, India must undertake major very sophisticated programs to strike a new balance. It cannot afford to reduce agricultural production so the government will try to keep the fertilizers and pesticides that work and are not environmentally threatening, and are moving to ban worst offenders. In a similar vein, increased irrigation has also been vital, but it consumes so much water that the availability for other uses is threatened. Even as canal irrigation projects have been largely unsuccessful, government budgets have allocated massive amounts to them – along with the mentality of heavy subsidy for fertilizer, pesticides, power and fuel, and attempts to cut subsidies usually results in cowardly politicians who react by raising them instead. The policy of "free water" is a disaster, and soon India will have to figure out how to manage increasingly inadequate water supplies. Electric power is often free, especially to encourage the pumping of irrigation water. In addition, many in both rural and urban areas are skilled at tapping illegally into water and power sources, and there does not seem to be any will or ability to stop it or punish the culprits. But strangely, all of these public subsidies have not led to financial stability for farmers: over half of them are into serious debt to the point that many are driven to suicide. Land degradation, water wastage, obsolete practices and corruption seem to cost India 20% of its agricultural output each year. [16]

And dramatically increasing the food supply did not really eliminate hunger, and more people still go hungry or malnourished than in any other country. There are said still to be 200 million malnourished children, both urban and rural. The solution to this problem is more economic than agricultural – how to make the economy provide food to these people and get it distributed.

Cities are becoming the new India and thus the urban environment is critical and cities are rapidly becoming more complex and multi-faceted environmental threats. Air quality in India's cities make them among the world's worst. Mumbai is the 5th most polluted city in the world, and New Delhi is not far behind, with 97% of their residents exposed to air that fails to meet World Health Organization standards." More and more, urban residents, even in better neighborhoods are forced to truck in water, even where they may be hooked up to the municipal water supply; there is simply not enough water in the pipelines.

The most modern elements of the new Indian city are still surrounded by massive slums, and these are environmental disasters in terms of pollution and threats to people's health. Every city in India now fails the government's own emission standards, which were set far below WHO standards. Then, the governments, both national and local, see little advantage in enforcing even these lax standards for fear of slowing industrial development and cutting their revenues. In other words, the urban environment is a great hazard physically, medically and environmentally, but it is most terrible in human terms.

India has a Central Pollution Control Board. The government enacted the National Climate Action Plan in 2008, the Environmental Sustainability Index in 2007, and earlier, the National Air Quality Monitoring Program and the Ambient Air Quality Standard. The real issue is whether these are further examples of mere rhetoric, or whether something – anything -- will actually be done. The Plan would require really drastic action and a lot of trauma, political and otherwise, and environmental regulations are hard to enforce when a very large proportion of economic activity is very small and concealed in the secretive informal economy. Illiteracy remains high, bureaucratic process is muddled, and most people do not trust the government to begin with. How do you enforce anything in such an environment?

China has 85 million enterprises of all kinds; India is not far behind. The difference is that China is top down and has heavy forces to enforce; India is bottom up and light on enforcement capabilities, much less the skill or political will do anything unpopular. In both countries, SOEs are notoriously exempted from most government regulations. Environmental impact statements in both countries are a joke, and are generally ignored.

Most areas of India centralize all water functions at the State level, where they are further centralized into a single ministry: policy, regulation, financing, construction and maintenance, and service delivery. "Within the work culture of the Indian bureaucracy, this bundling virtually guarantees poor performance." Indian performance is said to compare poorly even with other Asian developing nations. Often when a pipe is damaged, whole neighborhoods are without water for weeks. Economists strongly urge the unbundling of these functions and more competition from the private sector. They also urge greater delegation from the State governments to local communities. Many customers would pay for better service than hand pumps or communal pumps, but the socialist bureaucracy won't let them! Regulation should be independent and should be as free as possible from traditional political corruption and pressuring. There is apparently a substantial history to show that heavy subsidizing of water supplies is not necessary and simply leads to a lot of water wastage.

Despite obvious advances, it is felt that most Indian cities are still at risk in terms of both the safety of water supplies, and the availability of adequate sanitary facilities. According to the World Bank [17] water supply is available less than 2 hours a day in Chennai; 2-3 hours in Ahmadabad and Bangalore; 4 hours in Delhi, and between 5 & 6 in Mumbai. There is some data showing that the hours per day is shrinking. This time limitation is almost universal regardless of city size. Half of the supply in rural areas is hand pumped from wells. State agencies are supposed to maintain water supplies including these hand pumps, and often months will go by before a failed facility will be fixed, and as usual, the government's water facilities are seen as inadequate, incompetently managed and corrupt. Most urban dwellers have access to "safe" water, and 75% have access to piped water, but more than half of this piped water is through individual connections. Public sanitation is better, but still only 36% of urban dwellers have access to sewers, 27% to septic tanks, and less than 20% to latrines. In rural/village areas, access to "improved" sanitation is only about 20%.

According to another report, "India experiences more premature deaths due to air pollution than any other country, and New Delhi is one of the ten most polluted cities in the world. Government regulatory laws have been few, and implementation even worse. Even when the government does something, they often do it wrong. Everybody knows that the most serious pollution comes from industrial facilities, but there is not a city in India where waste water treatment is adequate. Presently, only about 10% of waste water is treated, and untreated water enters the underground water sources, much of which ends up as water for residential use. And it is increasingly true that the Indians are recognizing more dangers to health from these environmental problems. Diseases such as nervous, circulatory, cancerous, respiratory, digestive and endocrine afflictions are traced to chemical pollution and have been directly related to specific patterns of industrial development." [18]

CHINESE ENVIRONMENTAL PROBLEMS: THE WORST IN THE WORLD

(Note: much of this material has been taken from the author's book "Reforming the Chinese Government".)

Consider the judgments of official sources and expert opinions [19] both in China and from the outside, about China and the environment:

- Agricultural runoff is "the worst in the world"
- Soil erosion is "the worst in the world"
- Desertification is "the worst in the world"
- Air pollution: China is the world's largest producer of carbon dioxide
- China has 16 of the 20 world's most polluted cities
- China suffers from "the worst river water cessation in the world"
- The Yellow River is the most silt clogged in the world
- China is the world's largest user of coal, the world's largest producer of carbon dioxide, and acid rain falls in one third of the country
- Almost every river in the country is heavily polluted
- 25-40% of all mercury emissions in the world come from China
- Only 20% of waste water is treated
- In the last half century, 332 Chinese dams have failed, including "the worlds worst dam disaster" – the Banqiao and Shimanan dams in Henan Province which collapsed and killed an estimated 80,000 to 200,000 people.

In fact, in every one of these environmental disaster areas, the situation is getting worse and not better.

Economic development in China means breakneck urbanization, heavy concentration on manufacturing, greatly expanded coal fired electrical power generation pollutants, heavy metals dumped into the air, and nasty chemicals dumped into the water. Heavy metals in the water are highly concentrated – 2,000 times as high as the official government standard. Japan and Korea are suffering from acid rain produced by China's coal power electricity plants, and from dust storms carrying toxic dust. Scarce water resources are simply being recklessly dissipated. All of these problems are heavy contributors to environmental failures and crises, and all have been known by the government from the very beginning. The problem of environmental pollution was first addressed at a national conference on the subject in 1973, and six years later, the National People's Congress passed the Environmental Protection Law. Five years after that, in 1984, the National Environmental Protection Agency (NEPA) was formed. In 1998 it was promoted to ministerial level as the State Environmental Protection Administration (SEPA) under the State Council. The law was amended to require environmental impact studies for all major construction projects and for imposing stiff fines for violations. Many environmental groups were started, and public opinion polls were almost unanimous in calling for stricter enforcement.

But despite all of these official efforts, extraordinarily little has ever really been done. Environmental issues seem particularly difficult to resolve in the Chinese political system because of the continuing clash with economic development goals and understandable conflict with local governments over the money problem. So all environmental problems continue to get worse.

The Chinese Communist Party (CCP) has issued its 11th "Five Year Program" in 2005 which calls for a 20% improvement in energy efficiency by 2010. Energy efficiency is very expensive and a highly technical and long term activity, and there seems to be no adequate explanation of how the Chinese could achieve this goal. "Socialist industrialization" was highly wasteful; because land and water were government owned they were given away usually free in the name of economic development, and recklessly squandered. Water and energy have been supplied to favored cities either free or at highly subsidized rates. All governments and most State Owned Enterprises (SOEs) had positive motives to consume assets if it will produce more profit.

Nor is this really a matter of China being a poor country. The government now has large sums of money that it can deploy, but environmental problems continue to be low priority. As in India, the national government has avoided responsibility by delegating responsibility for environmental problems to local governments – provinces, townships, counties and cities. But at the time, all of these jurisdictions were still very poor and seriously disorganized after the Maoist neglect. The commune system displaced much of the normal government apparatus with amateur incompetents, and forced pathological practices on the country. For example, hundreds of thousands of valuable trees were simply cut down to provide fuel for hundreds of thousands of back yard iron smelting furnaces, which were a total failure. It is true that deforestation had been going on for centuries, but the Maoist era simply made it very much worse very fast. Unrealistic production quotas forced overproduction, land wastage, more forest clearing, production of the wrong things, and the wasting of huge sums of scarce funds. Terracing and irrigation were rapidly expanded, often with disastrous consequences. Dams, terraces, reservoirs and cisterns were so poorly built that many quickly collapsed or have been abandoned, since they often served marginal land that had low production potential and high costs. Activities in the hands of collectives have been better, but still amateurish and exposing low managerial abilities. Beijing has reacted typically: the government kept announcing bold new "30 Year Plans", but everybody knew that local governments have never had the money to implement them. In fact, there has never had a sufficiently sturdy source of funds for environmental problems, and the national government has never had any intention of filling the gap. The CCP likes to point out that it is "spending more than $10 billion on environmental concerns", which is a truly pitiful trivial sum. China's environmental problems stem as much from its corrupt and indifferent political system as from Beijing's continued focus on economic growth. Local officials and enterprise leaders routinely – and with impunity – ignore environmental laws and regulations, illegally reallocate environmental protection funds or simply steal them. [20]

In case after case, huge environmental problems have been documented, but this simply highlights the real issue: nobody in China seems capable or willing to deal with the enormity of these problems. Instead, the government continues to issue bland political promises, Five Year Plans, Thirty Year Plans, and new laws and regulations, and to criticize local governments because they have not yet "solved" the problems. These plans and pronouncements are political cover for the fact that governments choose to provide only pitifully inadequate funding. All of this is deliberate. The CCP fully recognizes the heart of their dilemma: environmental problems are enormously costly, and they are heavy potential counter demands against the dominant policy of spending on economic development which is at the heart of the CCP's survival strategy. Local governments feel that they have been unfairly stuck with these problems with absolutely no help from anybody else. The SOEs were never involved. The private sector doesn't want the added expense or the responsibility. The whole manufacturing sector of the economy is still highly inefficient. Many SOEs have long histories of running at a deficit and having to be propped up by the government. Many private enterprises are running on very thin profit margins and maintain that they can't afford any more expensive responsibilities. There are too many competitors struggling to stay alive, and they often feel they have to conceal their real situation from the government.

Many environmental problems are ancient: floods, droughts, overgrazing, desertification, soil erosion, mining wastes. But there are also new problems that are a direct consequence of the economic development programs such as hundreds of thousands of new industrial sites dumping pollutants into the air or water; millions of new automobiles; accelerating exhaustion of water resources; and wastage of energy and raw materials. Over expansion of cities has created rapidly growing urban problems. Lack of raw materials and energy tends to drive up prices. While China's government benefits greatly from foreign sales, it has not yet made satisfactory progress in meeting the consumer needs of its own people.

The success of economic development is vital to the survival of the CCP itself, and this cannot and will not be changed any time soon. Economic development has been the compelling and overpowering driver in China for almost 35 years. Because of this, China will not stop burning coal and creating acid rain. It will not willingly close industrial plants that pollute the air unless there is the risk of fatal political disaster. The CCP will not reverse its policy of dumping environmental problems on local governments, nor will it fund these governments. Neither the CCP nor anybody else has any idea of what to do about desertification, soil erosion and river silting, and even if they did, these problems are so enormous and complex that they are simply "mission impossible". Urban air pollution is not being dealt with, and in fact, is getting worse every day, and in more cities and lung diseases now kill more people than any other cause. The depletion of urban underground water aquifers is permanent and irreversible, and the exhaustion of these resources is speeding up. Urban expansion requires more water resources, urban sanitation, waste water treatment and other public services. It also means the rise in the number of households, millions of urban transportation trips, huge truck traffic to bring in supplies, vastly increased oil and gas consumption, and heavy and unremitting construction activity.

Most of the older industrial base and energy production facilities, and even the newer manufacturing plants were designed and built with absolutely no thought to their environmental impact. Many are highly inefficient, environmental issues aside. Most are energy guzzlers, using 8 to 10 times the energy per unit of output compared to that of modern plants elsewhere. In other words, "fixing" the environmental problems of SOEs is a monumental problem embedded in an even more monumental problem of upgrading the SOEs themselves. SOEs, which were the great bulk of industrial production through the early 90s, were never even permitted to deal with environmental concerns because of the potential costs; the government recognized that up to 50% of SOEs were operating at a deficit, and many others were economically marginal. Few could bear the additional costs of environmental protection. In fact, the government often subsidized these SOEs not only with money, but with free water, free land and highly subsidized energy. As a result, the industrial and energy sectors of the economy were highly wasteful and polluting, and environmentally ignorant.

Much of what is now being developed such as farming, pulp and paper mills, coal mining, chemical factories, tanning and dyeing plants, small scale manufacturing are high polluting enterprises, and their runoffs are going untreated into rivers and streams, and their solid waste is forming new mountains. There are hundreds of thousands of these little operations, mostly township/village enterprises (TVEs) run by government people or government sponsored collectives, and many of them are only marginally profitable. What is the prospect of fighting through local political resistance and getting all of these little marginal enterprises to clean up their act? It is nonsense to expect local governments to tackle more than local problems, and most of the worst problems are countrywide in scale, begging for national solutions. Every river basin encompasses dozens of provinces, counties and cities. Air pollution not only effects all 600 of the largest cities but has "fallout" consequences in Japan, the Koreas and even the United States and Canada. Farming takes place in every province, but if there is a solution for desertification and land silting and chemical runoffs, it will have to be paid for by eastern cities. Policing of hundreds of thousands of polluting factories cannot be left to the varying capacities of more than 700,000 local political jurisdictions.

THE MOST DESPERATE CRISIS: WATER

The enormity of the problems can best be illustrated by the almost desperate future China faces over water resources. ([21] For example:

- Two thirds of the water in underground aquifers in the 118 major cities is "severely polluted".
- 75% of all lakes and about half of the rivers are heavily polluted, in some cases, so badly that the water can't even be used for farming or industrial purposes.
- Only 20% of waste water, both rural and urban is treated (compared to 80% in developed countries).
- Water supply is already very low on a per capita basis – about 25% of the world average
- Those underground aquifers in cities are not only being polluted, but they are being exhausted. Almost every city in China faces an increasingly ominous future about the adequacy of its water supply. In some coastal cities, when underground aquifers are drawn down, they may be penetrated by seawater pollution which is permanent and irreversible.

- Water usage is highly inefficient. Irrigation consumes two thirds of China's water resources, and more than half of this water is wasted by terracing, faulty irrigation systems and poor water management. In addition, irrigation has produced high levels of salinity in more than 10% of all land.

Industrial plants have never been asked to be water efficient. And as a consequence, the unit cost of water is 15 times higher than in developed countries, 25 times higher than in Japan, and higher even than in India and Pakistan. Chinese factories use ten times more water than most developed countries to produce the same products, and Chinese irrigation uses twice as much. By contrast, the growth in the U. S. economy has been achieved largely without increasing water use.

The Chinese government certainly knows about these threats but has essentially chosen to ignore them until very recently. Even where the government is now acting, it is not certain that they will succeed. Take the case of the Yellow River, one of the two most important in China. "The Yellow River began to run dry at some times as early as 1985. Now, each year, it gets worse. In 1997, it ran out of water 600 miles short of the sea, for 9 months. In 2001 it had dried up again before reaching the sea – the 4th time in 10 years. The tributary Fen River is dry all year, except for a few weeks. The Yellow River valley contains 130 million people, and in total, a half a billion people depend on it for water and crop irrigation. As the rivers have dried up, people have had to go miles away from home to get drinking water from some neighboring town. This appears to be one of those big problems that never seem to be recognized by any government. There are many dams, and they displaced hundreds of thousands of residents, but 27 new dams are planned. In many cases, when populations are displaced, the government promises to take care of the displaced people, but then does so inadequately or not at all. And engineers agree that the Yellow River problems have yet to reach their peak. The CCP resisted these warnings for more than 40 years well into the 90s, and their policy did not begin to shift until the end of the decade. On the upper reaches of the river, lakes are disappearing and in the middle portion, irrigation canals are running dry, fields are lost, desert areas are growing, wind storms are common and cover vast areas of China, Japan and S. Korea. In Shandong on the river delta, more than half of the water for irrigation is now drawn from underground sources but these are being drained for urban use twice as fast as the river and rainwater are replacing it. [22] The Yangtze River, China's most important, is 60% polluted, including water from feeder rivers and its soil discharge exceeds the Nile and the Amazon combined. The slogan "when the Yellow River runs clear" has the same connotation as "when Hell freezes over".

The Chinese government is developing what is called the "South to North Transfer Project" which proposes to set up three transfer routes from the Yangtze River in the south to the Yellow River in the north. One transfer route is near the end of both rivers, where an existing reservoir will be enlarged and a 200 foot wide channel will be dug. The second route will be from Shandong to Tianjin. The third will be near the headwaters of both rivers where a 65 mile tunnel will be dug. But this whole scheme has a certain fantasy quality about it. It would take almost unthinkable amounts of money (about $16 billion has already been committed) and long periods of time for activation, and it is not yet been made clear how more water would solve the pollution problems that are the major dilemma. The main objective of the project seems to be to solve the water shortages in Beijing, but it is difficult not to conclude that the grand scheme is not likely to be a serious solution to anything.

PROTECTING THE LAND

The environmental problems stemming from China's land are as ancient and intractable as those of the waters. For hundreds of years, Chinese farmers had been farming the land in ways that produced a long term balance, but China has never had enough land to grow enough food, and Mao pushed farming to the limits by relying too heavily on destructive terracing of hillsides and excessive crop irrigation systems, especially for rice. Thus, whatever balance existed has been shattered in modern times. China's population has more than doubled in the Communist era despite the one child policy and this has created a genuine government urgency (i. e. panic) to increase production of food. Second, new farming technology created exactly this potential and the government thought/hoped to get it adopted.

Third, industrialization began to compete for land and water, especially in areas next to cities. The "socialist" nature of this industrialization was such that it was very wasteful and low efficiency and thus offered no incentive to conserve or to be efficient. Resources such as timber, coal, other minerals, and water were ruthlessly exploited, and have left the country with the serious consequences of this waste. A lot of the pollution in the past was caused by SOEs and collectives, all of which saw themselves as excused from environmental responsibilities, and since so many of them were loss making, the political leadership has been reluctant to increase their expenses. This discouraging situation has not developed because of a lack of agencies, laws, or regulations. On the contrary, China has a reasonably complete set of environmental protection laws and regulations and a fully articulated structure of government offices devoted to environmental matters, whose principal role is to maintain a façade of credibility.

China's provinces, towns, and villages have attempted to deal, however ineffectively, with these ancient land and water problems, but they can no longer cope with their escalation, and most are facing grim environmental futures. But local governments might still produce some limited solutions in the use and conservation of land because they are the creators of most problems. One third of Chinese land suffers from serious soil erosion, but provinces can, if they have the will, begin to prevent excessive terracing, and help farmers develop other land preservation techniques. Erosion is not just bad – it ranks among the worst in the world. Deforestation contributes heavily to erosion and it is losing huge areas of land to desertification; one quarter of China is now desert. Land losses reduce food production capacity just when it is most needed. Droughts seem to be getting worse; they used to occur every few years, but now occur almost every year. Irrigation is hugely wasteful of water, and it is now producing extensive salinity and pollution through runoffs of fertilizers and pesticides. Further losses of land stem from overgrazing, and the new modern threat – usurpation of farm land for urban and industrial expansion. Local governments at all levels are harsh exploiters of land which can be leased for economic development which produces major revenues, and they have little compunction about stealing land from farmers and ignoring the growing threats from environmental degradation.

DANGER IN THE AIR

The most "modern" of China's environmental disasters is in the air. The amounts of dangerous chemicals pumped into the air are now staggering. China is now the world's largest producer of carbon dioxide. Air pollution also includes excessive and illegal levels of sulphur dioxide, chlorofleurocarbons, smoke, dust and soil. Even the government's own State Environmental Protection Administration (SEPA) admits that this is true, and that air pollution is getting worse, not better. It is typical that the Chinese government has a full array of nicely drafted laws and regulations "controlling" air pollution, and there are standards setting limits for every form of emission. But two thirds of China's cities that have been tested cannot meet these standards, or similar standards set by the World Health Organization. Nor does anybody seem to have a clue how this pollution can be brought under control. On the contrary, the whole vast tide of industrialization and urbanization is guaranteed to make matters very much worse very fast. One needs only to think about the millions of new automobiles and trucks and airplanes, and the development of an additional 562 new coal fired power plants, and the addition of many thousands of new or expanded industrial facilities to realize what is making air pollution worse.

Finally, and most typically, these environmental disasters pose ever increasing threats to the health of China's citizens. An estimated 190 million Chinese have had illnesses connected with drinking contaminated water. Cities and villages alike have suffered from repeated epidemics of diarrhea, and heightened rates of cancer, tumors, poisoning from lead, mercury and other heavy metals. Air pollution alone is said to have been the cause of up to 300,000 deaths. Once again, China's record is worse than any other country on earth. Beijing has six times higher air pollution rates than New York. Past dust storms are so persistent and severe that many people in cities wear face masks against dust and chemicals. There are huge worker time losses from lung diseases, blood infections, heart diseases, strokes and diabetes. There are about 24 million cars today, but in 20 years there may be upwards of 100 million, most of them in already choked cities. 60-90% of rain in Guandong province is acid rain, and farmland losses would equal the farm land in Britain, Germany and France combined.

MISSION IMPOSSIBLE

One gets the increasing sense that environmental problems in total are mission impossible. Past sins are so grievous that they have put China in a massive hole. It would take the bulk of national resources to cure these past sins, much less improve the current situation. The CCP is simultaneously urging local governments to clean up the world, but at the same it continues to pressing forward at the maximum possible speed on economic development, creating hundreds of thousands of new pollution sources. The development of the 562 new coal powered plants is a classic case in point. Domestic coal is far cheaper than imported oil so environmental concerns are problems that will be handled by lip service and "correct" political rhetoric. But the economics of environmental losses may finally force them to change their policy. Even if this does happen, the situation remains the same – the gap is so enormous that it can't possibly be closed in the short run. So China will suffer for decades. Meanwhile, quietly, China has become the largest recipient of World Bank loans for environmental work, and the World Bank officially supports the huge Three Gorges Dam project despite its environmental threats, and in fact, has funded one of the upstream dams.

Overall, the economic consequences of China's air and water pollution have been estimated at 3-8% of GDP a year which approximates the highly touted growth rate of the whole economy. Great floods in 1996 were not only human disasters but cost $25 billion in damages, and the 1998 floods were even worse, impacting 240 million people and causing $70 billion in damages. Acid rain is said to cost $700 to 800 million each year, and air pollution an additional $55 billion per year.

China is the world's largest user of coal for all purposes – one third of world consumption. Between 1978 and 1995, cities swelled by 180 million approved citizens, plus some 50 million unregistered migrants from the countryside. In small communities, lack of power has forced the use of hundreds of thousands of small inefficient industrial/commercial boilers and generators which account for one-third to one-half of emissions. Coal still produces 75% of all residential energy. Beijing has about 10% of the numbers of cars as in Los Angeles but the emissions are about the same. Congenital obstructive pulmonary disease (COPD) is the leading cause of death in China, and it is five times more frequent than in the U. S. Recent increases in the price of oil have simply confirmed the government's faith in reliance on coal. The idea of a coal tax to constrain demand is stoutly resisted, since many coal users have no other options. World Bank reports describe many technological or managerial improvements that could be made, but they sound hollow, since all of them would take decades to disseminate very widely, and all would be extremely costly. The government likes to claim credit for closing down hundreds of thousands of small TVE establishments, but most of them were doomed anyway because they were so inefficient and amateurish. Besides, some of them competed with SOEs.

The medical insurance system covers less than 50% of the official urban population and less than 10% of the rural/small town population. Private spending on health care is the main source of funding – at least double that of public spending. But the costs of medical care are rapidly escalating and hundreds of millions of citizens simply do not have the money. Any serious health problems mean either no treatment or bankruptcy. The number of HIV infected exceeds the UN criteria for a "generalized epidemic", and the health care system can't cope. The health care system has almost no capacity to deal with such serious problems stemming from environmental problems as nervous system disorders, heart disease, stroke, diabetes, or lung disease. Only 44% of the population has even rudimentary sanitary facilities, and fresh water is not available to 23% of the population. Preventative medicine is very rudimentary, and there are huge economic losses from worker medical and health problems such as heart disease, stroke and diabetes. And China is the world's largest consumer of tobacco products, with 320 million smokers.

Political leaders have learned to say the right things and lots of laws and regulations have been issued, but funds are scarce, and enterprises still bribe officials to look the other way. Environmental laws are seldom really enforced, and everybody knows it. There is a famous old Chinese saying: "The mountains are high and the Emperor is far away."

But the disasters are building. Shanghai is in many respects modern China in miniature. Consider this example: in the late 90s, the river basin northwest of Shanghai, which contains 110 million people, suffered from a further massive pollution of an already polluted river. "Hundreds of thousands of people were left without drinking water, several thousand were treated for dysentery, diarrhea, and vomiting, and 26 million pounds of fish were killed." Pollution came from 1,000 factories: paper factories, leather, cloth dyeing, many more. Most were TVEs; most workers were migrants and moonlighters at slave wages. While the government forces the closure of these small business plants (60,000 in 1999), the larger SOEs are left alone. And still Shanghai continues to grow.

CHAPTER VIII

Military Capabilities

· 〰〰 ·

THE INDIAN MILITARY

THE GREAT OPPONENT OF THE Indian military is seen as Pakistan, and conflict with the Pakistani army is constant, ranging from small border insults to threats of nuclear holocaust. India and Pakistan have been in major conflict with each other over Kashmir for almost 60 years. Wars were fought in 1948 and 1965, and again in 1971 when India supported East Pakistan with both diplomatic and military assistance against Pakistan, to help it become Bangladesh. India is still fighting three anti-terrorist wars: in Kashmir; against the Maoist Naxalites in north east India; and against rebel groups in Assam supported by Pakistan and Bangladesh. In November, a large, well organized group of terrorists attacked targets in Mumbai killing many, destroying property, and terrorizing the population. India is convinced that this attack was sponsored and supported by the Pakistani Inter- Services Intelligence Agency (ISI), and it once again seriously damaged some hopeful peace negotiations at the time and is regarded as a mortal insult that will not soon be forgotten. The great fear for the future seems to be China, and the more the Chinese rattle their sabers, the more hysterical the Indians become. But one of the dominating problems which the Indians are reluctant to discuss is the fact that they have never been able to develop a satisfactory "military/industrial complex" and they are heavily dependent on the Russians, the Americans and others to provide them with modern weapons. In the last analysis, India's strategy seems mostly internal and defensive, and it is hard to see its military as ominous or threatening. India's political and military preoccupation continues to be Pakistan, and this relationship has made little sense for 60 years. All other foreign players – Russia, China, the U. S. and even Japan – are first and foremost measured by their relationship with Pakistan, and then, collaterally, with India itself. It is a game which nobody seems to know how to play, and each has its own set of rules.

India's strategic situation makes it hard to conceive of a major land based conflict with China over the mountain barriers that separate them. First of all, it is hard to conceive why China would ever consider invasion at all. Second, the mountains make such an invasion very difficult, with impossible supply lines, and terrain relatively easy to defend. An option for invasion might be for China to come through Pakistan, but this would be impossible if Pakistan were not an ally. Even if it were, the first point still applies – what could China hope to achieve even with a successful invasion of India? The same realities apply in reverse for India versus China and Pakistan. It is also probably true that the deterioration of Pakistan and its own internal conflicts have substantially reduced the likelihood of any serious offensive against India. In the end, offensives by the land forces of all three countries are marginalized, and their main roles are defensive and internal. In addition, the international community would bring enormous pressure against all three countries if insanity threatened to take over.

INDIAN MINISTRY OF DEFENSE

Responsibility for national defense lies with the Cabinet Committee for Political Affairs, chaired by the Prime Minister. India's military command has no joint defense staff or unified command apparatus. The Minister of Defense and the ministry staff provide management and operational control over the three main services. [1] There are important inter service organizations such as the Services Headquarters, Production Establishments, and R & D organizations—plus a Finance Division. A major study in 2000 resulted in recommendations – being implemented – to establish a Defense Procurement Board, a Defense Intelligence Agency, the National Defense University, a Strategic Forces Command, and an integrated headquarters in the Ministry of Defense. To enhance military planning, the Ministry of Defense (MOD) has created the Defense Coordination and Implementation Committee, and the Defense Planning Staff. All of these steps seem highly desirable, but what one wonders is why they have been so long in coming. 1

The Union Ministry of Home Affairs controls the nationwide Indian Police Service, most of the paramilitary forces, and the internal intelligence bureaus. It includes the Central Bureau of Investigation (reporting to the Dept. of Personnel), the Central Industrial Security Force, and the Indo-Tibetan Border Police. The separatist insurgencies, drug interdiction problems, and community unrest have led to a stronger role for paramilitary forces under the direction of the Home Ministry. Unfortunately, these paramilitary forces have a bad reputation for civil rights abuses. Each State has its own police force, reporting to a Director General (Police), and State forces are provided in the districts. The prison system is entirely State operated.

A Department of Defense Production was set up in 1962 after the disastrous war with China to shape up all defense procurement, and it was later merged with the Department of Defense Supplies in 1984. The basic policy is to move almost completely to domestic production of all needs. Presently 39 ordnance factories and 8 Defense Production Service Units (DPSUs) are in operation, but much is purchased from civilian suppliers. The Ordnance Factories (OF) are government owned and run by the Ministry of Defense. They produce ammunition, explosives, weapons, vehicles both regular and armored, and other ordnance equipment and maintenance. The 8 DPSUs are: Hindustan Aeronautics Ltd.; Bharat Electronics; Bharat Earth Movers; Mazagon Dock Ltd.; Garden Reach Shipbuilders and Engineers Ltd.; Boa Shipyard Ltd.; Bharat Dynamics Ltd.; Mishra Dhatu Nigam Ltd.

In the mid-1980s, the government established a Defense Research and Development Organization (DRDO) as an umbrella agency to exercise control over which weapons requested by the military services would actually be procured, including the decision to import as an alternative to domestic Indian development and manufacture. DRDO strongly favors local production vs. import since the government has long favored a general import substitution policy. But the DRDO record has been miserable. It still seems that Indian government owned producers lack the necessary technical and managerial skills to produce sophisticated weapons systems, and DRDO has produced a series of embarrassing failures. It has yet to produce an aircraft acceptable to the Indian Air Force. A locally produce Arjun tank is obviously inferior to Russian supplied T-72 and T-90 tanks. The highly touted guided missile program seems to have fizzled. The Prithvi which is in service, has a range of only 150 km and is liquid fueled. The larger Agni-II with a range of 2000 km has never been produced in quantity. DRDO itself is seen as poor planners, unable to control either time delays, almost inevitable cost overruns or long term, huge, and ubiquitous corruption. It is seen as too easily swayed by political pressure that favors locally produced weapons systems, whether they work or not.

The government has only recently begun to urge the private sector into the armaments market, presumably to try and split the costs, but so far, the private sector has been permitted only marginal participation through the provision of raw materials, semi-finished parts, components, services and some maintenance, which means that they contribute little to more sophisticated weapons systems R & D. FDI in any defense activity is limited to 26%. It also seems obvious that the failures of government producers has finally led to the admission that the private sector must be admitted to a broader range of procurement, hoping that they will do better.

The size of the budget is difficult to assess. The official military budget excludes military pensions (15% of actual total outlay), the Coast Guard, the nuclear weapons arsenal, and the huge paramilitary forces. All things considered including PPP calculations, the military budget is about $100 billion. [2] The terrorist attacks on Mumbai in 2008, also terrorized the political parties who had been very sluggish about the cost of modernization, and as a result, the military asked for and got a 34% increase in its main operating funds for 2009. India is the second largest weapons importer after the Chinese, which is a reflection not only of the desire to upgrade equipment, but also the inability to produce high technology weaponry domestically. Recent purchases of new items include the Adm. Gorshkov aircraft carrier purchased from the Russians, plus another new carrier now being built by a Russian shipyard. India is also purchasing new MIG 29s, Mirage fighters, Hawk trainers, submarines, multiple unit rocket launchers, light helicopters, long range artillery, plane-based radar, and it has increased funding for R & D. Funds are also included in the budget for the start of deployment of short range 700 km. Agni-I surface-to-surface missiles, and the intermediate range 2,000 km. Agni-II missiles. The Army is also seeking development of a "weapon locating "radar. The military is also seeking new "anti- terrorism" weapons – whatever that means. One of the most significant ways to redirect military expenditures would be to do what the Chinese did: radically cut back on the very large numbers of infantry troops and reinvest the money saved into high technology weaponry. This is especially true because, as a result of a recent Sixth Pay Commission report, major increases in pay, benefits and pensions will add large sums to an already tight budget. India can scarcely afford its very large standing army and paramilitary forces, but it seems extremely hard to reduce units with such grand traditions.

The Iraq war proved to be a great surprise to military planners and procurement officials because it demonstrated the great superiority of U. S. vs. Russian weapons systems which are heavily relied upon in the Indian armed forces. There is a growing feeling that scarce military funds will be better spent on U. S. and other western country weaponry. This fits in with other tides running in Indian foreign affairs – the decline of the Soviet Union as a potential ally, the surge of concern over the rise of China and its military modernization program, the decline of Pakistan, and the fact that the "on again, off again" relationship with the United States seems again to be "on". This is especially true because the Indian R & D community which was supposed to key the development of Indian domestic weapons development capability seems to have promised much, but delivered little. Soviet weapons systems were often disappointing, lacking promised performance and often proving to be of poor quality and reliability. Many Soviet suppliers have gone out of business and been replaced with post Soviet owners and managers, but some sources of replacement and repair parts have been lost, and it seems hard for Indian enterprises to fill these gaps. But still, the major purchases remain heavily oriented toward Russian sources which are said still to supply almost 70% of India's military hardware.

THE INDIAN ARMY

The Indian Army numbers over 1.4 million troops on active service plus 1.8 million reserve troops, making it the second largest standing army in the world and it is almost all volunteer and has long been able to maintain a large number of permanent long serving troops as its core. [3] But pay is low, morale is often poor, discipline is often weak, and there is a growing pattern of accusations of corruption. It also seems true that fewer young men are enlisting, more are opting out, and even appointments to the Indian Military Academy are less sought. But still, the government is attempting to find ways to modernize Army weaponry. Indian armored units, which have performed well against the Pakistan Army are being beefed up with the purchase of more than 1,600 new T-90 main battle tanks from Russian sources, along with more than 4,000 Milan 2T anti-tank guided missiles. It has been involved in four wars with Pakistan (1947, 1965, 1971, and 1999) of which it can be said to have won three. It has fought one war against the Chinese in 1962, which was a military disaster, and led to a new emphasis on military modernization that is still progressing slowly. It usually fields about 36 divisions, 97 armored regiments with more than 5,000 main battle tanks, 3,200 artillery pieces, 1,500 aircraft, and more than 2,000 battle field ballistic missiles. The Chinese realized, in the post Maoist period that its huge army was far larger – and far more expensive – than the country needed or could support, and it has spent 25 years reducing the size of its standing army and re-equipping the remaining forces. It is felt that perhaps India is facing the same problems, and they it may need to decide to trim back its standing forces, so that the money saved could be used to finance modernization. As with the other services, most of the Army's weapons are imported, but there are more small arms and ammunition being produced domestically.

THE INDIAN NAVY

It may well be that the most important service in the Indian military is not the Army, with its huge forces and glorious traditions, but the Navy, because it has a series of contemporary missions to perform, and more flexibility in its deployment. It would be the first line of defense if any country attempted either invasion or attack against the homeland. It would be the only feasible weapon of offense against another county if needed. It can and will play a critical role in either blockading or keeping open vital shipping lanes in the whole of Southeast Asia. And it has already established a solid record of offering help to other nations in the area such as its excellent record against Indian Ocean pirates operating out of East Africa.

The Indian Navy currently has about 65,000 personnel on active duty, and that makes it the fifth largest navy in the world in terms of personnel. It has about 150 ships, including one aircraft carrier, 8 destroyers, 15 submarines, 37 frigates and corvettes, and about 250 aircraft of all kinds. It operates mainly out of three naval bases at Goa and Karwar on the west coast about 400 miles south of Mumbai, and at Visakapatnam on the east coast about 400 miles north of Chennai.

The Indian Navy has always had one aircraft carrier in service starting with one purchased from the British in 1963 and running thru three replacements or retrofits. The current INS Vikrant has been in service since 1987, and is due for retirement in 2012 – but may be kept in some adapted role. But in direct response to constant Chinese rumblings about building a carrier, the Indians have done two things:

1. They purchased the aircraft carrier Adm. Gorshkov from Russia and it is currently being refitted in India for service "soon" (this is a valuable learning process for Indian technicians)
2. They signed a contract in 2005 for design and construction of an entirely new modern carrier which is being built by the Russians.

When these actions are completed, India will have two and possibly three carriers in operation and they will be the only carriers possessed by any Asian nation. The key to the military balance of power in S. E. Asia will then lie with the ability of the Indian Navy to operate three powerful aircraft carrier groups carrying the best military aircraft in the region, and contracts have been signed for purchase of 16 more MiG 29s, and there are apparently plans for purchase of an additional 29. This is very important; it represents the kind of force projection that the Chinese do not have. The capacity of the Indian Navy to disrupt supply lines and blockade the ports of other countries is very great, and could be devastating. The Navy has 8 destroyers, 13 frigates and 24 corvettes which are capable of independent operations but are critical as the carrier escort vessels in aircraft carrier groups.

The Indian Navy has 16 submarines only one of which is nuclear powered– but at any given time only about 6 are operational. They are diesel powered and obsolete by international standards. Half of these subs are approaching 22-23 years old, with a supposed life cycle of 30 years. General plans seem to be to start to replace these at the rate of 2 per year, and six are already scheduled, but it not certain that this schedule can be maintained. Training, refitting, maintenance and upgrading capabilities all seem very limited and difficult. India keeps saying that it wants to be self sufficient in weapons systems production, but in fact they seem technically to be another generation away, and meanwhile it keeps buying ships from the Russians, with more frigates and submarines to be purchased soon. In fact, one of the Navy's most serious problems is the talent shortage, both in the service and in its supporting military industrial complex. The Navy has been very dependent on military state owned enterprises because of long standing government policy of import substitution, and the domestic private sector has been largely excluded from the more technologically sophisticated systems. [4]

This may change. India is trying to build up its skill base, the Russians are increasingly reluctant to supply its top level technology, and the U. S. and other countries such as France, Israel, Japan and Brazil are ready to step into any gap, and appear more willing to share their technology knowledge.

THE INDIAN AIR FORCE

India's air force is the world's fourth largest with about 170,000 personnel and over 1,300 aircraft, including over 600 combat aircraft and more than 500 transports and helicopters operating out of more than 60 airbases around the country. [5] Its newest plane is the multi-role Sukhoi 30 which are obtained from Russia, and are capable of delivering strategic weapons. It now also operates a large number of MIG 29s and Dassault Mirage 2000 aircraft which have advanced electronics permitting night operation. MIG 27 aircraft are deployed for ground attack and ground support missions. The air force has many older MIG 21s which it wants to replace with a domestically produced light combat aircraft. Hindustan Aeronautics Ltd. (HAL) is major domestic aircraft manufacturer and it currently produces many of the Russian aircraft in India under license. It also produces several helicopters, and is designing the HAL Tejas domestically as the replacement for the obsolete MiG 21s.

The Indian Air Force is also responsible for the defense of the country against air attack, and it is moving to upgrade its land- based detection electronics and its ground to air missile systems, including the use of mobile missile trailers. It is also deploying three of the Phalcon Airborne Earl Warning radar system obtained from Israel Aerospace Industries considered among the best in the world. The Air Force also operates a large number of transport aircraft which gives it superior airlift capability.

PARAMILITARY FORCES OF INDIA

The military capability of India is supported by an extraordinary complex of police and semi-military organizations grouped under the general heading of the Paramilitary Forces of India. [6] The first and most important level of such forces are the Central Police Organizations which function as a national police force dealing with a whole range of law enforcement matters ranging from insurrections to parades. These organizations include the State Armed Police, which is a highly mobile and well armed force of more than 450,000 troops, and functions independent of the military, reporting to civilian bosses. It is supported and reinforced by the Central Reserve Police Force (CRPF) which is a volunteer force with more than 300,000 active members, plus a Home Guard and Civil Defense forces with almost one million more members. The Central Reserve Police Force also maintains a Rapid Action Force and the Anti-Riot Police to deal with particularly violent threats, and a new 10,000 man Rapid Action Battalion for Resolute Action (COBRA) has been formed under the CRPF specifically to deal with the Naxalite Maoist insurgents in northeast India.

Unfortunately, the police in India have a very bad reputation. According to an editorial in the Economic and Political Weekly of India "Indians view the police, the most visible arm of the State, with distrust and fear and consider it one of the most corrupt of the government agencies. It has the powers to detain and arrest citizens, and verify documents essential for citizen services. And as custodial deaths and rapes show, it is not uncommon for the police itself to break the law and even violate basic human rights. In the last 30+ years, there have been at least eight major assessments by the National Police Commission promising major reforms, but little has really happened. Changing the police's image as the pliable instrument of the rich and powerful will require a complete overhaul of the colonial mindset that colours its attitude towards the ordinary citizen."

At a next level are the Central Paramilitary Forces which are linked more closely with the Indian Army, and during wartime, would serve directly under the armed forces chain of command. It includes such units as the Coast Guard, the Border Security Force, the Central Industrial Security Force, the Tibetan Border Police, and many other special purpose units. The total population of all of these units exceeds 8.7 million troops. All of these organizations are headed by a senior Indian Police Service Officer apparently to provide some coherent leadership to a very complex array of military and police establishments, which are hugely expensive.

CHINA: THE PEOPLE'S LIBERATION ARMY

The People's Liberation Army (PLA) holds a special place of honor in China as its liberator, its protector, the stalwart defender of the Chinese Communist Party (CCP) and the guardian of the Revolution. Despite this honored position, the PLA has suffered from a strangely rocky history of alternating support and neglect, and has spent the last 20 years attempting to recoup its position from the mistakes of it's past. It was both neglected and ill-used for 20 years by the Maoist regime. It's strategies were muddled, its equipment obsolete, its funding has been uncertain, its officer corps is underpaid and under trained, and its troops are a non-professional transient population. In the 80s it was authorized to create or acquire state owned enterprises (SOEs) and other businesses in the hope that it could largely finance itself and save the political leadership from the necessity of raising more taxes. This policy was a disaster for both the PLA and the Chinese economy from which both are still laboriously recovering.

Military affairs are naturally highly political, and they are under the direction of the Central Military Commission (CMC), an extraordinarily powerful body that is chaired by the CCP General Secretary, who is also the head of the CCP and formal leader of the government and the country. The CMC has three vice chairmen, one of whom is the prime minister, plus seven other members who are the most senior military officers. It has four general departments: General Staff, Logistics, Armaments, and Political Affairs. The country is divided into 7 Regional Military Districts, and the PLA itself has five field Commands: Army (PLA), Navy (PLAN), Air Force (PLAAF), the Second Artillery (which is the nuclear missile command), and the Peoples Armed Police (PAP), which is officially under the dual command of the State Council and the CMC, but is generally considered to be an integral part of the military establishment.

The strategic thinking of the CMC and the PLA is almost entirely defensive except for Taiwan. Its major stated policies are first and foremost to defend the CCP, then to defend industrial centers, defend the capitol of Beijing, guard the borders and potential avenues of attack, protect key elements such as transport routes, lines of communication, harbors, and power sources; and to secure key locations providing internal security. None of these policies specifically emphasize the defense of the Chinese people. The authority of the PLA is wide open and its role is defined at any given time by the views of the political leadership. It is pursuing several major modernization programs: reduction in troop numbers, creation of medium and long range missile capability, an expanded and updated Air Force and Navy, creation of "multi- role" military units with rapid deployment capability, an upgraded command/field communications network, and an air defense system, and a coastal defense capability with naval and shore forces. But troop concentrations seem not to have changed much in 20 years and they are still deployed opposite Taiwan, along the Russian border, and in Tibet and Xinjiang.

As with so much else in the modern history of the Chinese, the death of Mao in 1976 broke the pattern of neglect and stagnation and permitted the CCP leadership to initiate a long, complex and multi-faceted reform of the PLA which, 30 years later, is still under way. Essentially three major arenas of reform were therefore considered vital:

First, the whole military establishment had to be "downsized" on a grand scale in terms of personnel, and its organizational structure had to be simplified and made more efficient and productive. It had to get rid of old obsolete types of forces, mainly massive ground units, so that it could afford new units more relevant to the nature of modern warfare.

Second, every aspect of PLA operations had to be modernized from new field communications, to weapons systems design and acquisition, to logistics, supply and transport and even to financial responsibility and control. An important policy was enunciated by Deng Xiaoping in 1985: the military should concentrate on modernization through R & D; but it was not necessary to then manufacture new weapons unless the actual military situation requires them. This is the same pattern that makes sense in the U. S. since R & D is relatively cheap, and manufacture is very expensive, especially with technologies that tend to become obsolete quickly. The difference for China is that, in many disciplines, Chinese education and technological development had never really developed, and this limits the skills available for military upgrades.

Third, the government made a decision about 1985 that probably seemed smart at the time, but which ultimately proved to be a disaster. The PLA was authorized to enter into business in a big way to create or acquire state owned enterprises (SOE) and other businesses. The political reasoning at the time was that the central government budget could not afford both the PLA and funds for economic development, so the PLA was largely cut loose to finance itself. The basic intent of authorizing PLA business activities was very quickly perverted. At its peak, the PLA controlled 30,000

SOEs employing 3 million workers. There was almost no accounting for either income or expenditure, and these commercial operations were a serious cause of corruption, including the diversion of military assets (such as trucks, fuel, food and labor) to its businesses. In many cases such as electronics or certain minerals, the PLA enterprises dominated whole sectors of the economy. The whole complex structure continues to suffer from the usual sins of corruption, patronage and incompetence, and it is likely that any development of major weapons systems, will take 12-15 years to complete, even if it is pursued steadily and not interrupted with funding shortages or political changes of mind. Only in the 90's did the Chinese appear to discover systems management and competitive bidding, and it is not clear how far they have advanced.

Despite years of hand wringing, it was not until 1999 that the political leadership finally got serious about this elaborate mess. The point had been reached where both the military and the political leadership realized that this PLA commercial activity was a failure. The essence of the agreement that emerged was that the government promised to substitute regular appropriated funds for the loss of SOE revenues, and the newly acquired wealth from the market economy made it feasible to promise the PLA adequate funding for the future. The PLA leadership recognized this was a good face saver, since most of its SOEs were operating at a loss, despite their subsidies. Therefore they could dump the failed commercial enterprises, return their officers to military roles, clean up much of the corruption, and assure a reasonable flow of funds for modernization. So the deal was struck.

But it is clear from subsequent events that the PLA and the rest of the government never really got out of the enterprise game. At present, it appears that there are still about 10,000 enterprises employing 700,000 workers under PLA control. There are about 2000 SOEs that are genuinely defense related, but there remain many others that are for mixed military/ civilian production. For example, the Aviation Industries of China, which produces both civilian and military aircraft is in fact a large holding company that includes more than 200 enterprises and trading companies and employs more than 500,000 people, of whom 200,000 are engineers and technicians. [7]

The other big source of PLA revenue is weapons sales. The PLA is reported to still own or control dozens of major SOEs that produce weapons for export. **[8]** Most of the weapons sales have been to international "bad guys" in the eyes of Western nations: Iran, Iraq, Syria, Libya, Nigeria, Cuba, Sudan, Pakistan and of course N. Korea. But predictions that Chinese aid would allow Iran to have nuclear weapons by 2000 were obviously exaggerated. In fact, the Chinese seemed to have been aiding Iran for 25 years to little effect.

In the fall of 2002, the State Council and the Central Military Commission directed local governments at all levels to include provision of "rear services" costs for the military establishment which allowed the PLA to reduce its own budgets. In addition, local governments bear some/all of the cost of military reserve units.

Adequate accounting procedures were not available until well into the 90s when the Ministry of Finance (MOF) developed standards which the PLA is required to use. Also, the MOF began serious budget reviews with a Zero Based Budgeting approach requiring more line item information and more account auditing. Thousands of PLA accounts were off budget, and much of the PLA budget was (and still is) concealed in other types of accounts. Huge debt levels were revealed – so substantial that they endangered the banks and local governments that had been coerced into backing the loans. Thus, it was clear in retrospect that the PLA had access to huge amounts of money, and it is a puzzle why they got so little real military capability out of these funds for more than 40 years.

MILITARY REFORMS

When all is said and done, the PLA seriously wants to be a lot smaller and a lot more technically advanced. Therefore, one major reform has been to shift the mix of units away from large ground units to more compact and multi-mission units. The number of divisions has been reduced in favor of more brigade size (1,000-2,500 troops) units to add flexibility. There are 13 infantry, 20 artillery, and 20 tank brigades. 59 divisions including 44 infantry, 10 tank and 5 artillery are still active. Efforts have been made to create at least one Rapid Reaction Unit (RRU) for each of the seven military regions, but airlift is scarce, and there are only about 130 transport helicopters in the whole PLA. Thus, most rapid deployments would still be by rail or truck. There are an estimated three RRUs actively deployed. Artillery is a big strength, with 30- 35,000 pieces of ordnance of many types, including 14,000 self propelled howitzers of 120 to 203 mm caliber. There are more than 6,000 tanks of varying age with 85-125 mm guns. **[9]**

The PLA has about 8,300 main battle tanks of different ages, but all of them, even the new T-90s under development, are obsolete by international standards, and those sold to Iraq were no match for the U. S. tanks. The history of tank design and production is a good illustration of how weak the Chinese military/industrial complex really is. A tank designated the T-69 was the first tank domestically produced. It was designed about 1970, but took another 10 years to reach production, and was not deployed in any numbers until the mid 80s by which time it was obsolete. The main battle tank is now considered to be the T-85, introduced in 1989, but it did not enter production until 1995, and not many have yet actually been deployed to the troops. **[10]**

The PLA has two very capable artillery pieces: the 155 mm and 203 mm mobile howitzers. The 203 mm howitzer has, at 50 km, the longest range of any weapon in the world but again, neither has really been built in any numbers.

Even before these reformed unit alignments, there was a serious reduction in troop numbers, over a 20 year period. Reductions have so far totaled 1.8 million from its peak of 4.5 million as recently as 1985 (5.5 million in 1950), and the active Army ground troops now number about 1.6 million. But in fact, many of the people "reduced" have been simply redeployed. A Reserve component has been created, largely for Army forces, and some active duty personnel have been transferred to the Reserves which now number about 800,000. Some have been moved into civilian jobs in the PLA and others have even been assigned to other government ministries. There are about 4 million military dependents and "several million" civilian employees of the PLA.

Taiwan is the keystone to military policy. The conflict with Taiwan is the only external situation that can be used to justify the high cost of the PLA. There is no credible land threat, now or in the foreseeable future. The major strategic posture is one of coastal defense. The military has virtually no force projection capability, beyond Taiwan. China wants to become the dominant regional power, and it needs "just enough" military potential to buttress that ambition. About 82% of the PLA total forces have been 3 year conscripts. The goals are to cut the conscript period to two years, but to reduce the percentage of conscripts to less than 65%.

Many personnel have been transferred to the People's Armed Police (PAP), created in 1983, including 14 PLA divisions more or less intact. This reflects a significant change in policy following Tiananmen Square; the leadership wants a far larger and more heavily armed internal security force to deal with potential civil insurrections but wants to avoid the visibility of using the army. The PAP force which was about 400,000 in 1982 and around 900,000 in the late 90's has climbed to what is estimated to be about and 1.5 million today (the official number is just 660,000). Its major roles are border control, internal security, civil unrest, customs and anti-smuggling and facilities protection. But it is still not clear who really controls the PAP. The CCP wants it both ways; they appear to want it linked to the military establishment, but want it to appear to be run as a civilian function.

Major modernization of forces has occurred in all of the services. Recently, most modernization funding is going to the PLA Air Force (PLAAF) and the PLA Navy (PLAN). While ground forces are being upgraded, only a limited number of units will be improved; the rest of the Army units will be low quality. There is an annual conscription program which is dysfunctional. 25% of all forces are one year people, and many of the rest have three year terms of service in a profession that is poorly paid and not very promising. All services suffer from a lack of capable NCOs. The Navy has no aircraft carriers, no heavy capital ships, only about 25 capable subs (only one nuclear powered nuclear missile capable sub and that is in its development/testing cycle. All 6 of the nuclear powered subs are obsolete). [11]

The Air Force has about 420,000 personnel and a growing number of planes, but most are based on 20 year old technology. It has about 150 first line planes including two fighter types bought from Russia, and one domestic plane based on good but 20 year old Israeli designs, but it has languished because of major technical problems with design, metallurgy, avionics, engine technology, and generally low manufacturing skills and quality control. The engines for the new J-18 fighter are actually being supplied by Sugat – a Russian company. More than 3,000 older aircraft (built in 1979 or earlier) of all types are so obsolete that they are being decommissioned. The Russian SU-27 is a good but old trainer that has been upgraded. The SU-30 is a good modern multi-task fighter-bomber with a range of 1600 nautical miles. There are about 120 old but good Russian "Badger" heavy bombers with a range of about 5,900 KM, and nuclear capability. None of these aircraft compare well against American and other country aircraft. The past reliance on Russian sources is now in question. Increasingly, the Russians are reluctant to part with new designs or production technology, fearing China not necessarily as an enemy but rather as a competitor as well as a customer, and they are now insisting on cash rather than bartered goods. [12] The PLAAF also operates a formidable Air Defense System with 220,000 air defense personnel in 100 sites, with surface to air missiles and about 16,000 anti aircraft guns. There is a large early warning radar network with ranges up to 100 km.

Missile forces are perhaps the strongest arm of the PLA, but they are still almost entirely ballistic. Seven ICBM missile systems entered development, but four have been cancelled and one is an old liquid fuel system. There are two modern systems: the DF-31 with a range of about 7,200 km; and the DF-31A with a range of 11,200 km, but the inventory for each is very small – less than 10. There are about 1000 air-to-air missiles, and another 1000 land based cruise type missiles, but the maximum range for any of them is about 85 NM. These are Russian designs that are being upgraded and switched to domestic production. The Chinese produce several short range attack missiles, have sold a lot to Iran, and wants to sell more to developing countries. There is a consolidated missile force with longer range missiles named "The Second Artillery". Long range missiles are really upgraded middle range missiles shifted from liquid to solid propellants.

There are at least ten theater missiles with ranges from 180 to 4,700 km. Most remain ballistic; and some are now equipped with upgraded guidance systems, but they remain scarce. China has 8-900 nuclear weapons, the third largest inventory in the world.

The People's Liberation Army Navy (PLAN) has a total of about 250,000 personnel. It has been trying hard to upgrade its submarine fleet as an attack force. It initiated five types of subs, of which two – the Type 92 Xia and the Type 94 Jin are nuclear capable, but neither is fully operational, and only 9-10 have so far been identified. Submarine missiles are old and limited in numbers. The JL-2 has a range of 7,200 km, but apparently has yet to be deployed for fleet operations. It has only one full range nuclear powered ballistic missile sub, plus 5 "attack" boats with ballistic missile capability. China has a very large merchant marine, but many of the vessels are coast or river based. It has two guided missile destroyers based on a 1990 Soviet design, and carrying 8 anti-ship cruise type missiles. It also has 2 smaller guided missile destroyers and 8 smaller frigates. All other ships in the Chinese navy are from the 1950's and are obsolete. [13]

The current budget is estimated at about $36 billion, but much of the funding for the military establishment remains concealed. Almost all R & D is carried in a separate national R & D budget category. The costs of some arms imports are budgeted separately and mostly off budget. The PAP is largely funded out of civilian accounts. The Reserve is funded from provincial budgets. A lot of the cost of military SOEs including deficits are covered by government subsidies and forced "loans" and the PLA has always had huge bank debts, much of which is not realistically expected to be repaid. Many of the prices of military goods are deliberately understated. There is a serious and deliberate lack of reliable data, and most of the statistical comparisons with world prices lack a Purchasing Power Parity (PPP) assessment. In fact, there is serious doubt that the Chinese themselves know how much they spend on their military establishment. The budget in 2000 was double that of 1978, but it has had persistent ups and downs – up for Korea and then down; up for the Vietnam War and then down. In effect, financing for the military establishment as a percent of the national budget is not much better than it was in 1978. A substantial part of the recent increase is to bring pay for both officers and men up to some reasonable standard after decades of underpayment. The quality of personnel has, for 30 years or more been poor since the military is not an attractive career. In addition, there is a track record of bad maintenance, a shortage of spare parts, and low performance reliability.

"China's reported 17.5% increase in its defense budget still leaves it a fraction of what the US spends each year on its armed forces. President Bush's last budget requested $515 billion for FY 2009 – a 7.5% increase – plus $70 billion for the wars in Iraq and Afghanistan." [9] A spokesman for the Chinese National People's Congress said that defense spending has increased at an annual average of 15.8% in the last 5 years, and while this seems ominous to some observers, it is actually less than the increase in general government revenues which have increased an average of 22.1%. He noted that the defense budget is equivalent of 1.4% of GDP, while the US spends at 4.6% and Britain spends 3%. He also stated that much of the increase was for higher military salaries, more training and rising oil costs rather than new weapons. However the Pentagon still manages to brood about nuclear force modernization and new high tech missiles.

END NOTES

CHAPTER I: Government Reform in India and China

1   Das, Gurcheran, "India Unbound", p. 95. New York, Anchor Books, 2002

2   Luce, Edward, "In Spite of the Gods: The Rise of Modern India", p 203. New York, Anchor Books, 2006.

3   Kohli, Atul, "Democracy and Discontent", p. 311. Cambridge University Press, 1990.

4   Economist Magazine, March 3, 2008.

5   Indian Ministry of Finance, "Economic Survey of 2005-06.

6   State Owned Enterprises (SOE) are often called Public Sector Undertakings. See Indiacatalog.com., and also Amritt Ventures.com, Wikipedia on government owned enterprises. Also see Search.Marketing. IN, Global Times, July 2, 2009.

7   See Government of India, Ministry of Industry, National Commercial Programme, 2005.

8   See AllBusiness, February 22, 2010.

9   Das, Gurcheran, "India Unbound", p. 94. New York, Anchor Books, 2002.

10 Ibid

11 Luce, Edward, "In Spite of the Gods: The Rise of Modern India", New York, Anchor Books, 2006.

12 Thardoor, Shaski, "India from Midnight to the Millennium and Beyond", pp. 290-292. New York, Arcade Publishing, 1997.

13 Mishra, Pankai, "Temptations of the West", p. 49. New York, Farrar, Straus and Giroux, 2006

14 Panageriya, Arvind, "India the Emerging Giant", Chap. 7. Oxford University Press, 2008.

15 Heller, Peter S., and Rao, M. Govinda, Editors, "A Sustainable Fiscal Policy for India". See article by Ricardo Hausmann and Catriona Purfield, "The Challenge of Fiscal Adjustment in a Democracy", pp 283-321, Oxford University Press, 2006.

CHAPTER II: China: Government From the Top Down

1   Bingman, Charles F., "Reforming China's Government" pp. 9, 162, 174., XLibris Corp. 2010. See also Schell, Orville, and Shambaugh, David, "The China Reader", p 362. New York, Vintage Books, 1999.

2   Becker, Jasper, "The Chinese", p. 208. Oxford University Press, 2000. See also Tsai, Lily, "Accountability Without Democracy", pp. 60-70. Cambridge University Press, 2004.

3   World Bank, "World Development Indicators – 2001", Washington, D. C., World Bank, 2001. See also Economy, Elizabeth C., "The River Runs Black" Chapter 3. Cornell University Press, 2004.

4   Ibid, p. 72, p. 85.

5   Saich, Tony, "Governance and Politics in China", p. 278-284. New York, Palgrave Macmillan, 2004. See also Becker, Jasper, "The Chinese", Oxford University Press, 2000.

6   Yang, Dali, "Remaking the Chinese Leviathan", chapter two, Stanford University Press, 2004.

7   Gittings, John, "The Changing Face of China" p. 175. Oxford University Press, 2006.

8   Yang, Dali, "Remaking the Chinese Leviathan", p. 1, p. 63. Stanford University Press. 2004.

9   Bingman, Charles F., "Reforming China's Government", p. 250. The following sources were used in the research for this statement: Becker, Jasper, "The Chinese", pp 33-41; Bergsten, Fred C. et al, "China's Rise", pp. 152-156; Chow, Gregory C., "China's Economic Transformation", pp. 187-192; Economy, Elizabeth, "China's Coming Environmental Crash", Foreign Affairs Journal, Sept./Oct. 2007; Friedman, John, "China's Urban Transition", pp. 124-126; Gittings, John, "The Changing Face of China", pp. 284-289; Harney, Alexandra, "The China Price", pp. 88-101; Hutchings, Graham, "Modern China" A Guide to a Century of Change". pp. 124-127; Pei, Minxin, "China's Trapped Transition", pp.175-176; Schell, Orville, and Shambaugh, David, "The China Reader". Pp. 376-393; Shirk, Susan, "China: Fragile Super Power", pp. 32-34; Starr, John B., "Understanding China", pp. 176-191; Word Bank, "China 2020", pp. 71-81.

10 Economy, Elizabeth, "China's Coming Environmental Crash", Washington, D. C., Foreign Affairs Journal, Sep./Oct. 2002

11 Bingman, Charles F., "Reforming China's Government" p. 64., XLibris Publishing Co., 2010

CHAPTER III: Economic Development in India

1 Kohli, Atul, "State Directed Development", p. 270-277. Cambridge University Press, 2004.

2 Ibid, p. 259, pp. 270-277.

3 Nilekani, Nandan, "Imagining India: The Idea of a Renewed Nation", p. 71. New York, Penguin Press, 2009.

4 Ibid, p. 74.

5 Economist Magazine, Nov. 12, 2009.

6 Government of India, "Statement on Industrial Policy", New Delhi, July 24, 1991.

7 Das, Gurcheran, "India Unbound", p. 73, p.83. New York, Anchor Books, 2002

8 Government of India, "Statement on Industrial Policy", New Delhi, July 24, 1991.

9 Das, Gurcheran, "India Unbound", p. 73, p.83. New York, Anchor Books, 2002.

10 Fernandez, Leela, "India's New Middle Class", p. 82. University of Minnesota Press, 2006.

11 Thardoor, Shaski, "From Midnight to the Millennium and Beyond', p. 281. New York, Arcade Publishing, 2006.

12 The Indian Institutes of Management are located in Kolkata, Ahmedabad, Bangalore, Lucknow, Kozhikode, Indore and Shillong. Indian Institutes of Technology are located in Kharagpur, Mumbai, Chennai, Kanpur, Delhi, Guwahati, Bhubaneswar, Gandhinigar, Hyderabad, Patna, Punjab, Rajasthan, Indore, Mandi, and Roorkee. The Indian Institutes of Information Technology are located in Madras, Gwalior, Hydrabad, Japalpur, Bubaneswar, Allahabad, Jabalpur, Kancheepuram, Kharagpur, Delhi, and Chennai. The Indian Institute of Science is located in Bangalore.

13 Panagariya, Arvind, "India the Emerging Giant", p. 238. Oxford University Press, 2008.

14 Fernandez, Leela, "India's New Middle Class", p. 107. University of Minnesota Press, 2006.

15 Government of India, Central Statistical Organization, "Economic Survey of India" 2008-09.

16 Economist Magazine, July, 9, 2009.

17 See Panagariya, Arvind, "India the Emerging Giant", Chapter 3. Oxford University Press, 2008.

18 Economist Magazine, "Tax Reform in India, Dec. 17, 2008.

19 Communist Party of India, "People's Democracy", No. 27, July 2, 2006.

20 Panagariya, Arvind, "India the Emerging Giant", p. 386. Oxford University Press, 2008.

21 Foreign Affairs Journal, Mar./Apr. 2010, Fiegenbaum, Evan A., "India's Rise, America's Interest", p. 76.

22 De Soto, Hernando, "The Other Path", preface, p. xxi. New York, Perennial Press, 1989.

CHAPTER IV: Economic Development in China: From the Top Down

1   Bingman, Charles F., "Reforming China's Government: Fixing the Worst Government in the World", p. 139. XLibris Publishing Co., 2010.
2   Saich, Tony, "Governance and Politics in China", pp. 80-86, New York, Palgrave Macmillan, 2004.
3   Ibid, Chapter 6, pp. 150-179.
4   "Reforming China's Enterprises", Organization for Economic Cooperation and Development, pp. 51-61, p. 38. Washington, D. C., OECD Publishing, 2000.
5   Bingman, Charles F. "Reforming China's Government", p. 154. XLibris Publishing Co., 2010.
6   Ibid, pp. 156-160. See also Lubman, Stanley B., "Bird in a Cage: Legal Reform in China After Mao", p.214. Stanford University Press, 1999.
7   Bingman, p. 158.
8   Haung, Yasheng, "Selling China: Foreign Direct Investment During the Reform Era", Introduction, and pp. 1-30. Cambridge University Press, 2003.
9   Bingman, pp. 165-166.
10 Ibid, p. 168. See also Pie, Minxin, "China's Trapped Transition", pp. 97-102. Harvard University Press, 2006.

CHAPTER V: Social Services in India and China

1   Das, Gurcheran, "India Unbound", p. 98. New York, Anchor Books, 2002.
2   World Policy Journal, Spring, 2007.
3   Panagariya, Arvind, "India the Emerging Giant", pp. 432-441. Oxford University Press, 2008. See also Nilekani, Nandan, "Imagining India", pp. 172-194. New York, Penguin Press, 2009.
4   Nussbaum, Martha, C., "The Clash Within: Democracy, Religious Violence, and India's Future", Harvard University Press, 2007.
5   India Today, October 13, 1997.
6   See references in #3 above.
7   UNESCO, Institute for Statistics, 2008.
8   India Today, October 13, 1997.
9   Nussbaum, Martha, C., "The Clash Within: Democracy, Religious Violence, and India's Future", pp. 264-272. Harvard University Press, 2007.
10 Panagariya, Arvind, "India the Emerging Giant", pp. 432-441. Oxford University Press, 2008.
11 Nilekani, Nandan, "Imagining India", pp. 174-177. New York, Penguin Press, 2009.
12 See footnote #12, Chapter III.
13 Becker, Jasper, "The Chinese", p. 241. Oxford University Press, 2000.
14 Ibid, p. 64.

15 UNESCO, Institute for Statistics, Education Report, 1995.

16 Shell, Orville, and Shambaugh, David, Editors, "The China Reader", pp. 215-223. New York, Vintage Books, 1999.

17 Panagariya, Arvind, "India the Emerging Giant", pp. 415. Oxford University Press, 2008.

18 Dreze, Jean, and Sen, Amaryta, "India: Economic Development and Social Opportunity", p. 101. Oxford University Press, 1995.

19 Economic and Political Weekly, Feb. 23, 2002, "State Adjusted Public Expenditure on Social Sector Poverty Alleviation Programmes".

20 Health Affairs Journal, July/August 2008.

21 InfoChange India News, February, 2010.

22 World Bank Policy Research Paper WPS 491, "How Well Do India's Social Services Programs Serve the Poor?"

23 Indian National Commission on Macroeconomics and Health, 2002.

24 Panagariya, Arvind, "India the Emerging Giant", pp. 420-427. Oxford University Press, 2008.

25 Ibid, p. 425.

26 Reason Magazine, September 4, 2009, Walker, Jesse, "A Different Sort of Health Care System".

27 Ibid.

28 Harvard Gazette, Powell, Alvin, "In China and India, Health Care Burden Shifts to the Poor", October, 2006. See also Indian Child Magazine, "Health Care in India", 1995.

29 Yip, Winnie, and Mahal, Ajay, "The Health Care Systems of China and India: Performance and Future Challenges", Heath Affairs Journal, 27(4), pp. 921-932.

30 Becker, Jasper, "The Chinese", p. 241. Oxford University Press, 2000.

31 Ibid, pp. 243-244. In 2002, the Chinese government introduced another Rural Cooperative Medical Scheme, but the coverage is very limited. The government expressed "hopes" to expand the program to 40-60% of the rural population by 2007, but that date has come and gone, with little result.

32 Gifford, Rob, "China Road", p. 74. New York, Random House, 2008.

33 Panagariya, Arvind, "India the Emerging Giant", pp. 251-255. Oxford University Press, 2008

34 Nilekani, Nandan, "Imagining India", pp. 387-389. New York, Penguin Press, 2009.

CHAPTER VI: Urbanization

1 Government of India, "National Health Profile – 2005", New Delhi, Central Bureau of Health Intelligence, Ministry of Health and Family Welfare, 2005.

2 InfoChangeIndia, News and Features, Srivstata, Rahul, "Urban India", January, 2005. See also WaterAid India, "The State of Slums in India"; and Government

of India Press Release, May 12, 2010, Statement of the Secretary for Housing and Urban Poverty Alleviation.

3   Government of India, National Sample Survey Organization survey, 2002.
4   Economist Magazine, August 31, 2007, and June 11, 2009, "The Nano Home".
5   Government of India, "Urban Poverty Report 2009", report of the Ministry of Housing and Urban Poverty Alleviatilon.
6   Economist Magazine, December 11, 2008, "Creaking and Groaning: Infrastructure is India's Biggest Handicap".
7   Government of India, Pranod, Dr. K., "Government of India Scheme for Governance of Health Service Infrastructure in Rural India", Ministry of Heath and Family Welfare. (no date).
8   Panagariya, Arvind, "India the Emerging Giant", p. 428. Oxford University Press, 2008.
9   Kohli, Atul, "Democracy and Discontent", p. 123. Cambridge University Press, 1990.
10   Panagariya, p. 428.
11   Paryvaran Mitra Foundation, "Pollution in India", 2007.
12   UNESCO, Kundu, Amitable, Dr., "Urban Development Infrastructure Financing and Emerging System of Governance in India", 2000.
13   National Institute of Urban Affairs, "Urban Governance Decentralization in India", 2004. See also State Finance Commission, recommendations and follow-up actions, Vol. 1, 2006.
14   Bingman, Charles F., "Reforming China's Government", p. 265. XLibris Publishing Co., 2010.
15   Pei, Minxin, "China's Trapped Transition", p. 203. Harvard University Press, 2007.
16   Campanella, Thomas, J., "The Concrete Dragon: China's Urban Revolution", p. 15. New York, Primator Architectural Press, 2008.

CHAPTER VII: Rural Life and the Environment

1   Wolpert, Stanley, "India", (4th Edition), p. 120. University of California Press, 2009.
2   Pinstrup-Anderson, Per, "Reshaping Indian Food and Agricultural Policy to Meet the Challenges and Opportunities of Globalization", EximBank Commencement Day Annual Lecture, Mumbai, India, April 22, 2002.
3   See New York Times, June, 22, 2008.
4   Kundar, Mira, "Planet India", pp. 169-185. New York, Scribners Publishing, 2003.
5   Sen, Amaryta, remarks made at a public hearing on hunger and the right to food, New Delhi University, January, 2003.
6   Pinstrup-Anderson, Per. See note #2 above. Pinstrup-Anderson is the Director General, International Food Policy Research Institute and 2001 World Food Prize Laureate.

7   Economist Magazine, October, 2, 2006.

8   Varshnay, Ashutosh, "Democracy, Development and the Countryside", pp. 82-88. Cambridge University Press, 1998.

9   Sen, Amaryta, speech reported in IndiaTogether, March 14, 2010.

10 Economist Magazine, "When the Rains Fall", September 10, 2009.

11 Ibid, July 3, 2008.

12 CARE Report. See the Hindu newspaper, March 5, 2010.

13 Economist Magazine, November 5, 2009.

14 Thaardoor, Shaski, "The Elephant, the Tiger, and the Cell Phone", pp. 91-93. New York, Arcade Publishing, 2007.

15 Panagariya, Arvind, "India the Emerging Giant", pp. 427-431. Oxford University Press, 2008.

INDIA'S 10 TOP AGRICULTURAL

COMPANIES:Monsanto (high yield crop varieties and hybrid crops); Rallis (domestic agribusiness, international business, contract services; H. J Heinz (food and dairy products); Advanta India Ltd. (Germplasm and intellectual properties; sunflower, rice, corn, mustard, cotton, vegetables, etc.); Phalada Agro Research Foundation Ltd. (organic agriculture); Poabs Organic Estates (organic farming); National Agro Industries (seed, fertilizer); DuPont India (food and crop production); Rasi Seeds (seeds and cotton industry); ABT Industries (Shakti Group) (manufacturing and production of agricultural products).

16 Nilekani, Nandan, "Imagining India", pp. 414-418. New York, Penguin Press, 2009.

17 The World Bank Report 2006.

18 Payyvaran Mitra Foundation, 2007.

19 Bingman: see end note #1, Chapter V.

20 Economy, Elizabeth, "China's Coming Environmental Crash", p. 56. Washington, D. C., Foreign Affairs Journal, Sept./Oct. 2007.

21 Pei, Minxin, "China's Trapped Transition", Harvard University Press, 2006.

22 Gittings, John, "The Changing Face of China", p. 286. Oxford University Press, 2006.

CHAPTER VIII: Military Capability

1   Wikepedia: Indian Army; Indian Air Force; Indian Navy; Paramilitary Forces of India. See also GlobalSecurity, Ministry of Defense.

2   OpenSalon.com. Report of the Indian Defense Budget, Feb. 7, 2010. See also GlobalSecurity "Military Budget". See also Medhani in The Trajectory, "India's Defense Spending: Facts Beyond the Figures", July 10, 2010.

3 GlobalSecurity, July, 2009.

4 Wikipedia, "Indian Navy".

5 Wikipedia, "Indian Air Force"

6 GlobalSecurity, Union Ministry of Home Affairs, 2010, and Wikipedia, "Paramilitary Forces of India"

7 Shambaugh, David, "Modernizing China's Military", p. 202. University of California Press, 2004.

8 Ibid, p. 221, and pp. 225-283. See also Frankenstein, John, and Bates, Gill, "Current and Future Challenges Facing Chinese Defense Industries", in Shambaugh, David, and Yang, Richard H., Editors, Oxford University Press, 1997.

9 Karmel, Solomon, M., "China and the People's Liberation Army", Chapter 4, pp. 123-154. New York, St. Martins Press, 2000.

10 Ibid, pp. 252-255.

11 The Chinese Navy has fewer than 10 nuclear submarines, only one of which is armed with strategic ballistic missiles, and it is not operational. Although the PLAN keeps announcing plans for the development of new ships, even if true, the actual development cycle for such systems to reach production can be 15-20 years.

12 Karmel, Solomon, M. "China and the People's Liberation Army", pp. 158-161. New York, St. Martins Press, 2000.

13 Shambaugh, David, "Modern China's Military", University of California Press, 2006.